DANCE CLASS

HERMES HOUSE

PAUL BOTTOMER

DANCE CLASS

HOW TO WALTZ, QUICK STEP, FOXTROT, TANGO, SAMBA, SALSA, MERENGUE, LAMBADA AND LINE DANCE – STEP-BY-STEP!

Contents

This edition is published by Hermes House

Hermes House is an imprint of Anness Publishing Ltd
Hermes House, 88–89 Blackfriars Road, London SE1 8HA
tel. 020 7401 2077; fax 020 7633 9499

www.hermeshouse.com; www.annesspublishing.com

If you like the images in this book and would
like to investigate using them for publishing,
promotions or advertising, please visit our website
www.practicalpictures.com for more information.

© Anness Publishing Ltd 1998, 2006

A CIP catalogue record for this book is available from the
British Library.

Publisher: Joanna Lorenz
Senior Editor: Lindsay Porter
Photographer: John Freeman
Clothes Stylist: Leeann Mackenie
Hair and Make-up: Karen Kennedy
Designers: Clare Baggaley and Mark Stevens

10 9 8 7 6 5 4 3 2 1

Introduction

Dancing is both the most artistic of social pastimes and the most social of artistic pastimes. In all societies, dancing forms an integral part of the lifestyle. Dancing is not only a reflection of life but is a basic human expression of life itself. While the initial motivation to dance is often a social one, once past the hurdle of actually learning to dance, many find in the music, the atmosphere and the dance, the opportunity to take on a new persona. In an instant, the dancer can be mentally and emotionally transported to almost any scenario of their choosing – a Texas Dance Ranch, an elegant Gala Ball in Vienna, a Caribbean beach party, a smart dinner dance in London's West End, a backstreet bar in Buenos Aires, a carnival in Copacabana, a bodega in old Havana, a bull-fight in Valencia, a New York night spot or a Parisian café. The music and venue create the atmosphere but it is the dancer who expresses their own individuality through the language of the dance.

In this unique volume, the most internationally popular dances are brought together in a practical and easily understandable way. The book is divided into three sections.

The Club Dance section deals with dances that are normally danced at special nightclub-style venues and where one dance or dance style predominates throughout the evening. These are Tango Argentino, Salsa (including Cumbia, Vallenato and Pachanga), Merengue, Lambada, Samba Reggae and American Line Dancing.

The International Latin-American Dance section covers the partner dances that originated in Latin countries but whose style and technique were later internationally standardized. The international style and technique often differs from the original indigenous style but, since it is the international style which is most widely danced and which is most durable, it is this style that is described here. These dances include Mambo, Rumba, Cha Cha Cha, Samba and Paso Doble. We have also included the Jive family of dances – Lindy Hop, Boogie Woogie and Rock 'n' Roll in this section because, in international competition, Jive is included in Latin dancing.

The International Standard Dance section introduces those dances formerly known as ballroom dances. The descriptions used in this book represent a simplified version of the internationally standardized style and technique used throughout the world. These dances include the Social Foxtrot, Waltz, Quickstep, Slow Foxtrot and Modern Tango. There is no uniformly standardized technique for Viennese Waltz, so in this book it is presented as an easy style enjoyed by ordinary social dancers rather than the more demanding style danced in championships.

With the International Standard and Latin-American dance competitions now part of the Olympic programme, these styles look set to reach and inspire an even wider audience and attain even greater popularity.

Whatever your musical taste or individual preferences, the huge variety of dances ensures that there is something to suit you. You do not need to be a good dancer to enjoy the dancing, the music, the mood, the atmosphere and, of course, the social life. Dancing is accessible to everyone irrespective of age or ability. Some of the most touching and rewarding moments I have experienced in the world of dancing have been with physically and mentally handicapped dancers.

Dancing is a fabulous way of keeping fit both physically and mentally and is recommended by the medical profession. If, however, you have a condition which would prevent you from taking a brisk walk, you should consult your medical practitioner before embarking on your dance programme.

As you work through the book, relax and learn steadily at your own pace. If necessary, read through the relevant section several times until you become totally familiar with the move. Remember too that some of the most important information is in the introductory section to each dance. Focus on what you know rather than what you don't and avoid setting your expectations too high in too short a timescale. Everyone needs time. To make progress in any style of dancing, you will need commitment, application and as much practice as possible but the rewards for these can deeply enrich the quality of life in so many varied and worthwhile ways. And the great thing is that it's so much fun!

So, enjoy this introduction to some of the world's most popular dances and remember the sooner you learn to dance, the longer you'll have to enjoy it. It won't be long before you, like so many others, have become completely dance crazy!

Paul Bottomer

Club Dances

Dance clubs are a popular way of enjoying a particular dance style. At such clubs, one dance or one dance style tends to predominate. This focus usually means a more rapid progress from beginner to experienced dancer. Dancers tend to be single – though couples are equally welcomed and the age range is often wider than one might suspect. Tuition is frequently offered before the start of the club night.

At a Tango club, the event will be largely devoted to Argentine Tango but may also include an occasional Milonga and Tango-Waltz in which Tango is danced to Waltz time. Most Salsa clubs play non-stop Salsa interspersed with an occasional Merengue.

Rock 'n' Roll clubs may feature live music and may also offer different styles of Jive including Lindy Hop, Boogie-Woogie, Swing and the so-called French Jive on different evenings.

One of the most popular club dance styles of the decade is American Line Dancing. Line Dancing events are called Dance Ranches, tuition is often included and you don't need a partner. There are, however, tens of thousands of different Line Dances and it may take several visits to build up a repertoire of dances. Nonetheless, you can have a lot of fun while you learn, and the moves included in this book will provide a sound basis on which to develop your skills.

As well as nightclubs, many universities, colleges and high schools have dance clubs which also welcome non-students. Check out your local press for details, then get out there and join the club!

Tango

Passionate, sensual and tantalizing, the Tango is many things to many people. In the European and International styles, there are many dances from which to choose to suit the mood of the moment – the romance of the Waltz, the ebullience of Rock 'n' Roll, or the carnival atmosphere of Samba. Despite its reputation as a melancholy dance, Tango captures all these moods and more. Born of life's experience in the back street gutters of Buenos Aires, the Tango rose from its humble beginnings to dazzle at high class Parisian soirées, yet the back street bars remained its true home among the people who had given it life.

In the closing years of the nineteenth century, Europe had been ravaged by wars, famine and economic uncertainty. With few prospects and little hope of a stable life in the land of their birth, many young men emigrated to begin a new life in South America. Many hundreds of thousands disembarked in the new federal capital of Argentina, the port of Buenos Aires on the Rio de la Plata.

Despite a high degree of prosperity in Argentina at this time, life was hard for the immigrants, who were forced to live in the squalid outskirts of the city. Despite this, the immigrants kept coming, and by 1914 they outnumbered native-born Argentinians in Buenos Aires by three to one. About half of the immigrants were Italian, and about a third Spanish. The old port area of Buenos Aires, la Boca, where many Italians settled, is a colourful reminder of the Italian contribution to the history of Tango.

By the advent of the immigrants, the life of the famous Argentinian cowboys, known as "gauchos", had all but disappeared, so the image we have of Rudolph Valentino dancing a theatrical version of the Tango in the 1924 film, *The Four Horsemen of the Apocalypse*, is erroneous. However, in the days when gauchos did roam the prairies, news was carried by *payadores*, who were a type of travelling minstrel. From these came a style of song, and later a dance, called the Milonga. The records for this period are vague, but we do know that the Milonga enjoyed great popularity in Buenos Aires, particularly among the poorer classes.

The word "Tango" is thought to be African in origin, and denotes a "meeting place" or "special place". This does not mean the Tango itself is of African origin. The Cuban Habanera, the Spanish Contradanza and the Afro-Argentinian Candombé all influenced the evolution of the Tango, but no dance more than the Milonga. Milonga means "party" or "fiesta" and the music itself was lively, vivacious and joyful. What evidence there is suggests that *compadritos* frequently visited

Afro-Argentinian dances and may have borrowed some of the moves and adapted them to the Milonga, paving the way for the Tango-Milonga variant.

The new Argentinians of European descent shared a common bond, but one that often found currency in despair and disillusionment. This poured out into song: the song of sadness, nostalgia and longing, but also of hope and aspiration. The passion of the song demanded further expression in a dance, and so it was that in the back-street gutters of Buenos Aires, the Tango was born.

The vast majority of the immigrants to Argentina were young men, who eventually outnumbered women by fifty to one. These young men were often frequent visitors to the *academias* (from "dance academy") and *pregundines*, low-life cafés where the waitresses could be hired for dancing. In order to attract the women, it became very important for the young men to become good dancers. With no real dance academies, men would teach each other the Tango, exchange steps and practise together before exercising their skills to attract the women. Freed from the conventions of European dances, the men would devise very practical and often unique ways of skilfully leading the women.

The first instruments to accompany the Tango were the guitar, flute and violin. Eventually, though, the bandoneon became the crucial instrument. It is often remarked that the bandoneon is the soul of the Tango, and Tangos have been written which pay homage to that "instrument of the devil". The bandoneon is a sort of squeeze-box concertina with keys at both ends, and notoriously difficult to play.

With the exception of some vocal Tangos, most feature the bandoneon. "La Cumparsita", perhaps the best known Tango in the world, dates from 1916, and was composed originally as a march by Gerardo Matos Rodriguez. Later adapted as a Tango, "La Cumparsita" means a small street band or procession in a carnival. Another very famous Tango composed in 1905 by Angelo Villoldo is "El Choclo". This has endured as one of the most popular Tangos of all time, and, in the 1950s, had a new lease of life when the release of a new arrangement, "Kiss of Fire", launched it into the American popular charts.

With the deep, sonorous and breathy notes of the bandoneon, the Tango became more earthy, intense and brooding, and even sometimes, but not always, melancholy. Words were added to the melodies, which reflected the preoccupations of the people. The principal themes evoked by the Tango lyricists adopted a fatalistic view and focused on the trials of life as they saw them. Carlos Gardel became the greatest Tango singer of all time. Gardel was the archetypal Latin lover, and was killed tragically in an air crash in 1935. His grave in the cemetery of La Chacarita in Buenos Aires has since become a place of pilgrimage. Many of Gardel's vocal Tangos had only a guitar accompaniment, reflecting the style of the old *payadores*. The first Tango to be performed by Gardel was "Mi Noche Triste" ("My Sad Night") in 1917. The sentiments express the sorrow of an abandoned lover consoling himself with drink.

Enrique Santos Discepolo, one of the foremost Tango poets and composers, said "Tango is a sad thought expressed in dance". To me, however, Tango is not so much a thought as an impulse that challenges the dancers to explore their inner feelings through dance.

The Universal Suffrage Law of 1912 gave a new freedom to the people, and an impetus to the Tango. Now, it was not only the lower classes who wanted to dance the Tango, but it also became fashionable for high society to throw Tango parties, and Tango salons were quickly established in the upper-class areas of Buenos Aires. The fame of Tango soon spread from South America to New York, London and Paris, where Tango tea-dances became the rage.

However, the uncompromising and daring character of the Tango placed it in immediate conflict with authority figures. In Paris, Cardinal Amette declared that "Christians should not in good conscience take part in it" and the following year, Pope Benedict XV complained "It is outrageous that this indecent, heathen dance, which is an assassination of family and social life, is even being danced in the Papal residence". In 1914, Kaiser Wilhelm II forbade his officers to dance the Tango while in uniform, describing the dance as "lascivious, and an affront to common decency".

As the First World War raged on, people sought distractions from its horror and, despite the turmoil of the time, the Tango was far from forgotten. The mood of the time was changing and there was a new sense of freedom in the air. The adventure of the Tango reflected that mood, and the demand for it continued to grow. As the war came to an end, Tango entered its golden age of the 1920s. As it became more and more popular in Europe and North America, in Buenos Aires its popularity had reached unprecedented heights. Some musicians strived to interpret it in new and innovative ways as a musical art form. These musicians and composers were greatly admired and became household names in Buenos Aires and beyond. Bandoneon players became almost like gods. But it was not only the musicians who captured the imagination – the great dancers too, were adulated by the people. Perhaps the best known and most enduring reputation was held by the legendary El Cachafaz (José Ovidio Bianquet). Dancing with Carmencita Calderon, El Cachafaz was revered by the public. The greatest Tango dancers of recent times must be Juan Carlos Copes and Maria Nieves. They are the embodiment of the dance, and never fail to inspire and touch those who witness their Tango.

In more recent times, there have been many Tango dancers made famous by their appearance in spectacular shows around the world. Their style, however, is Show Tango, and over the years, it has grown less and less to resemble the authentic Tango of Buenos Aires. This is in no way to diminish the expertise and quality of the performance, but this chapter is about how two ordinary people can come together to dance the authentic Argentine Tango.

A military coup on 6 September 1930 in Argentina heralded a period of unsettled government during which the authorities, nervous and anxious to control any possible criticism, started to ban any Tango which had any political innuendo or sang of social injustice.

In Europe, the Tango had undergone a massive evolution. The Argentine Tango did not accord with the long-held European ideas about dancing, and the authentic style was quickly and ruthlessly changed. Walks were introduced to make the dance progress around the ballroom floor, and the seductive character of the Tango was suppressed beneath a faster, harsher, more aggressive beat. Drums, which were hardly used in the Argentinian *Orquesta Tipica*, added to the staccato, march-like quality of this "modern" Tango, and encouraged a sharper interpretation, including the highly stylized head jerks associated with the modern international style of competitive Tango.

During the 1950s in Buenos Aires, the Tango went into decline. Peron fell from power, and the health of the economy moved precariously downwards. The immigrants no longer viewed themselves as immigrants, but as Argentinians, and the power of the Tango to console nostalgic longing had waned. With economic decline, there were less funds to promote the huge Tango events and orchestras typical of the 1940s. Tango was still played by smaller groups, but now the audience listened rather than danced. By the 1960s, musicians and composers were experimenting with "el nuevo Tango", a new style of Tango music for listening to. As this grew in popularity, so the interest in Tango as a dance declined. Some notable orchestras and composers, including the celebrated Osvaldo Pugliese, continued to play for audiences both in Argentina and abroad. During the 1980s, large-scale productions went on tour around the world, stimulating a revival of interest outside Argentina. Such was their effect, that a new generation discovered Tango for the first time. Now, Tango clubs, salons and schools are once again springing up throughout North America, Europe and the Far East.

The Tango has come a long way from its humble beginnings, but it has a long way to go yet. Its history is rich with legend, romance and nostalgic reminiscence. Tango is a supremely sensual dance, which captures the full gamut of human emotion, of hope, disappointment and life itself. *Esto es Tango* – This is Tango.

The woman dances the sensuous Ocho.

Getting Started

If you have danced any other Tango before, it would be as well not to transfer the characteristics of that dance to Tango Argentino, as this is a very different dance. It does not have the angry staccato interpretation of the modern international-style Tango, but is smoother and much more sensuous and seductive. This Tango is to be danced by two people for each other rather than to be performed. The dance is more important than the dancers and, if this is respected, the dance will repay the dancers' respect a thousandfold.

During the course of the book, we will be introducing and working through some of the basic popular moves of Tango Argentino. Each element is fully explained. By following the instructions exactly, you will find that the moves are not difficult and, with practice, you will soon be dancing Tango in the authentic style of Buenos Aires.

Figures or moves are explained step by step and then joined together with other figures to build up a complete group of figures. These groups can then be repeated or followed by any of the other groups of figures in the book. As you learn one group and

progress to the next, you will find that the elements of the next group are already familiar to you. It is particularly important therefore to ensure that you are completely happy and comfortable with each element before moving on. In this structured way, you will quickly increase both your vocabulary of moves and your pleasure in dancing them.

The most important aspect of any dance is to enjoy what you are doing at whatever level. While technical excellence can yield enormous pleasure, it is equally possible to find pleasure in learning to Tango with each new step. Now relax and try the first group.

Above and right: Tango Argentino is a much more intimate style of dance than modern Tango, and is well suited to dancing in small settings.

Left: Today, Argentine Tango retains the intimacy of the original dance.

Tango Tongue Twisters

El Retroceso – *retro-ssessoe*

La Salida – *sall-eeda*

La Cunita – *kun-eeta*

La Resolucion – *reso-loo-see-on*

El Ocho – *ó-cho*

El Ocho Abierto – *o-cho abbey-air-toe*

La Ronda – *ron-da*

El Pepito – *pep-ee-toe*

Los Tres Ochos – *tress o-choss*

La Trabada – *tra-ba-da*

La Parada – *pa-ra-da*

La Llevada – *zhay-va-da*

La Sentada – *sen-ta-da*

Los Ochos Largos – *o-chos lar-ghos*

La Media Luna – *may-deeya loona*

Group One

El Retroceso – La Salida – La Cunita – La Resolucion

The first group of figures combines some of the basic moves in Tango Argentino. Once this basic group has been mastered, you will be able to dance, practise and enjoy Tango continuously. While dancing Group One, you will make approximately a quarter turn (or 90°) to the left.

El Retroceso (The Reverse Start)

The opening movement of the Tango is called the Salida. However, the Salida incorporates many varied starting elements, so the opening move is separated here from the rest of the Salida for the sake of clarity. The Retroceso, or the Reverse Start, is one of the most easily led, practical and popular starts. The man and woman start with their feet together. The man is standing on his left foot and the woman corresponds by standing on her right foot.

1

COUNT – SLOW

Man Walk forward with the right foot between yourself and the woman. Ensure there is no turn.

Woman Walk backwards with the left foot.

1

COUNT – SLOW

Man Walk backwards with the right foot, taking a short step.

Woman Walk forward with the left foot.

2

COUNT – SLOW

Man Step to the side with the left foot, taking a wider step than the woman.

Woman Step to the side with the right foot, taking a shorter step than the man.

La Salida (The Continuation of the Start)

For the man it is very important not to turn in Step 1 of the Salida. Turning can be avoided by ensuring that the woman does not take too wide a side step during the Retroceso. In Step 2, the man squeezes the woman between his hands, leading her to move away from him.

2

COUNT – QUICK

Man Walk forward with the left foot, turning the body slightly to the right.

Woman Walk backwards with the right foot, taking a slightly longer step and turning slightly to the right to ensure the shoulders remain parallel with the man's.

3

COUNT – QUICK

Man Close the right foot to the left foot and end standing on the right foot.

Woman Cross the left foot in front of the right foot – this need not be a tight cross. End standing on the left foot.

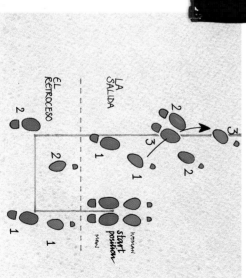

La Cunita (The Cradle)

This simple figure comprises a step followed by a crossing tap, producing a gentle rocking motion which gives the step its name. This figure is particularly useful because it can be repeated, allowing the couple to avoid others and to manoeuvre into a clear space on a crowded floor. From the end of the Salida, the couple gently rotate anticlockwise on the first step of the Cunita, so that this figure is danced almost side by side. There is then no danger of treading on your partner's feet.

1 COUNT – SLOW

Man Walk forward with the left foot.

Woman Walk backwards with the right foot.

2 COUNT – &

Man Standing on the left foot, tap the right foot across and behind the left foot.

Woman Standing on the right foot, tap the left foot across and in front of the right foot.

3 COUNT – SLOW

Man Walk backwards with the right foot.

Woman Walk forward with the left foot.

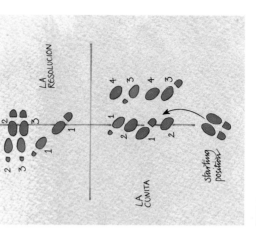

4 COUNT – &

Man Standing on the right foot, tap the left foot across and in front of the right foot.

Woman Standing on the left foot, tap the right foot across and behind the left foot.

La Resolucion (The Closing Finish)

In this movement, the man and woman "resolve" the previous moves in a conclusion which once again brings them together. This movement is also sometimes called "El Cierre". This group, like many of the best Tangos, should be allowed to resolve itself gently, as in a caress, and under no circumstances should the feet be stamped or closed strongly. While there is a variety of movements that can be used to end a figure, this one is the most common and most practical, as it leaves the dancers standing on the appropriate foot, ready to start the next group with the Retroceso.

1 COUNT – QUICK

Man Walk forward with the left foot, starting to turn to the left.

Woman Walk backwards with the right foot, starting to turn to the left.

2 COUNT – QUICK

Man Step to the side with the right foot, continuing the turn.

Woman Step to the side with the left foot, continuing the turn.

3 COUNT – SLOW

Man Close the left foot to the right foot.

Woman Close the right foot to the left foot.

Dance Tip

In Step 3, the foot is "peeled", heel first, from the floor and then placed gently, heel last, to close with straight legs. On slow counts, the ball of the foot usually touches the floor first.

Group Two

El Retroceso – La Salida – El Ocho – La Resolucion

In the second group, the Cunita is replaced by one of the most popular figures in Tango, the Ocho. "Ocho" is simply the Spanish word for "eight" and the figure is so-called because the woman seductively describes a figure of eight on the floor in front of the man. In Tango, there are many figures in which the movement alternates from the man to the woman and vice versa. The Ocho is one such figure, where the members of the couple are not dancing the opposite of their partner's steps. First dance the Retroceso and the Salida. The man now has his feet closed and is standing on the right foot. The woman has crossed the left foot in front of the right foot and is standing on the left foot.

El Ocho (The Eight)

1

COUNT – &

Woman Release the right foot and lift the lower right leg parallel to the floor, ensuring that the knees remain firmly together. Move the right foot to the right, causing the body to rotate anticlockwise (counterclockwise) as you swivel on the left foot.

2 ▶

COUNT – SLOW

Woman Still with the knees together, point the right foot forward between yourself and the man and outside the man's right side.

3 ▲

COUNT – &

Woman Transfer your weight forward to stand on the right foot, knees still together. Standing on the right foot, lift the left foot so that the lower left leg is parallel to the floor. Move the left leg to the left, causing the body to rotate clockwise as you swivel on the right foot.

The Man's Movements

While the woman dances the Ocho, the man can remain in position with the feet closed, relaxing the knees slightly to await the completion of the woman's move. Alternatively he can join in the movement, in which case the figure becomes the Doble Ocho.

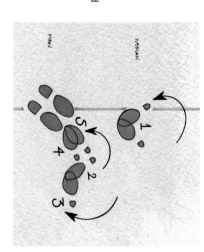

5

COUNT – &

Woman Transfer your weight forward to stand on the left foot, knees still together. Lift the right foot just clear of the floor and swivel on the left foot to face the man.

4

COUNT – SLOW

Woman Still with the knees together, point the left foot forward between yourself and the man.

El Doble Ocho (The Double Eight)

In this figure, the woman's steps remain the same. When the man feels the woman turning at the beginning of the Ocho, he joins her.

Music Suggestions

"Delusion" by Orchestra Tango Café (Sounds Sensational) is an excellent Tango with a clear beat and a steady tempo ideal for the first-time dancer.

5

COUNT – &

Man Hold the position while guiding the woman to face you.

4

COUNT – SLOW

Man Close the right foot to the left foot, legs straight.

3

COUNT – &

Man Complete the transfer of your weight back onto the left foot and straighten the leg in preparation for a close.

2

COUNT – SLOW

Man Point the left foot backwards, matching the woman's right foot and leg.

1

COUNT – &

Man With the feet still closed, swivel on the right foot to maintain the shoulders parallel to the woman's.

Conclude Group Two with the Resolucion.

Now try dancing Groups One and Two alternately following each other. If danced correctly, you will be dancing along the four sides of a square.

Leading

A lot of nonsense is often talked about leading. Leading, contrary to the popular image, is not a case of the man making the woman dance a particular figure or move. Rather, a good lead from the man merely makes clear his intention to the woman, who then follows. The Tango dancer Juan Carlos Copes once remarked about leading, "The man should always remember that he is dancing with a lady". This is sound advice.

Keeping Parallel Shoulders

The first ingredient of a good lead is for the man to dance his own moves clearly and confidently. Clarity from the man is all-important, as it enables the woman to detect the speed, direction and feel of a figure early enough to respond appropriately.

The woman will generally be aware of where and how the man is moving by following the alignment of his shoulders and trying to maintain a parallel position between her shoulders and his. Try dancing Groups One, Two and Three without holding your partner, using only the maintenance of parallel shoulders as a guide.

A Steady Framework

The man's arms and upper body make a firm frame in which the woman is gently held. The man must not allow his arms to move independently of his upper body, as this destroys the frame. He must never be seen to "steer" the woman with his arms. Leads are a subtle but clear communication between the dancers and should not be visible to others.

The woman should not try to anticipate the man's intentions but should wait to accept and follow the man's lead.

In some specific figures, the man will squeeze the woman firmly between his hands to produce, for example, a turn, as in the Parada. Specific leads such as these are dealt with in the sections on the particular figures in which they are used.

As we explore Tango Argentino, there is always something new and unexpected. Uniquely in Tango, some leads may be given with the foot or leg. These are called Sacadas.

The upper body and arms of the man provide a "frame" with which to lead the woman.

Orientation

It is important, especially in the early stages of learning to Tango, that you try to adhere to the given orientation or "alignment" of the figures, as distortions look as well as feel awkward. In Step 2 of the Retroceso, the man steps to the side with no turn. The position of his left foot now determines the line of travel of the remainder of the group.

The woman follows the alignment of the man's shoulders as a lead.

Group Three

El Retroceso – Modified Salida – El Ocho Abierto – La Resolucion

Having had some practice at dancing the Ocho, you can now try a more expressive version, the Ocho Abierto, or the "open eight".

Begin this group with the Retroceso, then dance a modified Salida. Note the change of timing as the Salida is modified.

Modified Salida

1
COUNT – QUICK

Man Walk forward with the right foot between yourself and the woman.

Woman Walk backwards with the left foot.

2
COUNT – QUICK

Man Walk forward with the left foot but turn your body one-eighth of a turn to the right.

Woman Walk backwards with the right foot keeping parallel shoulders with the man.

3
COUNT – SLOW

Man Hold the position with the right foot behind. Flex the left knee and swivel to the left on the left foot, maintaining parallel shoulders with the woman. Do not extend either arm, as the woman goes on to dance the Ocho.

Woman Walk forward with the left foot, crossing past the right foot onto the man's line.

El Ocho Abierto (The Open Eight)

1
COUNT – &

Man Hold the position. Swivel on the left foot to maintain parallel shoulders.

2
COUNT – SLOW

Man Hold the position. Swivel on the left foot to maintain parallel shoulders.

3
COUNT – &

Man Hold the position. Straighten the left leg.

4
COUNT – SLOW

Man Close the right foot to the left foot with straight legs.

1–5
COUNTS – &, SLOW, &, SLOW, &

Woman Dance an Ocho in front of the man.

5
COUNT – &

Man Hold the position, while guiding the woman to face you.

Conclude Group Three with the Resolucion.

To help clarify exactly when the man closes, it is helpful to count the man's steps, starting at the beginning of the group. The group has ten steps and the man will close on Step 7.

Styles of Tango

While it is sometimes said that there are as many styles of Tango as there are bars in Buenos Aires, in reality there are only three predominant styles.

Show Tango

Perhaps the style most widely seen by the general public is show Tango, which is the breathtaking version seen in the series of Broadway and West End Tango productions of recent years. This is a stylized stage variant and it is the remaining two styles which are the most commonly seen in Buenos Aires and in the many Tango clubs, schools, salons and *milongas* around the world. These come under the broad heading of the "Tango de salon" and it is in this style that the real magic of Tango can be found.

Tango de Salon

In this style, the movements are built up moving along a line such as those in Groups One, Two and Three. It can also be danced, by not turning the Resolucion, to track anticlockwise (counterclockwise) around a medium to large floor such as a ballroom. This "Salon Tango" is a slightly more formal style of Tango than the Tango Orillero.

Tango Orillero

This is a style more suited to smaller floors such as those of Tango cafés and bars. In this type of Tango, the man and woman weave intricate figures around each other while taking up very little space. This style is definitely more intimate.

Group Four

El Retroceso con la Ronda – La Revolucion – El Doble Ocho – La Resolucion – Los Tres Ochos

The next new figure to be introduced is the Revolucion, which requires very little space and in which the man and woman move around each other in intimate exploration. As before, the group also includes some moves with which you are already familiar. This move is typical of the Orillero style.

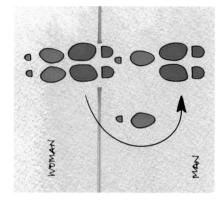

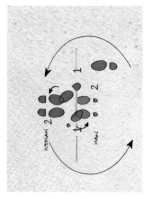

Summary of the Turn
El Retroceso con la Ronda – *no turn*
La Revolucion – *half turn (or 180°) anticlockwise (counterclockwise)*
El Doble Ocho – *quarter turn (or 90°) anticlockwise*
La Resolucion – *quarter turn (or 90°) anticlockwise*
By the end of the group, you will have made one complete turn.

Style Tip
It is not necessary and not good style to power the turn in Step 2.

Continue to turn a further quarter turn anticlockwise (counterclockwise), and complete the group by dancing the Doble Ocho and the Resolucion described earlier or Los Tres Ochos.

El Retroceso con la Ronda (The Reverse Start with the Circle)

1
COUNTS – SLOW, SLOW
Man Walk backwards with the right foot with the knee flexed, leaving the left foot in place.

1-2
COUNT – SLOW, SLOW
Woman Dance the Retroceso as usual.

2
COUNT – SLOW
Man Circle the left foot anticlockwise (counterclockwise) to close to the right foot, without transferring your weight onto the left foot. As this is part of a continuing movement, the knees remain flexed.

La Revolucion (The Full Turn)

1
COUNT – SLOW
Man Extend the left foot forward past the woman's left side and point it at the woman's back foot.

Woman Extend the left foot forward past the man's left side and point it at the man's back foot.

2
COUNT – SLOW
Man Transfer your weight forward onto the left foot, swivelling to face the woman and closing the right foot to the left foot, legs straight. End standing on the right foot.

Woman Transfer your weight forward onto the left foot, swivelling to face the man and closing the right foot to the left foot, legs straight, without transferring your weight onto the right foot. End standing on the left foot.

Los Tres Ochos (Three Eights)

This figure comprises three Doble Ochos. Dance the Retroceso con la Ronda and the Revolucion.

The Woman's Movements

Dance three Doble Ochos as normal, but turning a little more on the left foot to match the man. Make the forward steps with the right foot a little shorter and the forward steps with the left foot a little longer, to finish facing the man at the conclusion of each Ocho.

COUNT – &

1

Man Continue to make a further quarter turn (or 90°) anticlockwise (counterclockwise) by swivelling to the left on the right foot.

COUNT – SLOW

2

Man With your shoulders parallel to the woman's, point the left foot straight back, keeping your weight on the right foot.

COUNT – &

3

Man Transfer your weight back onto the left foot.

Style Tip

The man should ensure that he uses his right forearm to keep the woman dancing the Ochos in front of him and not under his right arm.

COUNT – &

5

Man Hold the position, guiding the woman to face you.

Repeat moves 1–4 twice more, curving very gently to the left. No more than a half turn should be made by the man during this figure.

COUNT – SLOW

4

Man Close the right foot to the left foot. Straighten the legs and end standing on the right foot.

Complete this variation of Group Four with the Resolucion.

Cortes

We have already touched on the drama of the Tango as the dancers explore their relationship through the dance. Each in turn may take the lead and many moves can be improvised, although improvisations must maintain the character of the Tango. It is during these improvisations that a conflict of intention may arise. In these circumstances, the dance may come to a sudden halt while the conflict is resolved. Such a halt, though not a figure in itself, is called a "Corte". To an onlooker, this often serves to heighten the suspense before the drama moves on. In reality, the man must now indicate and clarify his intentions to the woman – or vice versa. There are many ways of doing this within the character of the dance and many elaborate devices have been invented over the years.

▶ The Shoeshine

Let us suppose that the couple has danced the Retroceso, when suddenly the man feels that the woman is in doubt as to which foot she is to use in the next move. The couple stop – a Corte. The man now indicates to the woman which foot he has free and, in so doing, he shows her which foot she must use next. In the Shoeshine, the man remains on his left foot with the knee slightly flexed and rubs his right foot slowly up and down the calf of his left leg, as if polishing his shoe. There is no timing for this gesture. Suffice it to say that the couple resume the dance in time with the music.

▶ La Puntada del Pie (The Foot Tap)

In a similar gesture to the Shoeshine, the free foot can be tapped repeatedly against the floor. The Puntada may also be performed by the woman while the man is dancing the Shoeshine, just to show her irritation at being kept waiting!

Music Suggestion

"El Amanecer" by Carlos di Sarli (MH/Sicamericana Corp). Meaning "the dawn", legend has it that the composer, Roberto Firpo, was inspired to write this magical Tango while walking home after performing at an all-night party. Listen to the violins as they recreate the dawn chorus.

La Levantada

A very useful corte for the woman is the Levantada. When the couple comes to a standstill with the feet apart, the woman may perform a Levantada by lifting the free foot so that the knees are together and the lower leg is parallel with the floor. She then gently swings the free foot from side to side in an expectant gesture.

Amague

A different type of embellishment is an Amague, where a threatening gesture is made. An Amague is also sometimes danced to express frustration or to warn of a following figure which may be fast, sharp and dramatic. A stamp or harsh tap called a "frappé" executed immediately before the next dramatic movement is a good example of an Amague. While less experienced dancers may enjoy interspersing their dancing with a peppering of Amagues, the effect is lost if the following figure does not live up to its dramatic announcement. Good Tango dancers therefore use this type of embellishment sparingly and only in the proper context of announcing the severe or powerful nature of the following move.

Group Five

El Retroceso – La Parada – El Sandwich – El Ocho – La Resolucion – La Llevada

Another classic Tango figure is introduced here. The Parada is a super figure, allowing even inexperienced dancers to feel the magic of Tango in the Orillero style. Again, this group starts with the Retroceso. The man has ended standing on his left foot and the woman on her right. To dance the next figure, the woman's right foot should be roughly opposite a point halfway between the man's feet.

La Parada (The Stop)

In this figure, the man "stops" the woman with a combination of his right hand and confirmatory contact of his right foot with her left foot.

1
COUNT – SLOW

Man Hold the position. Lead the woman by squeezing her with your right hand towards your left hand. Keep the left hand and arm still and firm and do not rotate the body. Apply base of hand pressure with the right hand to turn the woman for the Parada.

Woman Facing square to the man, cross the left foot loosely behind the right foot to a point opposite the man's left foot to aid balance. End standing on the left foot.

2
COUNT – SLOW

Man Leading the woman back across yourself a quarter turn (or 90°) towards the right, slide the right foot forward in a curve. Keep the foot in contact with the floor but without weight and, with the inside edge of the ball of the right foot, make contact with the outside edge of the ball of the woman's left foot. End with the knees together, left knee flexed and right leg straight.

Woman Swivel a quarter turn (or 90°) to the right on the left foot and step backwards onto the right foot. Flex the right knee with the left leg held forward, knees together.

El Sandwich

This figure is also known as "La Mordita" ("the bite"). During the move, the woman's left foot is sandwiched between the man's feet.

1
COUNT – SLOW

Man Transfer your weight forward onto the right foot and close the left foot to the right foot, sandwiching the woman's left foot. End facing the woman with legs straight.

Woman Hold the Parada position.

2
COUNT – SLOW

Man Swivel a quarter turn (or 90°) to the right on the left foot and step backwards onto the right foot. Flex the right knee with the left leg held straight forward, knees together.

Woman Transfer your weight forward onto the left foot.

Group Six

El Retroceso – La Sentada – El Ocho – La Resolucion

The Sentada is another popular and classic figure in Tango Argentino. The woman moves to a position on the man's left side which suggests that she is sitting on his knee, hence the name Sentada, or "chair".

Start with the by now familiar Retroceso but, to lead the Sentada, the man takes a slightly wider step and moves the left foot a little forward in Step 3. The left knee flexes, while the right leg remains straight.

La Sentada (The Chair)

The lead in the Sentada is different from the lead in the Parada. In the Parada, the couple remains facing in Step 3 and the man squeezes the woman between his hands. In the Sentada, the man rotates his frame, causing the woman to turn.

1 COUNT – SLOW

Man Hold the feet in position. Lead the woman to turn by rotating the frame anticlockwise (counterclockwise).

Woman Standing on the right foot, swivel a quarter turn (or 90°) to the left. Step back underneath the body with the left foot and relax the left knee.

3 COUNT – SLOW

Man Hold the position. Lead the woman to turn by rotating the frame clockwise.

Woman Lower the right foot to the floor, making a small forward step.

Music Suggestion

"A Media Luz" by Olivia Molina (Indoamerica). This gentle yet passionate Tango is captured perfectly in this excellent vocal version. For a non-vocal version try Gran Orquesta Tipica (Orfeon).

2 COUNT – &

Man Hold the position.

Woman Continue turning slightly on the left foot and relax down to contact the man's left knee as if to sit, but without weight. Lift the right foot to contact the outside of your left knee, toes pointing to the floor.

4 COUNT – &

Man Holding the feet in position, straighten the left leg.

4–6 COUNT – &, SLOW, &

Woman Continue by dancing an Ocho, ending on the left foot and facing the man.

5 COUNT – SLOW

Man Close the right foot to the left foot with legs straight. End standing on the right foot.

6 COUNT – &

Man Hold the position, while guiding the woman to face you.

Continue with the Resolucion or the Doble Ocho or Tres Ochos, as danced following the Revolucion in Group Four.

Merengue

The Merengue (pronounced me-rren-gay) has now established itself as one of the most popular Latin American dances. It comes from the Dominican Republic in the Caribbean, which has become a favourite holiday destination in recent years. The mood of the Merengue reflects that holiday atmosphere and, since the rhythm and steps could not be simpler, demand for it in Latin clubs and dance schools continues to grow. The music of the Merengue is lively and is popular even with people who do not dance it. One of the artists responsible for the best Merengue music is Juan Luis Guerra and his band 4.40. His hits "La Bilirrubina" and "El Costo de la Vida" have quickly become Merengue standards.

The Merengue beat is a strong one-two rhythm, which is interpreted as two dance steps using the characteristic pumping action of the Merengue. There are no deviations from this simple rhythm so the steps themselves are very easy – an advantage which has resulted in many people being able to get up and just dance the Merengue without any formal tuition. If you can walk, you can Merengue. The dance does not progress around the floor but remains very much on the spot, with the man leading his partner to dance a variety of very gentle, slow turning moves, usually over eight steps. More expert dancers may spice up their Merengue by dancing the moves over just four steps. It is how these turns are put together plus the fabulous music that provide much of the enjoyment of Merengue.

Merengue Action

Most steps use the characteristic Merengue action. On the first step, the foot is placed in position with pressure onto the floor through the inside edge of the ball of the foot, the body weight is not transferred onto the foot. On the second step, the body weight is transferred onto the foot that has just been placed while releasing the heel of the other foot from the floor, allowing the knee of that leg to move across the knee of the standing leg. The Merengue pumping action should not be exaggerated. Merengue steps are usually danced with the feet a little apart.

The lively Merengue is a favourite all over the world and the simplicity of the basic steps makes it easy to learn.

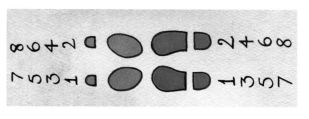

The Merengue Basic can be repeated and gradually rotated in either direction over the eight counts.

Basic Merengue

The basic one-two rhythm of Merengue music makes the steps very simple – in a way, rather like marking time. You will find yourself enjoying the infectious Merengue beat in no time. Start in a close contact hold with the man standing on the right foot and the woman on the left foot. Importantly, the Merengue Action is used.

1

COUNT – SLOW

Man Step in place with the left foot.

Woman Step in place with the right foot.

2

COUNT – SLOW

Man Step in place with the right foot.

Woman Step in place with the left foot.

3–8

Man & Woman Repeat Steps 1–2 up to the count of eight.

Style Tip

As you dance the Merengue, the look and feel of your dancing will be considerably enhanced by keeping the upper part of your body as still as possible and focusing all the Merengue Action into the legs, which will result in a seductively attractive hip movement.

Merengue Side Steps

You can dance the Merengue Side Steps in either a close contact hold or a double hand hold. This figure moves first to the man's left and then to his right. To start, the man is standing on the right foot and the woman on the left foot. Use the Merengue Action to give these simple steps extra style.

1
COUNT – SLOW
Man Move sideways, a small step, onto the left foot.

Woman Move sideways, a small step, onto the right foot.

2▶
COUNT – SLOW
Man Close the right foot to the left foot.

Woman Close the left foot to the right foot.

3—4
COUNT – SLOW, SLOW
Man & Woman
Repeat Steps 1–2.

5—8
COUNTS – SLOW, SLOW, SLOW, SLOW
Man Step in place with the left foot. Move sideways, a small step, onto the right foot. Close the left foot to the right foot. Move sideways, a small step, onto the right foot.

Woman Step in place with the right foot. Move sideways, a small step, onto the left foot. Close the right foot to the left foot. Move sideways, a small step, onto the left foot.

Right: When the party really gets going, a dancer may perform the Melt-Down while leaning back like a Limbo dancer and "shimmying".

Merengue Melt-Down

The Merengue Melt-Down is not so much a figure in itself as an embellishment of the Basic Merengue.

Left: To dance this fun move, flex your knees and sink down to an almost sitting position before rising again to normal height as you dance the Basic Merengue. During the Melt-Down, the couple may rotate the Basic Merengue.

Separation to Double Hand Hold

To move into this hold, the man simply eases the woman away from him, allowing his right hand to slide down her left arm to take up the double hand hold. During the "Separation", carry on dancing the Basic Merengue, gradually moving backwards away from each other as you change hold. The Separation should last the usual eight counts.

Copy-Cat Turn

In this typical Merengue move, the man leads the woman to dance a turn underneath their joined hands, then the man copies the woman. Start in a double hand hold. As usual, the man is standing on the right foot and the woman on the left foot. Continue dancing the Basic Merengue steps as you turn. During Steps 1–8, the man remains facing in the same direction, while the woman turns. During Steps 9–16, the woman remains facing in the same direction, while the man turns.

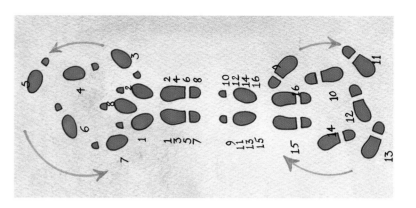

Leading Turns

Note that the lead for the turn initially moves in the opposite direction to the turn, suggesting that the man leads the woman by creating some turning momentum through his arms and swinging her into the turn. Having understood this convention, it is not then necessary to use any forceful swinging action in the arms or to pull the woman in any way.

1–2

Man Bring your hands together and swing them down and over to your left as an indication to the woman that she is about to be turned.

Woman The man will bring your hands together and swing them to your right. This is your lead that he is about to turn you to the left.

3–8

Man Continue to dance the Basic Merengue steps facing the woman. Circle your hands, still together, anticlockwise (counterclockwise) above head height, returning them to waist height by count 8. Your hands are now crossed.

3–8

Woman Continue to dance the Basic Merengue steps, turning anticlockwise to end facing the man on count 8.

9–15

Man Continue to dance the Basic Merengue steps. Turn clockwise, circling your joined hands, still together, above head height and down again to waist height.

Woman Continue to dance the Basic Merengue steps facing the man, allowing him to turn in front of you.

16

Man End facing the woman.

Woman End with your hands at waist height.

You can now dance the Copy-Cat Turn again or continue into any other Merengue move. A popular alternative ending to the Copy-Cat Turn is La Yunta.

La Yunta

La Yunta, or "the Yoke", is a slick, suave and seductive conclusion to the Copy-Cat Turn. To create the best effect, dance the complete Copy-Cat Turn, then repeat Steps 1–8, but this time, leave the joined hands above the woman's head. The woman's arms now resemble a yoke, hence the name of this impressive move.

1-8

Man & Woman The man releases hold with his right hand, and using only his left hand, he moves the woman's still joined hands over his own head and places them on the back of his neck, resuming close contact.

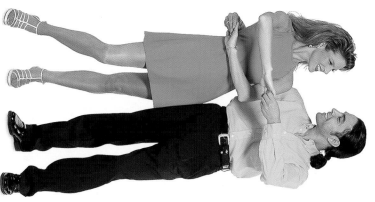

9-16

Man & Woman Over these eight counts, the man takes the woman's right hand in his left hand and...

...the couple gradually resume a close contact hold.

You can return to your programme with any of the basic Merengue moves, but a particularly good one to dance here is Steps 1–3 of La Cucaracha (described in the Mambo section of the book) with a Melt-Down action, before continuing with Steps 4–8 of the Basic Merengue.

Turns

Merengue is all to do with the action and turns, so let's have a look at some more of the standard Merengue turns. As usual, in the following turns, the man starts with the left foot and the woman with the right foot. The turns can be danced over four or eight counts, depending on how they fit in with other moves.

Half Turn to the Left

In the Half Turn to the Left, the man raises his left hand, while keeping his right hand at waist height. The man then leads the woman to turn by moving his left hand to the right. By Step 8, the woman will have turned left into the man's right arm on his right side. To exit, simply reverse the process to a further eight counts.

Half Turn to the Right

In the Half Turn to the Right, the man raises his right hand, while keeping his left hand at waist height. The man then leads the woman to turn by moving his right hand to the left. By Step 8, the woman will have turned right into the man's left arm on his left side. To exit, reverse the process to a further eight counts.

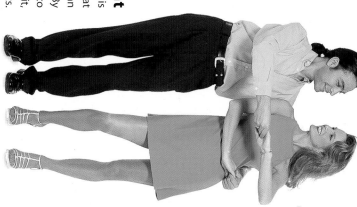

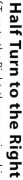

Combining the Turns

Half Turn to the Left with Armlock Turn to the Right

Dance the Half Turn to the Left over eight steps, then exit over four, ensuring that the woman is facing the man by the end of Step 12. His left hand is still raised and his right hand is still at waist height. The man now leads the Armlock Turn to the Right over four steps to finish by Step 16. Exit as normal.

Half Turn to the Right with Armlock Turn to the Left

Dance the Half Turn to the Right over eight steps, then exit over four, ensuring that the woman is facing the man by the end of Step 12. His right hand is still raised and his left hand is still at waist height. The man now leads the Armlock Turn to the Left over four steps to finish by Step 16. Exit as normal.

Armlock Turn to the Left

In the Armlock Turn to the Left, the man raises his right hand, while keeping his left hand at waist height and pressing the woman's right hand away from him. The man leads the woman to turn to the left by rotating his right hand. During the move, the man may turn up to a quarter turn (90°) to the right while the woman makes a half turn (180°) to the left. To exit, reverse the process.

Armlock Turn to the Right

In the Armlock Turn to the Right, the man raises his left hand, while keeping his right hand at waist height and pressing the woman's left hand away from him. The man leads the woman to turn to the right by rotating his left hand. During the move, the man may turn up to a quarter turn (90°) to the left while the woman turns a half turn (180°) to the right. To exit, reverse the process.

El Nudo

Not the "Nude" but the "Knot", this title accurately describes the fun you might have as you learn to solve the challenge of getting into and out of this more advanced move. To dance El Nudo, start in a double hand hold with the man standing on the right foot and the woman on the left foot.

1–8

Man & Woman Dance the Armlock Turn to the Right over eight steps, this time with the man turning a half turn (180°) on the spot to the right, lifting his right hand over his head to end back to back with the woman on his left.

9–12

Man & Woman Move to the left to end with each partner on the right of the other, still back to back.

13–16

Man & Woman Reverse Steps 9–12 by moving to the right, still back to back. The man raises his left arm over the woman's head by Step 16.

17–20

Man & Woman The man now leads the woman towards him and behind his back as he takes his left hand over his head and gradually turns on the spot to the right to face the woman.

21–28

Man & Woman By keeping his left hand raised, the man leads the woman into a Half Turn to the Right on the spot over four steps. Releasing hold with the right hand, the man now turns the woman on the spot underneath his left hand, before resuming a double hand hold.

Steps 25–28 can be danced without resuming double hand hold and then repeated before finally taking up the double hand hold, or close contact hold if you prefer.

La Silla Giratoria

La Silla Giratoria ("the Swivel Chair") introduces a new feel to your Merengue and is an excellent figure to enjoy when you are dancing on a crowded floor. The woman dances a series of swivels around the man as the move rotates steadily anticlockwise. Start in close contact hold with the man standing on the right foot and the woman on the left foot. Don't forget to use the Merengue Action throughout the move.

1
COUNT – SLOW

Man Step in place with the left foot.

Woman Step in place with the right foot.

2
COUNT – SLOW

Man Move sideways onto the right foot, turning a little to the left to lead the woman to swivel to her right.

Woman On the right foot, swivel to the right to end at a right angle to the man, and place the left foot forward, a small step.

3
COUNT – SLOW

Man Close the left foot to the right foot, leading the woman to face you.

Woman Transfer your body weight onto the left foot and swivel to the left to face the man, placing the right foot slightly forward.

4
COUNT – SLOW

Man Move sideways onto the right foot, turning a little to the left to lead the woman to swivel to her right.

Woman On the right foot, swivel to the right to end at a right angle to the man, and place the left foot forward, a small step.

5–7
COUNT – SLOW, SLOW, SLOW

Man & Woman Repeat Steps 1–3.

8
COUNT – SLOW

Man Step in place with the right foot.

Woman Transfer your body weight onto the left foot and end facing the man.

Style Tip
For the woman, the turn to face the man will be a little sharper than the turn away from him. Some women choose to dance the step with the left foot with a short kicking action. Try it when you feel comfortable with the move.

Salsa

SALSA

When in 1928 Ignacio Piñeiro used the phrase "Echale Salsita !" as the title of a new piece of music with lyrics, he could not have known the impact that that commonplace expression would have half a century later. Meaning "spice it up", the phrase was later simplified to "Salsa". Various singers and musicians included references to Salsa in their music and by the mid-1960s the Venezuelan radio presenter, Danilo Phidias Escalona, used the word in the title of his programme. It was not until the early 1970s that the phrase was recoined as a generic term for a diverse mixture of Latino music styles and rhythms previously known as "son"– guaracha danzón, cha cha cha, pachanga, rumba, mambo etc. This simple word suddenly made Latin music more marketable and demand for it took off. With the music, the dance inevitably followed.

The Latin countries of the Caribbean – Cuba, Puerto Rico, Haiti, the Dominican Republic and those of Central and South America – Mexico, Venezuela, and Colombia – share a common Latin culture and a fierce Latin pride. However, the influence and contribution of Afro-Caribbean music to Salsa is unmistakable. While many of the original styles of music were products of the Cuban countryside, economic necessity at various points in Cuba's history prompted migration to the cities, bringing the musical culture of the country into the towns. Like the Tango of Argentina, Salsa and its predecessors became a reflection of life in the barrios or poorer districts of town. Everyone could identify with it, and, in it, find an expression of their own, a reflection of their life, or an opportunity to forget their mundane preoccupations and lose themselves in the song, the rhythm and the dance.

Cuba's war of independence from 1868–78 against Spanish colonial rule virtually destroyed the important sugar industry and was followed in 1868 by the subsequent abolition of slavery. Afro-Cubans, having seen the destruction of their economic base, found their way into towns to seek ways to eke out a living. With them came the *Guajira*. At first the Guajira was considered vulgar, but it eventually gained acceptance and took its place in the unfolding story of Salsa.

Then came Son, a new style of Afro-Caribbean music which was to have a profound effect on the direction of all future Cuban music development. Son managed to combine the musical traditions of both Afro-Cuban and Latin-Cuban music in a new form which satisfied the people and which gained overwhelming popularity around the time of the First World War. The authorities, however, were not so happy about the lyrical themes which dwelt upon the privations of the ordinary people, and by 1917 Son was prohibited. But the popularity of the music and dance ensured their survival, and in 1920 the prohibition was revoked, with even the upper classes now captivated by its rhythm. Son continued to thrive through the next two decades, receiving even greater impetus after the Second World War with the advent of television. By this time though, other influences were beginning to bear on the original style of Son. During the 1930s, Jazz started to influence the purity of traditional Cuban music, and after the war, Jazz bands played Cuban music more in their own style than that of the Cubans. Perez Prado, originally a Cuban, but then based in Mexico, managed to combine both the flavour of Cuba with the tradition of Jazz. The *danzón*, another Cuban dance, absorbed other rhythmic influences and its music, in the hands of Perez Prado, evolved into what we now call Mambo. In 1948, a new composition by Enrique Jorrin called *Engañadora*, suggested a new rhythm which was immediately seized upon by the dancers and the Cha Cha Cha was born. When it was finally recorded and distributed in the early 1950s, its catchy rhythm assured its enduring popularity. In 1959, the revolutionary troops of Fidel Castro entered Havana. An era came to an end, and while many Cuban singers, musicians and composers chose to stay on, many also left, closing one chapter in Cuba and opening another in New York.

In New York, the music of Cuba became inextricably mixed with the musical variations of Puerto Rico and American Jazz. New styles of music were produced by new types of groups, bands and orchestras. Trombones found a place alongside trumpets, while traditional Caribbean instruments were retained in the rhythm sections, giving a wild new dimension to the development of Salsa. Then, in 1962, with the release of "Love Me Do", The Beatles changed everything. They became the new sensation of the era and as their fans grew, Latin music fell into decline. By the early 1970s, Fania records needed to promote their artists and repertoire. To do this they needed a name with which their product could be easily recognized, and so Salsa was born. Since those days, however, the USA has not had the monopoly on Salsa nor on new innovations. Puerto Rico continues to be a major source of Salsa music, and the influence from Colombia has also been increasingly marked.

The popularity of today's vibrant Salsa scene shows no sign of waning.

The Musical Count

Salsa music generally has a rhythm of four equal beats in one musical bar. This is interpreted in the dance by three steps and a tap, corresponding to the four musical beats. However, as you progress from the more basic Salsa moves, the rhythm of four beats may be interpreted in the dance by only three steps per musical bar. In this case, the dancers will use a count of "quick, quick, slow". A "quick" equals one beat of music, while a "slow" equals two beats. This sounds complicated, especially to a beginner, but if you listen to the rhythm, you will quickly become accustomed to it and dancing in time will become second nature.

Occasionally you may see Salsa dancers dancing the first step of each movement on beat two, which means that the tap will have occurred on count one. This does not necessarily mean that they are dancing out of time with the music. Salsa is a distillation of a variety of music and dance styles. In some types of music, the second beat is accentuated and some dancers like to respond to this rhythmic accent. Because of the diversity of Salsa music, it is not possible to define a standard beat, one or two, on which the dance should start and, in any event, this is really more of a technical issue than one which would concern the beginner or the club dancer who is just out for a great time. It is much more important to get a feel for the music and then get out onto the floor and enjoy it.

Left: In 1950s New York, trumpets were included in Salsa bands together with traditional Caribbean instruments.

Left and above: Percussion instruments such as the bongos and maracas give Salsa music its rhythm.

The Moves

Because Salsa moves have often not been invented by professional dancers, they rarely have names. For the purposes of this book, descriptive titles for the figures have been invented or existing names for figures have been borrowed from other dances or styles. So do not be surprised if, in your own Salsa club, the dancers have no idea what you

mean if you use names given in this book. On the other hand, if they do, it is probably because they have read the book, too.

The descriptions of the figures are not intended to indicate the only style used but are merely a basis for understanding the moves of a style seen in many of the Salsa clubs.

Salsa style is greatly enhanced by practising the leg action until it feels completely natural. The same holds true for moves such as the Figure of Eight with Double Hand Hold.

The Dance

It is not clear how Salsa moves evolved or exactly where they came from. Salsa, as a dance, mirrors Salsa as a musical form. It is a distillation of many similar dances and rhythms. Inevitably, some moves were taken from traditional dances, some were adapted from other dance styles and some were invented. New moves are appearing all the time. The style of the dance is Afro-Caribbean, which gives a relaxed feel to the moves. The rhythm is a standard four beat repetition interpreted by the dancers changing weight on three counts, and either tapping on the fourth, or incorporating the fourth beat into the third to make a third slow count. The moves themselves are simple enough but, as is always the case in dancing, it's not what you do, it's the way that you do it. In Salsa, the upper body is held still and upright throughout the dance, while the hips swing and sway rhythmically as a result of the leg action used. Note that the hip movement is a by-product of a good leg action, rather than an action in itself.

1

The dancers step to the right or left on the first count. Their movements mirror one another.

2

The weight shifts onto the opposite foot...

3

...and back to the first.

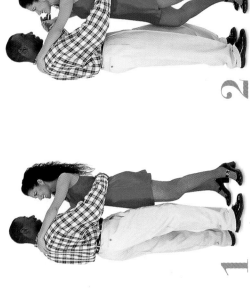

4

The last step is a tap.

Holds

There are two general types of hold in Salsa, one in which the couple are in close contact and the other in which the couple are dancing apart or in an open position.

Close Contact Hold

The man holds the woman around the waist with the right hand. The man's right hand need not close against her back. The woman places her left hand on the man's upper right arm, shoulder, back or neck. Her right hand is in the man's left, at eye level. The woman stands slightly to the right, so his left foot is outside her right foot and his right foot is between her feet.

Open Hold

This hold varies. The couple stand an arm's length apart. The woman's arms are toned, so when the man leads through the arm she feels it. They may hold hands, left to right, right to left, or take a double hold. In Cuban style, the man may hold the woman's wrist; in Colombian, double holds are preferred. If only one hand is used, the free arm should be flexed and held out to the side.

Basic Salsa Move

Take up a close contact hold. The man is standing with his weight on the right foot and the woman with her weight on the left foot. It is customary for the man to initiate the dance by dancing a left foot tap on count four. Keep the steps small and under the body; the objective is not to move around the floor in this move.

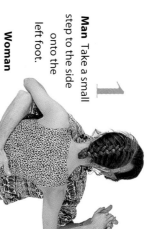

1

Man Take a small step to the side onto the left foot.

Woman Take a small step to the side onto the right foot.

2▼

Man Move the right foot sideways towards the left foot (it is not necessary to close).

Woman Move the left foot sideways towards the right foot (it is not necessary to close).

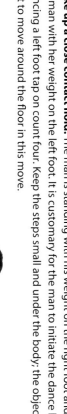

3

Man Take a small step to the side onto the left foot.

Woman Take a small step to the side onto the right foot.

4

Man Tap the floor with the inside edge of the ball of the right foot.

Woman Tap the floor with the inside edge of the ball of the left foot.

5

Man Take a small step to the side onto the right foot.

Woman Take a small step to the side onto the left foot.

6

Man Move the left foot sideways towards the right foot (it is not necessary to close).

Woman Move the right foot sideways towards the left foot (it is not necessary to close).

7

Man Take a small step to the side onto the right foot.

Woman Take a small step to the side onto the left foot.

8▼

Man Tap the floor with the inside edge of the ball of the left foot.

Woman Tap the floor with the inside edge of the ball of the right foot.

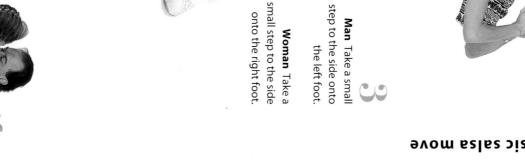

Music Suggestion

"Yamulemao" by Joe Arroyo (World Circuit) is a popular Salsa with a steady and relaxed tempo — ideal for practising the Basic Salsa Moves.

Getting the Salsa Feeling

The Salsa feel is given to the basic movement by a combination of keeping the upper body perfectly still and concentrating the energy into the waist and legs. The leg action is all-important because it is this which gives the characteristic hip movement of the dance. However, this hip movement is a by-product of the correct leg action and is not an independent movement.

The Leg Action

Let's look at the essential leg action using Steps 1–4 of the man's Basic Salsa Move. This is the same as Steps 5–8 for the woman. The same action is then repeated on the remaining steps of the move, which go in the opposite direction.

1
Take a small step to the side onto the left foot. Do not lift the foot far from the floor but lightly skim it. Flex the left knee, so that only the inside edge of the ball of the left foot is in contact with the floor. Keep the right knee fairly straight but not rigid. Imagine that, as you lower your weight onto the left foot, you are encountering some resistance and are having to push the foot down onto the floor. As you transfer your weight onto the left foot, the left knee becomes straighter, while the right knee flexes slightly.

2
Move the right foot sideways towards the left foot. The right knee is already flexed. Keep it flexed and move the right foot closer to the left without closing. Let the inside edge of the ball of the right foot rest on the floor. Imagine some resistance as you push down onto the right foot. As you transfer your weight onto the right foot, the right knee becomes straighter, and the left flexes.

3
Repeat Step 1.

4
Tap the floor with the inside edge of the ball of the right foot. The right knee is already flexed.

Style Tip

Generally, the rule is that when the body weight is moved onto the foot in a Basic Action, the same knee will straighten a little and the other knee will flex. When transferring body weight onto a foot, the body weight is never allowed to "drop" into place. The lowering is controlled through the knee and ankle to produce a feeling of "pumping" the legs. A good Basic Action is vital to Salsa, but it can be a little tricky to begin with. Practice not only makes perfect, it makes it possible, so practise until it becomes second nature. You can do this on your own without a partner but, with or without a partner, be sure to keep the upper body still. When practising alone, use your arms with your hands at waist height.

Eliminating the Tap

In a number of moves, particularly when the body weight is moving forward or backwards, it is desirable to eliminate the tap. When this occurs, the third step of the musical bar becomes a "slow" count. However, to maintain the Salsa Action, the foot is placed in position on the third count but the transfer of body weight onto the foot is delayed until the fourth count. This illustrates the importance of the tap occurring on count 4 rather than on count 1 as sometimes proposed. Count 4 is added to count 3 to become a "slow". If the tap were to occur on count 1 and count 1 were to join count 4 to become the "slow", then it would go over the bar of music and the dancer would be "out of rhythm".

Backwards Salsa Basic

This move is used to initiate many other figures. The man has just tapped the left foot and the woman her right at the end of the last move. The man stands on the right foot and the woman on the left. To start this move, the man gently pushes the woman away into an open position.

1

Man Move the left foot back, leaving the right foot in place, releasing the heel of the right foot and flexing the right knee. The left leg straightens as the body weight moves over the foot.

Woman Move the right foot back, leaving the left foot in place, releasing the heel of the left foot and flexing the left knee. The right leg straightens as the body weight moves over the foot.

2

Man Transfer your body weight forward onto the right foot, pressing the body weight onto the right foot. The right leg straightens as the body weight moves over the foot.

Woman Transfer your body weight forward onto the left foot, pressing the body weight onto the left foot. The left leg straightens as the body weight moves over the foot.

▲5

Man Move the right foot back, leaving the left foot in place, releasing the heel of the left foot and flexing the left knee. Straighten your right knee as you transfer your weight.

Woman Move the left foot back, leaving the right foot in place, releasing the heel of the right foot and flexing the right knee. Straighten your left knee as you transfer your weight.

3

Man Close the left foot to the right foot using the Salsa Action.

Woman Close the right foot to the left foot using the Salsa Action.

4

Man Tap the inside edge of the ball of the right foot next to the left foot.

Woman Tap the inside edge of the ball of the left foot next to the right foot.

▼6

Man Transfer your body weight forward onto the left foot, pressing the body weight onto the left foot. Straighten the left leg as you transfer your weight onto it.

Woman Transfer your body weight forward onto the right foot, pressing the body weight onto the right foot. Straighten the right leg as you transfer your weight onto it.

▲7

Man Close the right foot to the left foot using the Salsa Action.

Woman Close the left foot to the right foot using the Salsa Action.

▲8

Man Tap the inside edge of the ball of the left foot next to the right foot.

Woman Tap the inside edge of the ball of the right foot next to the left foot.

Forwards and Backwards Basic Move

This move can be danced in either a close contact hold or an open hold. If you are using a double hand hold, the man can resume the close contact hold by releasing the woman's right hand and drawing her towards him as he draws closer to her during the last movement of the preceding figure. The man is standing on his right foot and the woman on her left.

1

Man Move onto the left foot, leaving the right foot in place.

Woman Move back onto the right foot, leaving the left foot in place.

2

Man Transfer your weight back onto the right foot, leaving the left foot in place.

Woman Transfer your weight forward onto the left foot, leaving the right foot in place.

3

Man Move the left foot back to the right foot (it is not necessary to close).

Woman Move the right foot forward to the left foot (it is not necessary to close).

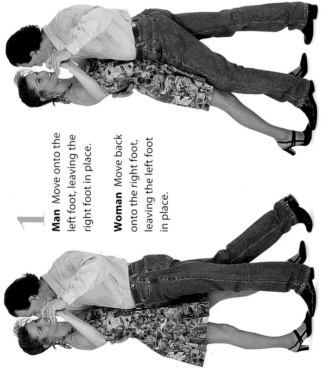

4

Man Tap the inside edge of the ball of the right foot next to the left foot.

Woman Tap the inside edge of the ball of the left foot next to the right foot.

5

Man Move back onto the right foot, leaving the left foot in place.

Woman Move forward onto the left foot, leaving the right foot in place.

6

Man Transfer your body weight forward onto the left foot, leaving the right foot in place.

Woman Transfer your body weight back onto the right foot, leaving the left foot in place.

7

Man Move the right foot forward next to the left foot (it is not necessary to close).

Woman Move the left foot back next to the right foot (it is not necessary to close).

8

Man Tap the inside of the ball of the left foot next to the right foot.

Woman Tap the inside of the ball of the right foot next to the left foot.

Style Tip

During the Forwards and Backwards Basic Move, the Salsa Action should be used. However, the feel is slightly different when moving forward or backward. When you move forward, try rolling your body weight around the edge of your foot, starting with the inside edge of the ball of the foot and ending with the leg pressing against the outside edge of the foot. As your body weight moves onto the outside edge of the foot, straighten the knee a little. This has a feeling of "looping the hip" around the foot. Try the same action when moving backwards.

Preparing to Turn

Having practised and become familiar with the various basic moves, it is now time to explore some of the basic variations as we get into some more serious Salsa.

Turns are a key component of Salsa and the best Salseros will generate a turning move during a preceding move so that it leads quite naturally into the turn. In a basic variation, this may be built up gradually by repeating a preceding move three or four times with the music, each time increasing the turning momentum and thus giving the woman a clear signal of what is to follow. The idea of repeating the same move occurs again and again in Salsa and reflects the often repetitive nature of the music in each musical phrase. By listening to the music, you will become accustomed to matching your dancing to the musical phrasing.

In this move, allow the natural movement of the figure to do the work for you, gradually building up into the next move and making the transition virtually effortless.

Dance three or four Backwards Salsa Basics with the following modifications.

Above: On Step 5, the man should use the right hand to ease the woman gently backwards and away from him.

Above: On each successive Step 5, the man should gently but firmly push the woman's left side away and increase his own turn to the right.

Right: On the next Step 1, the man places his right hand on the woman's left hip.

Woman's Movements

On Step 5, allow the man to push you away from him, matching his turn. When the amount of turn has been developed to a point where the couple are moving backwards to a side-by-side position, you can move easily into the next figure.

Figure of Eight

This figure is a standard and popular turn in Salsa. In it, the man dances a turn across and in front of the woman. Then it's her turn. The couple adopt a double hand hold but are holding only lightly to enable the hands to reposition during the move. The man is standing on his left foot and the woman on her right foot having first danced Steps 1–4 of the Backwards Salsa Basic.

1

COUNT – QUICK

Man Move back onto the right foot, leaving the left foot in place. Use the right hand to move the woman backwards and away from you, ensuring that the right hand is free.

Woman Move back onto the left foot, leaving the right foot in place, ensuring that the left hand is free.

2

COUNT – QUICK

Man Transfer your body weight forward onto the left foot, starting to turn to the left. Start moving the free right hand across your body above the joined hands.

Woman Transfer your body weight forward onto the right foot, starting to turn to the right.

3

COUNT – SLOW

Man Move to the side with the right foot, making a quarter turn (90°) to the left, ending with your back to the woman. Keep hold with the left hand.

Woman Move to the side with the left foot, making a quarter turn (90°) to the right, ending facing the man's back. Keep hold with the right hand.

4

COUNT – QUICK

Man Make a further quarter turn (90°) to the left. Release hold with the left hand, and move back onto the left foot. Take the woman's left hand in your right hand.

Woman Continue turning, making a further quarter turn (90°) to the right and move back onto the right foot, leaving the left foot in place. Hold the left hand at waist height.

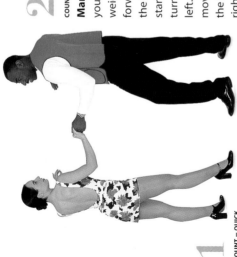

5

COUNT – QUICK

Man Transfer your body weight forward onto the right foot, starting to turn to the right, while leading the woman to turn anticlockwise (counterclockwise) in the same way as you turned on Step 2.

Woman Transfer your body weight forward onto the left foot, starting to turn to the left. Start moving the free right hand across your body above the joined hands.

6

COUNT – SLOW

Man Move to the side with the left foot, making a quarter turn (90°) to the right, ending facing the woman's back. Keep hold with the right hand.

Woman Move to the side with the right foot, making a quarter turn (90°) to the left, ending with your back to the man. Keep hold with the left hand.

SALSA: figure of eight

7

COUNT – QUICK

Man Continue turning clockwise, making a further quarter turn (90°) to the right. Release the right hand and move back onto the right foot, leaving the left foot in place. Take the woman's right hand in your left hand.

Woman Continue turning anticlockwise, making a further quarter turn (90°) to the left. Release the left hand and move back onto the left foot, leaving the right foot in place. Hold the right at waist height.

8

COUNT – QUICK

Man Transfer your body weight forward onto the left foot. At this point, take up an appropriate hold, depending on the next figure.

Woman Transfer your body weight forward onto the right foot.

Music Suggestion

"Lloraras" and "Me Dejo" by Oscar D'Leon (Codiscos). Oscar D'Leon is one of the most popular artists on the international Salsa scene. "Lloraras" is a club favourite. "Me Dejo" is a little slower and excellent for practice.

9

COUNT – SLOW

Man Move the right foot forward next to the left foot.

Woman Move the left foot forward next to the right foot.

(Note how the tap has been eliminated by the "slow" count.)

Figure of Eight with Double Hand Hold

Once you have mastered the Figure of Eight, let's introduce a new hold. Start as for the basic version of the figure. The man is standing on the left foot and the woman on the right foot, having danced Steps 1–4 of the Backwards Salsa Basic. The double hand hold is retained but the man has the palms facing up and the woman has the palms facing down. Contact is maintained through the fingers and thumbs.

1

COUNT – QUICK

Man Move back onto the right foot, leaving the left foot in place and gently but firmly using both hands to move the woman backwards and away from you.

Woman Dance the man's steps 4–6 followed by the man's steps 1–3. Dance a Backwards Salsa Basic starting with the left foot and eliminating the tap.

2

COUNT – QUICK

Man Transfer your body weight forward onto the left foot, starting to turn to the left. Raise the right arm.

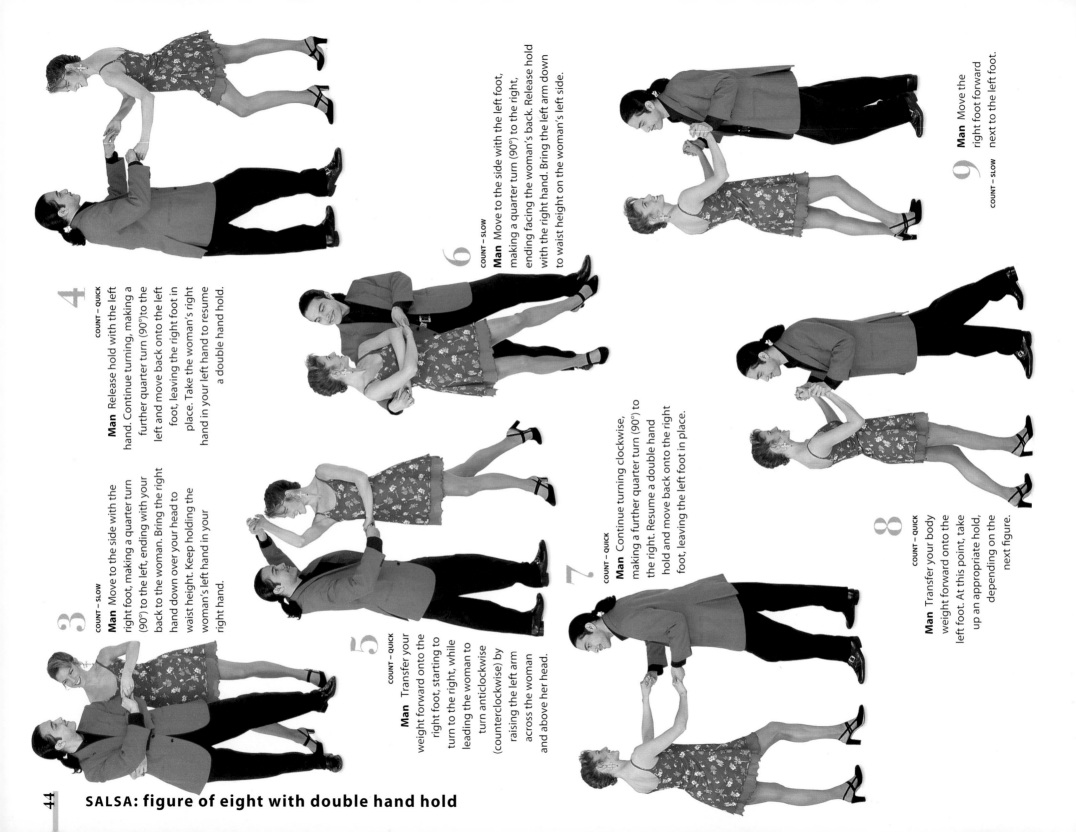

3

COUNT – SLOW

Man Move to the side with the right foot, making a quarter turn (90°) to the left, ending with your back to the woman. Bring the right hand down over your head to waist height. Keep holding the woman's left hand in your right hand.

4

COUNT – QUICK

Man Release hold with the left hand. Continue turning, making a further quarter turn (90°) to the left and move back onto the left foot, leaving the right foot in place. Take the woman's right hand in your left hand to resume a double hand hold.

5

COUNT – QUICK

Man Transfer your weight forward onto the right foot, starting to turn to the right, while leading the woman to turn anticlockwise (counterclockwise) by raising the left arm across the woman and above her head.

6

COUNT – SLOW

Man Move to the side with the left foot, making a quarter turn (90°) to the right, ending facing the woman's back. Release hold with the right hand. Bring the left arm down to waist height on the woman's left side.

7

COUNT – QUICK

Man Continue turning clockwise, making a further quarter turn (90°) to the right. Resume a double hand hold and move back onto the right foot, leaving the left foot in place.

8

COUNT – QUICK

Man Transfer your body weight forward onto the left foot. At this point, take up an appropriate hold, depending on the next figure.

9

COUNT – SLOW

Man Move the right foot forward next to the left foot.

SALSA: figure of eight with double hand hold

44

Changing Places Turn

2
COUNT – QUICK

Man Transfer weight forward onto the right foot, starting to turn to the right, leading the woman to turn anticlockwise (counter-clockwise) by raising the left arm across the woman and above her head.

Woman Transfer your weight forward onto the left foot, starting to turn anticlockwise.

3
COUNT – SLOW

Man Move to the side with the left foot, making a quarter turn (90°) to the right, ending facing the woman's back. Bring the left arm down to waist height, turning the woman to face you.

Woman Turning to the left under the man's arm, step onto the right foot, ending facing the man.

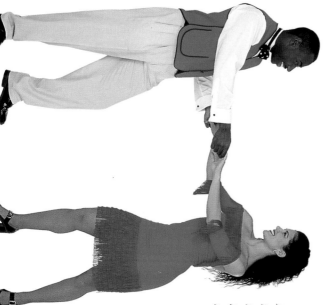

1
COUNT – QUICK

Man Move back onto the left foot, leaving the right foot in place and holding the woman's right hand with your left hand, palm up.

Woman Move back onto the right foot, leaving the left foot in place.

Leading and Following

In contrast to other dance styles, where a couple may be used to dancing together on a regular basis, Salsa is more frequently danced with a variety of partners. It is therefore very important for the man to be able to lead his partner clearly and comfortably.

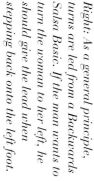

Left: If the man wants to turn the woman to her right, then the lead will be given when the man is moving back on his right foot.

Right: As a general principle, turns are led from a Backwards Salsa Basic. If the man wants to turn the woman to her left, he should give the lead when stepping back onto the left foot.

Armlock Turn to the Left

Another of the characteristic turns of Salsa, this typical move can be called the Armlock Turn for reasons which will become apparent as you dance through the steps. Start in a double hand hold. The man is standing on the right foot and the woman on the left foot.

1
COUNT – QUICK

Man Move back onto the left foot, leaving the right foot in place. Lead the woman backwards and away from you, ready for the turn.

Woman Move back onto the right foot, leaving the left foot in place.

2
COUNT – QUICK

Man Transfer your body weight forward onto the right foot, turning slightly to the right. Gently depress the woman's right hand away from you, while raising the right arm and turning the woman's left hand away to initiate the woman's turn to the left.

Woman Transfer your weight forward onto the left foot, starting to turn to the left.

3
COUNT – SLOW

Man Move to the side onto the left foot, making a quarter turn (90°) to the right. Keep the right hand up and continue turning the woman in an anticlockwise (counterclockwise) direction. As the woman rolls into her right arm, the right arm will assume a position similar to an armlock. End holding the woman's left hand in your right hand with your left forearm across the woman's back.

Woman Move to the side onto the right foot, making a quarter turn (90°) to the left, ending with your back to the man.

4
COUNT – QUICK

Man Move back a small step onto the right foot, leaving the left foot in place.

Woman Make a further quarter turn (90°) to the left, allowing your right arm to move into the "armlock" position. Move back a small step onto the left foot, leaving the right foot in place.

5
COUNT – QUICK

Man Transfer your body weight forward onto the left foot.

Woman Transfer your body weight forward onto the right foot, starting to turn to the right.

Style Tip

In Step 3, the man should give the woman plenty of space for the rest of the figure.

6
COUNT – SLOW

Man Move to the side onto the right foot, making a quarter turn to the left. Move the left hand to the left, leading the woman to unwrap. Lower the right hand to waist height.

Woman Move back onto the left foot, making a half turn to the right.

7
COUNT – QUICK

Man Move back onto the left foot, leaving the right foot in place.

Woman Move back onto the right foot, leaving the left foot in place.

8
COUNT – QUICK

Man Transfer your body weight forward onto the right foot.

Woman Transfer your body weight forward onto the left foot.

9
COUNT – SLOW

Man Move the left foot forward next to the right foot.

Woman Move the right foot forward next to the left foot.

You can now continue by dancing into the Backward Salsa Basic. If you wish to repeat the Armlock Turn, dance Steps 1–7, then Steps 2–9.

Variation

On Step 4, it is possible for the man to dance a Cucuracha onto the right foot. Some men choose to dance back onto the right foot with a quarter turn to the right and then a quarter turn to the left as they step back onto the left foot. While the turn is possible, it can be uncomfortable for the woman, as it tightens the "armlock". The technique described in the steps previously is therefore preferable.

Music Suggestion

"Que Bueno Baila Usted" by Oscar D'Leon (Rodven). This is a very catchy number with a feel and style particularly suitable for a Colombian interpretation. It is impossible to stand still to this track.

Armlock Turn to the Right

This figure is the same as the Armlock Turn learned earlier, but with the woman turning to the right rather than to the left. Start in a double hand hold. The man and woman do not change hands during this move. The man is standing on the left foot and the woman on the right foot.

1
COUNT – QUICK

Man Move back onto the right foot, leaving the left foot in place. Lead the woman backwards and away from you, ready for the turn.

Woman Move back onto the left foot, leaving the right foot in place.

2
COUNT – QUICK

Man Transfer your body weight forward onto the left foot, turning slightly to the left. Gently depress the woman's left hand away from you, while raising the left arm and turning the woman's left hand away to initiate the woman's turn to the right.

Woman Transfer your body weight forward onto the right foot, starting to turn to the right.

3
COUNT – SLOW

Man Move to the side onto the right foot, making a quarter turn to the left. Keep the left hand up and continue turning the woman in a clockwise direction. As the woman rolls into her left arm, she will assume a position similar to an armlock. End holding the woman's right hand in your left hand.

Woman Move onto the left foot, making a quarter turn to the right, ending with your back to the man.

4
COUNT – QUICK

Man Move back a small step onto the left foot, leaving the right foot in place.

Woman Make a further quarter turn to the right, allowing your left arm to move into the "armlock" position. Step backwards onto the right foot, leaving the left foot in place.

5
COUNT – QUICK

Man Transfer your weight forward onto the right foot, starting to turn right.

Woman Transfer your body weight forward onto the left foot, starting to turn to the left.

6
COUNT – SLOW

Man Move to the side onto the left foot. Move back onto the right foot making a quarter turn to the right. Transfer your weight forward onto the left foot. Move your right foot forward to the left foot.

Woman Move to the side onto the right foot, making a quarter turn to the left.

7–8
COUNT – QUICK

Man Move back onto the right foot, leaving the left foot in place and making a quarter turn to the right. Transfer your body weight forward onto the left foot.

Woman Continue to make a quarter turn to the left, moving back onto the left foot and leaving the right foot in place. Transfer your body weight onto the left foot.

9
COUNT – SLOW

Man Move the right foot forward next to the left foot.

Woman Move the left foot forward next to the right foot.

SALSA: armlock turn to the right

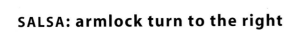

Pachanga Heel Taps

The Colombian style of Salsa places great emphasis on intricate footwork improvisations, which tend to make the Colombian style tighter than the Cuban style. Moves have always been borrowed from other dances, and here's one that has the exciting feel of the Pachanga.

Start in a double hand hold, palm to palm, and dance a complete Backwards Salsa Basic to a count of "quick, quick, slow, quick, quick, slow." On the last step, the man moves closer to the woman, but still without body contact, and he draws the woman towards him, moving his hand onto her waist and ensuring that she has transferred all of her weight onto the left foot. The toning of the woman's arms is critical in accepting the man's lead.

2
COUNT – SLOW

Man Standing on the right foot, swivel a quarter turn (90°) to the right to face the woman and step onto the left foot. Lead the woman to face you by pulling her right hand to turn her right side forward and using your right hand to turn her at the waist.

Woman Standing on the left foot, swivel a quarter turn (90°) to the left to face the man and step onto the right foot.

1
COUNT – & SLOW

Man Standing on the right foot, swivel a one-eighth turn to the right, then a three-eighths turn to the left with the knees together and the lower left leg held parallel to the floor. Lead the woman to turn by gentle pressure through the left hand and by turning her clockwise with the right hand. End touching the woman's raised foot with yours.

Woman Standing on the left foot, swivel a one-eighth turn to the left, then a three-eighths turn to the right with the knees together and the lower right leg held parallel to the floor. If the man places his hand on your waist, respond by placing your left hand on his upper arm. End touching the man's raised foot with yours.

3
COUNT – QUICK

Man Step backwards onto the right foot, leaving the left foot in place to dance a Backwards Salsa Basic. Either release the right hand or resume a double hand hold.

Woman Step backwards onto the left foot, leaving the right foot in place to dance a Backwards Salsa Basic.

4
COUNT – QUICK

Man Transfer your weight forward onto the left foot.

Woman Transfer your weight forward onto the right foot.

5
COUNT – SLOW

Man Move your right foot forward next to your left foot.

Woman Move your left foot forward next to your right foot.

Continue with a Backwards Salsa Basic.

Pachanga Cross Swivels

Time now for some more captivating, complex Colombian moves, featuring a little tricky footwork for those so far undaunted. Again, we borrow a move from the exotic Pachanga. Dance a Backwards Salsa Basic in a double hand hold. The man is now standing on the right foot and the woman on the left foot.

1

COUNT – QUICK

Man Standing on the right foot, swivel a little to the right, pointing the left toes towards the right toes and holding the left foot clear of the floor.

Woman Standing on the left foot, swivel a little to the left, pointing the right toes towards the left toes and holding the right foot clear of the floor.

2

COUNT – QUICK

Man Standing on the right foot, swivel a little to the left, bringing the left foot to cross the lower right leg and holding the left foot clear of the floor.

Woman Standing on the left foot, swivel a little to the right, bringing the right foot to cross the lower left leg and holding the right foot clear of the floor.

3

COUNT – SLOW

Man Pointing the left foot at your partner, move the left foot across the right foot and stand on the left foot.

Woman Pointing the right foot at your partner, move the right foot across the left foot and stand on the right foot.

4

COUNTS – QUICK

Man Standing on the left foot, swivel a little to the left, pointing the right toes towards the left toes and holding the right foot clear of the floor.

Woman Standing on the right foot, swivel a little to the right, pointing the left toes towards the right toes and holding the left foot clear of the floor.

5

COUNT – QUICK

Man Standing on the left foot, swivel to the right, bringing the right foot to cross the lower left leg and holding the right foot clear of the floor.

Woman Standing on the right foot, swivel to the left, bringing the left foot to cross the lower right leg and holding the left foot clear of the floor.

6

COUNT – SLOW

Man Pointing the right foot at your partner, move the right foot across the left foot and stand on the right foot.

Woman Pointing the left foot at your partner, move the left foot across the right foot and stand on the left foot.

Half Turns

The Half Turn is also known as the Cuddle Turn and you may decide to stay in the cuddle for a while before reluctantly exiting. Start in a double hand hold.

1
COUNT – QUICK

Man Move back onto the left foot, leaving the right foot in place. Lead the woman backwards and away from you ready for the turn.

Woman Move back onto the right foot, leaving the left foot in place.

2
COUNT – QUICK

Man Move your body weight forward onto the right foot. Lead the woman to turn to her left by raising your left hand and drawing it towards the right across yourself and above the woman's head. Keep the right hand at waist height, leading the woman to turn into your right arm.

Woman Move your body weight forward onto the left foot, starting to turn to the left.

3
COUNT – SLOW

Man Move forward onto the left foot with the left arm still raised, turning to the right.

Woman Move to the side onto the right foot, making a quarter turn (90°) to the left.

4
COUNT – QUICK

Man Move forward onto the right foot, leaving the left foot in place. Lower the left hand to waist height in front of the woman to continue turning her. End in a side-by-side position with the woman on your right, your right hand holding the woman's left hand and your right forearm across her back.

Woman Move back, a small step, onto the left foot, leaving the right foot in place and making a further quarter turn (90°) to the left. End in a side-by-side position with the man on your left.

5
COUNT – QUICK

Man Move your body weight backwards onto the left foot and use your right forearm to lead the woman forward. Raise the left hand to allow the woman to pass beneath it.

Woman Move your body weight forward onto the right foot, starting to turn to the right.

COUNT – QUICK

Man Transfer your body weight forward onto the right foot.

Woman Transfer your body weight forward onto the left foot.

8

COUNT – QUICK

Man Move the left foot back, leaving the right foot in place.

Woman Move back onto the right foot, leaving the left foot in place and making a quarter turn to the right.

7

COUNT – SLOW

Man Move the right foot backwards next to the left foot. Lower the left hand to the normal position as the woman ends facing you.

Woman Move to the side and back onto the left foot, making a quarter turn (90°) to the right.

6

COUNT – SLOW

Man Move the left foot forward next to the right foot.

Woman Move the right foot forward next to the left foot.

9

Music Suggestion

"Mexico, Mexico" by Grupo Niche (Sony). This track, with its medium-fast tempo for the more experienced dancer, proved a hit for this popular group. For a fabulous blend of African and Caribbean rhythms, try "Africando" and "Yay Boy" by Africando (Stern's Africa). These tracks not only illustrate the common ancestry of Salsa, but are also great to dance to.

Steps 7–9 may be replaced with the Changing Places Turn, which makes a good exit.

Half Turn and Changing Sides

COUNT – SLOW

Man Move to the side onto the right foot, crossing behind the woman and leading her to move across in front of you to the left by slightly extending the arms and moving the woman within their frame. Position the woman slightly forward of a side-by-side position on your left.

Woman Move to the side onto the left foot, crossing in front of the man to end slightly forward of a side-by-side position with the man on your right.

2

This figure, also known as the Double Cuddle, is great fun. Dance Steps 1–4 of the Half Turns before continuing into the new move.

1

COUNT – QUICK

Man Return you body weight back to the left foot, keeping both hands at waist height.

Woman Move your body weight forward onto the right foot.

3

COUNT – QUICK

Man Move forward onto the left foot, leaving the right foot in place. End standing in a side-by-side position with the woman on your right.

Woman Move back onto the right foot, leaving the left foot in place. End standing in a side-by-side position with the man on your left.

◀6

Man Move forward onto the right foot, leaving the left foot in place.

Woman Move forward onto the left foot, leaving the right foot in place.

4

COUNT – QUICK

Man Transfer your weight back onto the right foot, leading the woman to transfer her weight forward.

Woman Transfer your body weight forward onto the left foot.

Continue with Step 5 of the Half Turns or stay in the Cuddle by repeating the move, remembering to include step 4 of the Half Turn.

Extra Salsa Style

You can liven up some quite basic moves by incorporating some exotic extras. Try the first moves without overdoing them, then build them up to their full dramatic effect when you feel comfortable.

5

COUNT – SLOW

Man Move to the side onto the left foot, crossing behind the woman and leading her to move across in front of you to the right by slightly extending the arms and moving the woman within their frame. Position the woman slightly forward of a side-by-side position on your right.

Woman Move to the side onto the right foot, crossing in front of the man to end slightly forward of a side-by-side position with the man on your left.

Half Turn with Brazilian Head Throw

Add a little extra "salsita" to the Half Turn by using an extra Brazilian Style point. This deliciously exotic move occurs on Step 4 of the Half Turn. When the woman moves back onto the left foot, she can perform a head throw by throwing her head back and lifting her right foot to knee height, pointing the toes to the floor. To facilitate this action, the man will replace his forward movement with a quarter turn to the right, extending the right leg straight, to create a "lunge line". A strong lead will be needed from the man's left hand while his right arm supports the woman. Try this first without overdoing it, then build up to the full extent for a special and fabulous effect.

Changing Places Turn with Overhead Cuban Sink

You might want to spice the Changing Places Turn up a little. Here, the man starts the figure with a double hand hold, but brings his hands together so that they are touching. This hold is maintained while the woman turns under the hands. This is just the right moment for the Overhead Cuban Sink.

1
COUNT – QUICK

Man Move back onto the left foot leaving the right foot in place.

Woman Move back onto the right foot leaving the left foot in place.

2
COUNT – QUICK

Man Transfer your body weight forward onto the right foot starting to lead the woman to turn by swinging your hands to the right.

Woman Transfer your body weight forward onto the left foot starting to turn to the left.

3
COUNT – SLOW

Man Still on the right foot, allow the left foot to close towards the right foot. Continue to swing the hands up until overhead then bring the joined hands down over your own head placing the woman's hands on the back of your neck. This is helped by relaxing your right knee.

Woman Still on the left foot, spin a full turn anticlockwise under the joined hands and place them over the man's head onto the back of his neck.

4
COUNT – QUICK

Man Resuming close hold and lowering into the right knee, move a short step to the left and circle your left knee anticlockwise around your left foot in a circular hip roll.

Woman Lowering into the left knee, move a short step to the right and circle your right knee clockwise around your right foot in a circular hip roll.

5
COUNT – QUICK

Man Transfer your weight onto the right foot.

Woman Transfer your weight onto the left foot.

6
COUNT – SLOW

Man Close your left foot to your right foot.

Woman Close the right foot to the left foot.

Swing Step

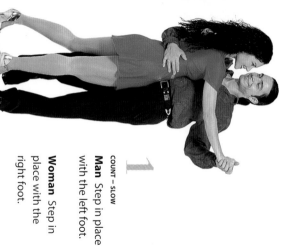

The Swing Step is a basic move but it is often used in combination with other moves and as part of the entry into some of the classic Lambada turns. Feel the swing through the hips as you get another chance to dance the raunchy Lambada hip roll. Start in the Lambada Hold described above and with your body weight on the same foot as before.

1

COUNT – SLOW

Man Step in place with the left foot.

Woman Step in place with the right foot.

2

COUNT – QUICK

Man Move sideways on to the right foot with the clockwise Lambada hip roll, moving your right side forward.

Woman Move sideways on to the left foot with the anticlockwise (counterclockwise) Lambada hip roll and moving your left side forward.

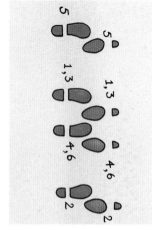

3

COUNT – QUICK

Man Transfer your body weight on to the right foot, completing the Lambada hip roll and moving your left side back to its normal position.

Woman Transfer your body weight on to the left foot, completing the Lambada hip roll and moving your right side back to its normal position.

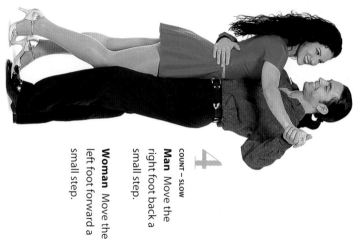

4

COUNT – SLOW

Man Move the right foot back a small step.

Woman Move the left foot forward a small step.

5

COUNT – QUICK

Man Move diagonally back on to the left foot, rolling your hips anticlockwise around the outside edge of your foot.

Woman Move diagonally forward on to the right foot, rolling your hips clockwise around the outside edge of your foot.

6

COUNT – QUICK

Man Transfer your body weight on to the right foot.

Woman Transfer your body weight on to the left foot.

6

COUNT – QUICK

Man Transfer your body weight on to the right foot, completing the Lambada hip roll and moving your left side back to its normal position.

Woman Transfer your body weight on to the left foot, completing the Lambada hip roll and moving your right side back to its normal position.

Continue with any basic Lambada move.

5

COUNT – QUICK

Man Move sideways on to the left foot with the anticlockwise (counterclockwise) Lambada hip roll and moving your left side forward.

Woman Move sideways on to the right foot with the clockwise Lambada hip roll and moving your right side forward.

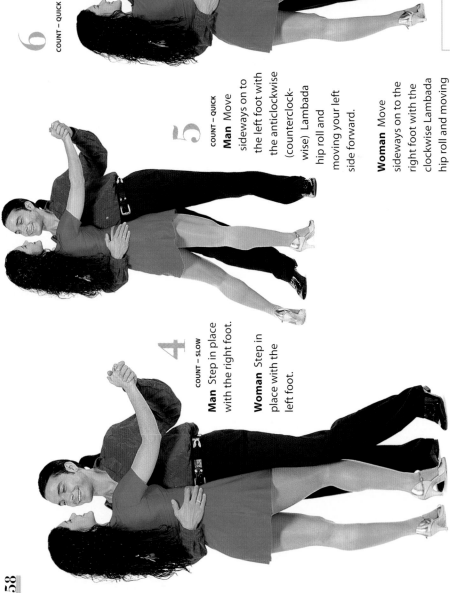

4

COUNT – SLOW

Man Step in place with the right foot.

Woman Step in place with the left foot.

Using Your Head

The woman's use of the head is crucial to looking her best when dancing the Lambada. While she will want to use her head in her own way to express both herself and the fluidity of the movement, there are a few useful guidelines to follow.

• All head movements are a natural extension of the move being danced.
• In the normal Lambada hold, the woman does not look at the man.
• The woman looks at the man only at the start and finish of each move.

Right: To move her head from right to left, she will roll it, circling it across with chin up.

Left: To move her head from left to right, the woman will roll it, circling it across with chin down.

Left: The woman begins and ends each move with her head inclined to the side.

Basic Lambada Turns

You can now try spicing up your Lambada with some exciting turns. This group of moves is complete in itself, so you can include it in your routine as soon as you have had a little practice. Start by dancing Steps 1–3 of the Basic Lambada, but on Step 2, the man should indicate his intention to dance the turns by turning his body a little to the left as he steps forward.

Man's Swing Step to the Left
The woman will open out during this move.

4

COUNT – SLOW

Man Step in place with the right foot.

Woman Move forward a small step, on to the left foot.

5

COUNT – QUICK

Man Move sideways on to the left foot with the anticlockwise (counterclockwise) Lambada hip roll and turning your upper body to the right.

Woman Pivoting on the ball of the left foot, make almost a half turn (180°) to the right to end on the man's right side and step back on to the right foot.

6

COUNT – QUICK

Man Transfer your body weight on to the right foot, completing the Lambada hip roll and turning your upper body to the left to resume its normal position.

Woman Transfer your body weight forward on to the left foot, starting to turn to the left.

Man's Swing Step to the Right
As before the woman will open out.

7

COUNT – SLOW

Man Close the left foot almost to the right foot, leading the woman to turn square to you.

Woman Move sideways on to the right foot to end facing the man square on.

8

COUNT – QUICK

Man Move sideways on to the right foot, keeping your body weight between your feet and turning your upper body to the left to lead the woman to continue turning anticlockwise.

Woman Pivoting on the ball of the right foot, make almost a half turn (180°) to the left to end on the man's left side and step back (part weight) on to the left foot.

9

COUNT – QUICK

Man Transfer your body weight fully on to the left foot, leading the woman to start her turn to the right.

Woman Transfer your body weight forward on to the right foot, starting to turn to the right.

Continue with the Basic Lambada.

LAMBADA: bailarina/a cadeira

Bailarina with Underarm Turn

The man prepares to turn the woman while she executes a Bailarina turn.

10

COUNT – SLOW

Man Close the right foot to the left foot, leading the woman to turn square to you.

Woman Move sideways on to the left foot, turning to the right to end facing the man square on.

11

COUNT – QUICK

Man Move sideways on to the left foot, with the anticlockwise Lambada hip roll and turning your upper body to the right.

Woman Pivoting on the ball of the left foot, make almost a half turn (180°) to the right to end on the man's right side and step back on to the right foot.

12

COUNT – QUICK

Man Transfer your body weight on to the right foot, completing the Lambada hip roll and turning the woman to the left, across you and underneath your raised left arm to end facing each other.

Woman Transfer your body weight forward and pivot on the left foot, turning to the left underneath the man's raised arm to end facing him.

Pivot

A pivot is a turn made on only one foot. As you pivot, both legs will be straight but you will be standing on only the left foot. During the pivot, it is important to allow the right foot to close naturally to the left foot, so that you pivot with both feet under the body. This will not only give you better balance but will also allow the right foot to end in the best position to continue into the next move.

A Cadeira

The name of this classic Lambada move means "The Seat" in Portuguese, although it has now become so popular with photographers that it is sometimes called "The Photo" instead. In this move, the man leads the woman to a position in which she appears to be momentarily sitting on his knee.

1

COUNT – SLOW

Man Move sideways on to the left foot, leading the woman to open out to your right.

Woman Swivelling a half turn (180°) on the left foot, move back on to the right foot.

2

COUNT – QUICK

Man Transfer your body weight on to the right foot, leading the woman to turn to the left towards you.

Woman Transfer your body weight forward on to the left foot, starting to turn to the left.

3

COUNT – QUICK

Man Move the left foot forward without any weight.

Woman Move forward across the man on to the right foot.

Lambada Drop

The Drop is an exotic and effective move which has justifiably become the trademark of the Lambada. In this move, the man holds his position while leading the woman to perform a body ripple which culminates in a flick of the hair. It is precisely for this purpose that dedicated female dancers grow their hair long to maximize and enhance the effect.

1
COUNT – SLOW

Man Move forward a small step on to the left foot.

Woman Move back a small step on to the right foot.

2
COUNT – QUICK

Man Move diagonally forward on to the right foot, with the Lambada hip roll.

Woman Move diagonally back on to the left foot, with the Lambada hip roll.

3
COUNT – QUICK

Man Transfer your body weight back on to the left foot, leaving the right foot in place with the right knee slightly raised. Use the quick transfer of weight to bring the woman towards you to ensure close contact.

Woman Transfer your body weight forward on to the right foot and, pulled by the man, move the left foot close to the right foot, sandwiching the man's right knee between your legs. (If the man does not support your back properly, you may need to grip with your knees.)

4
COUNT – SLOW

Man Hold the foot position.

Woman With the feet in place, swivel a half turn (180°) to the left to end on the right foot with the man on your right.

5
COUNT – QUICK

Man Press the ball of the left foot down on the floor but do not lower the heel, raising the left knee as you lower through the right knee. Raising the left arm, continue to turn the woman, allowing her to lower on to your left knee.

Woman Flex the right knee and lift the left foot to the outside of the right knee to create the illusion that you are sitting on the man's knee.

6
COUNT – QUICK

Man Stand up and close the left foot back to the right foot, leading the woman to face you and resuming the normal Lambada hold.

Woman Stand up and turn to the right to face the man, ending with your weight on the right foot.

Continue with any of the Lambada moves you have learned.

4–6
COUNT – SLOW, QUICK, QUICK

Man As the woman performs her body ripple, hold your position and support the woman's lower back with your right hand, but do not restrict her movement.

Woman To perform your body ripple, contract your waist, inclining your upper body slightly forward and bending your knees. Bend backwards, pushing your hips forward. Progressively accelerate the roll of your back forward to resume the normal body position, straightening your knees and finishing with a flick of your hair.

Continue with Steps 4–6 of the Basic Lambada, with the man moving the right foot back to the left foot on Step 4.

Samba Reggae

Samba Reggae is a fun variant of the Samba which even non-dancers can get straight into. This is a dance you can enjoy solo as there is no need for a partner. Coming from the Bahia region in the north-east of Brazil, the music is a cross between Samba and Reggae. With its vibrant and catchy beat it is a popular option for singles as well as a wider audience of Latin music and dance enthusiasts. The effect is not unlike an aerobics event, with the solo dancers facing front, either scattered randomly or in lines. In Brazil, open-air Samba Reggae can attract large crowds of participants, all following the moves of the leader. Now it's time to relax and get those hips moving with a short routine of typical moves.

Passo Basico

This is the basic Samba Reggae move and is very similar to the Side Basic Samba but without the weight change. Start standing with your feet a little apart. Feel the rhythm and interpret it by adding your own expression to the basic move. Use the whole of your body to dance with the beat.

1
COUNT – SLOW
Move sideways on to the left foot.

2
COUNT – SLOW
Tap or touch the right foot next to the left foot.

3 ▶
COUNT – SLOW
Move sideways on to the right foot.

4 ▶
COUNT – SLOW
Tap or touch the left foot next to the right foot.

Dance the Basic Samba Reggae four times.

Passo de Mike Tyson

This move includes the type of defensive shoulder shrug used by boxers like the world-class heavyweight champion Mike Tyson. Go to Bahia and everyone will know the Passo de Mike Tyson. There is no need to take steps in this move. Start with your feet apart, standing on your right foot.

1
COUNT – SLOW, SLOW
Transfer your body weight on to the left foot and move the left shoulder forward, while making a fist with your hands.

2
COUNT – SLOW, SLOW
Transfer your body weight on to the right foot and move the right shoulder forward, while making a fist with your hands.

O Pente

Everyone wants to make a good impression when out on the dance scene, and personal style is important. In this move, the dancers' movements resemble combing the hair, hence the name the "Comb". In O Pente, there are no steps, so your feet do not move. Start with your feet apart, standing on the right foot.

1
COUNT – SLOW, SLOW
Transfer your body weight slowly on to the left foot, as you turn your upper body to the right. Draw your left hand over your head as if combing your hair.

2
COUNT – SLOW, SLOW
Transfer your body weight slowly on to the right foot, as you turn your upper body to the left. Draw your right hand over your head as if combing your hair.

Passo de Pele –

Brazil is well known as a sport-loving nation, so it is not surprising that sporting heroes should be made a part of the other national pastime, dancing. Here, tribute is paid to one of Brazil's soccer superheroes in the "Pele Step".

1
COUNT – SLOW
Move forward on to the left foot.

2
COUNT – SLOW
Kick the right foot forward (as if kicking a football).

3
COUNT – SLOW
Move back on to the right foot.

4
COUNT – SLOW
Tap the left foot behind but without transferring your body weight.

Abrir a Cortina

This means "Opening the Curtains". It is the same as the Passo Basico but with arm movements to mime opening the curtains.

◀1
COUNT – SLOW
Move sideways on to the left foot, extending the left arm and moving it outwards to end opposite the left foot. Rest the right hand on the right hip.

2
COUNT – SLOW
Tap or touch the right foot next to the left foot.

◀3
COUNT – SLOW
Move sideways on to the right foot, extending the right arm and moving it outwards to end opposite the right foot. Rest the left hand on the left hip.

4
COUNT – SLOW
Tap or touch the left foot next to the right foot.

A Bailarina

This is the "Ballerina Step" and has a very similar pattern to that of the Samba Whisk described in the Samba section of the book. During the move to the left, rotate the arms clockwise to end extended on the right side. During the move to the right, rotate the arms anticlockwise (counterclockwise) to end extended on the left side.

◀1
COUNT – SLOW
Move sideways on to the left foot.

◀2
COUNT – SLOW
Tap or touch the right foot behind the left foot, turning the right foot out. Avoid lowering the right heel but maintain pressure through the toes.

3▲
COUNT – SLOW
Move sideways on to the right foot.

4▲
COUNT – SLOW
Tap or touch the left foot behind the right foot, turning the left foot out. Avoid lowering the left heel but maintain pressure through the toes.

Line Dancing

The enormous popularity of American Country Line Dancing is growing and growing with an enthusiasm, energy and drive which seems unstoppable. Not only in North America, but in Europe, too, people have discovered the fun of stretchin' denim on the dance floor. The choice of the USA among Europeans as a holiday destination, coupled with inexpensive transatlantic flights, have brought more and more people into contact with Country music in the many clubs to be found in almost every American town from Florida to Washington. The increase in popularity of Country music must also, in no small way, be due to the arrival of Country Music Television in Europe by satellite and the ever-increasing number of commercial radio stations and magazines devoted to Country music and style.

By the end of the 1980s, Country music had begun to change, with the formerly well-defined borders becoming blurred by a cross-over of styles. Soft rock was being incorporated and the lyrics, which were once predominantly sad, simple or sugary, were now acquiring a more up-to-date and intelligent sophistication, which appealed to an audience previously untouched by Country. The cowboy image of Stetsons, boots and belt buckles gradually lost its Hicktown associations and added a fun element, while music videos helped to broadcast the image of what has become known as New Country.

This process was considerably aided by the emergence and promotion of new and very talented stars of the New Country music scene: Mary Chapin Carpenter, Trisha Yearwood, Lorrie Morgan, Carlene Carter, Suzy Boguss, Michelle Wright, Shania Twain, Shelby Lynne, Ronna Reeves, Dwight Yoakum, Alan Jackson, Garth Brookes, Billy Ray Cyrus, John Berry, Vince Gill, Travis Tritt, Toby Keith, Hank Flamingo, John Michael Montgomery, Joe Diffie, Shawn Camp and a good many more. These performers realized that the music is only half of the phenomenon of Country and so produced music of an excellent quality not only for listening but also for dancing. A new phrase, the "Dance Ranch", was coined for Country music dance parties. During the 1980s,

attendances rocketed and more Dance Ranches were quickly established at Country & Western clubs throughout the world. Singles do not need to worry about not having a partner and the relaxed and exuberant atmosphere ensures that everyone has a great time. The music makes you just want to dance.

American Country Line Dancing owes some of its popularity to the Disco Line Dancing of the 1970s, following the Saturday Night Fever boom. However, the traditional moves of American Country dancing were not forgotten and some of them have been adapted for Line Dancing. Men in discos were never very comfortable with the idea of using their arms and dancing in the style of John Travolta, so the less ostentatious, more laid-back style of Country dancing, where thumbs are left firmly tucked in the tops of jeans, was bound to be a winner.

As its name suggests, American Country Line Dancing comprises pre-set routines of moves performed in lines. Everyone starts at the same time, dances the same steps in synchronization with everyone else (or that's the theory) and finishes with the end of the music. A lot of the music used for dancing has a moderate tempo or walking pace and most of the dances are suitable for any age group. Dancing keeps you fit and mentally alert and is a great way of making new friends. The moves are

American Country Line Dancing – good exercise and boot scootin' fun.

Above: Western-style bandanas and bootlace ties add a fun cowboy touch to any outfit.

Getting Started

Start with the feet together facing the same way as everyone else. Be aware which move you are going to do first and ensure that you are standing on the appropriate foot. Avoid putting your hands behind your back, on your hips or down by your sides. Place your thumbs inside the waistband of your jeans or skirt and you're ready to go.

Orientation

In most dances, you will turn to face a new wall during the routine, as the beginning is repeated. Sometimes this is a quarter turn (or 90°), sometimes it is a half turn (or 180°). If you are a newcomer to American Country Line Dancing, avoid standing at the back of the dancers. You could, at the end of the dance, find yourself at the front! The middle is the safest place for the beginner. Now let's get down to some serious fun and start dancing!

The Music

A lot of the American Country Line Dances are danced to music with a regular 4/4 time signature and a tempo of 30 to 34 bars of music per minute, so many of the dances can be danced to a wide variety of popular music.

On the following pages you will be taught a number of the most popular American Country Line Dances. Each numbered step represents a count in the music. If a number is followed by "&" this represents a half beat. Dance the figures at your own pace – you'll soon get the hang of it!

Avoid putting your hands down by your sides when dancing. Tuck them in your belt when not clapping with the music.

Boots or flat shoes are fine but avoid wearing trainers (sneakers) as these can be dangerous.

the same for both men and women and you will find that the steps often reappear in more than one dance. While, at first, the prospect of learning many line dances may seem a little daunting, as your vocabulary of moves rapidly grows, you will find new dances relatively easy to pick up by remembering the sequence of moves rather than the individual steps. The dances themselves vary in length and may not always fit exactly with the musical phrasing but no one really seems to care. It is enough to be out there, slappin' leather and stompin' with the best of them.

Occasionally a popular piece of music spawns many different dances all with the same name – the Achy Breaky is a good example. This can lead to confusion, so if you are unsure whether the dance which has been announced is the one you know, it is as well to sit out and watch the first sequence before joining in. It is not smart to dance a different dance to everyone else.

The organization of the dance party may also vary from event to event. In some clubs, an announcer may determine the choice of dance. In others it will be whoever is first on the floor who decides. Sometimes, several different dances are performed by different groups of people at the same time, although this is not recommended and a good organizer will avoid this sort of problem.

In this introduction to American Country Line Dancing, the moves are introduced as they appear in the dances and are fully explained. In some of the supporting photographs, the dancers may have their backs to you to make it easier for you to follow the moves at home.

The Electric Slide

This dance incorporates some of the basic moves common to many American Country Line Dances. The Electric Slide refers to the slide used on an electric guitar to produce the characteristic sound associated with Country music. The first move is called the Grapevine, although this is usually shortened to the Vine. The Vine is a frequent figure in many dances.

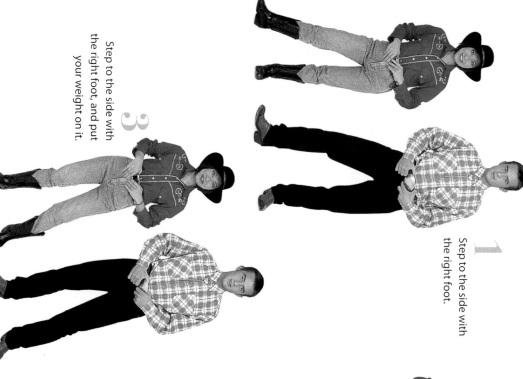

Vine to the Right

Start with the feet together, standing on the left foot.

1
Step to the side with the right foot.

2
Cross the left foot behind the right foot. Start with the ball of the left foot, as this is more comfortable.

3
Step to the side with the right foot, and put your weight on it.

4
Tap the floor with the heel of the left foot. (Some dancers stomp or scuff this step and that's OK, too.) End standing on your right foot.

Vine to the Left

5
Step to the side with the left foot.

6
Cross the right foot behind the left foot.

7
Step to the side again with the left foot.

8
Tap the floor with the heel of the right foot. End standing on your left foot.

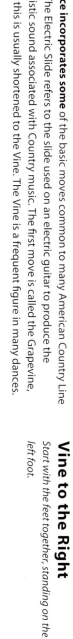

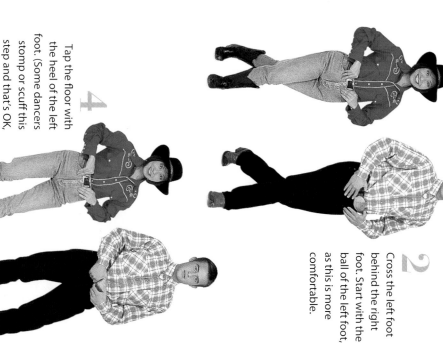

Walking Backwards to Tap

9
Walk backwards onto the right foot.

10
Walk backwards onto the left foot.

11
Walk backwards onto the right foot.

Style Tip
Steps 9–11: It is the sign of a good dancer to step backwards onto the heels, releasing the toes and "fanning" the toes out to the side, but this may take a little practice.
Step 14: It is good style to incline the left side forward and tip your hat – even if you don't have one!

12
Cross the left foot back across the right foot and tap.

Step Taps

13
Walk forward onto the left foot.

14
Tap the right foot across and behind the left foot. Turn the right knee out a little to make it easier.

Music Suggestion
Enjoy the easy tempo and have fun with Joe Diffie's "Prop Me Up Beside the Jukebox" (Sony). Then you can really get moving to John Michael Montgomery's "Be My Baby Tonight" (Atlantic). "Cotton Eye Joe", by Rednex (Internal Affairs), which topped the charts in 1995, though not mainstream Country, is a faster version which you can have some fun with.

Honky Tonk Stomp

The next dance uses the Vine that you learnt in the Electric Slide but with a Hitch Turn for real Dance Ranchers. You will also learn the popular Stomp. This is a great dance, especially for newcomers to American Country Line Dancing. The routine is quite short, easy to remember and the honky tonk music just makes you want to dance. Start with the feet slightly apart, standing on the left foot and facing the front.

Toe Fans

1
Standing on the left foot, keep the right heel in contact with the floor and "fan" the toe out to the side.

2
"Fan" the right toe back to its original position, roughly parallel with the left foot.

3–4
Repeat Steps 1 and 2. ➤

The Scuff

15
Walk backwards onto the right foot.

16
Cross the left foot back across the right foot and tap.

17
Walk forward onto the left foot and flex the knee slightly.

18
Swing the right leg forward so that the right heel scuffs the floor. As you do this, swivel on the left foot to do a quarter turn (90°) to the left. Don't put your right foot down. To maintain balance, make sure that you hold your body weight over your left foot and do not allow it to follow the scuffing foot.

Start the dance again facing the wall that was previously on your left. You are now dancing the Electric Slide.

Forward and Backwards Double Taps

5–6
Move the right foot forward and tap with the heel. Repeat once.

7–8
Move the right foot backwards and tap with the toe. Repeat once.

Taps and Stomps

9
Tap the right heel forward.

10
Close the right foot back to the left foot and stand on the right foot.

11–12▲
Stomp the left foot, lifting the knee and placing the foot down flat on the floor. Repeat once.

13
Tap the left heel forward.

14
Close the left foot back to the right foot and stand on the left foot.

15–16
Stomp the right foot. Repeat.

Vine to the Right

17
Step to the side with the right foot.

18
Cross the left foot behind the right foot.

19
Step to the side again with the right foot.

20
Tap the left foot.

Vine to the Left with Hitch Turn

21
Step to the side with the left foot.

22
Cross the right foot behind the left.

23
Step to the side with the left foot.

24▶
Standing on the left foot, swivel a half turn (180°) to the left. At the same time, raise the right knee, making a right angle at the ankle. This is call the Hitch.

25–28
Repeat Steps 17–20.

29–31
Repeat Steps 21–23.

32
Tap the right heel, with the feet far apart.

Now begin the dance again with the Toe Fans, starting with the right foot.

Music Suggestion

"Honky Tonk Attitude", by Joe Diffie (Columbia), is a real honky tonkin' number for stompin'. Another great track is The Tractors' version of "Baby Likes to Rock It" (Arista) – this is guaranteed to get you moving.

Tennessee Twister

The Tennessee Twister will really get you moving, with some twists and a new type of turn. This dance is still very suitable for new Dance Ranchers. You will be dancing to the right of the floor. As usual, start facing the front, with your feet a little apart and your weight evenly distributed over the balls of both feet.

Tennessee Twists

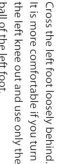
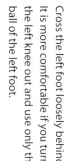
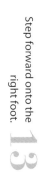

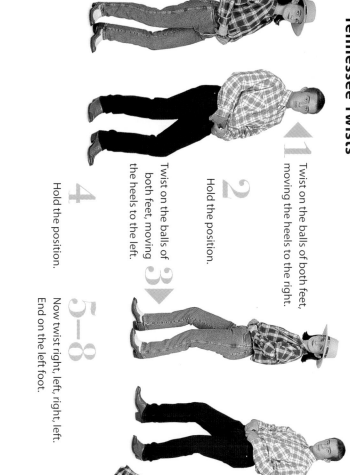

◄1
Twist on the balls of both feet, moving the heels to the right.

2
Hold the position.

3▶
Twist on the balls of both feet, moving the heels to the left.

4
Hold the position.

5–8
Now twist right, left, right, left. End on the left foot.

Forward-Backwards Double Taps

9–10
Moving the right foot forward, tap with the heel. Repeat once.

11–12
Moving the right foot backwards, tap with the toe. Repeat once.

Crosses, Starting with the Right Foot

13
Step forward onto the right foot.

14▼
Cross the left foot loosely behind. It is more comfortable if you turn the left knee out and use only the ball of the left foot.

15–16
Repeat Steps 13 and 14.

Swivel Turn to the Right

17
Step forward onto the right foot, flexing the knee for stability.

18
Standing on the right foot, swivel a half turn (180°) to the right. If necessary, use the left foot to steady yourself after the turn but do not stand on the left foot.

Crosses, Starting with the Left Foot

19
Step forward onto the left foot.

20▼
Cross the right foot behind. It is more comfortable if you turn the right knee out and use only the ball of the right foot.

21–22
Repeat Steps 19 and 20. ➔

Swivel Turn to the Left

23–24

Step forward onto the left foot, flexing the knee for stability. Standing on the left foot, swivel a half turn (180°) to the left. Use the right foot to steady yourself after the turn but do not stand on the right foot.

Vine to the Right with Hitch Turn and Vine to the Left

25–32

You now complete the dance simply by dancing the familiar Vine to the Right with a Hitch Turn making a half turn (180°) to right on the right foot, and a Vine to the Left.

You can now enjoy dancing the Tennessee Twister.

Music Suggestion

"Close but no Guitar", by Toby Keith (Mercury) is a slow track offering a gentle introduction to the dance.

"Get in Line", by Larry Boone (Columbia) is also excellent.

"Baby I'm Burnin'", by Dolly Parton (RCA) is great for a twistin' time with the Tennessee Twister.

I Feel Lucky

Occasionally, when a dance is devised with a particular piece of music in mind, the dance takes the same name as the music track. This popular dance is performed to the hit "I Feel Lucky" by Mary Chapin Carpenter. Start facing the front, with your feet together and standing on the left foot.

Walking Backwards and Forward to Tap and Clap

1
Walk backwards onto the right foot.

2
Walk backwards onto the left foot.

3
Repeat Step 1.

4
Tap the left foot and clap your hands.

5
Walk forward onto the left foot.

6
Walk forward onto the right foot.

7
Repeat Step 5.

8
Tap the right foot and clap your hands.

Turn to the Right

9
Making a quarter turn (90°) to the right, walk forward onto your right foot.

10
Making a quarter turn (90°) to the right along the same line, step to the side onto the left foot. You now have your back to the front.

11
Making a half turn (180°) to the right along the same line, step to the side onto the right foot. You are now facing the front.

12
Tap the left foot on the floor and clap your hands.

Points, Taps and Claps

13–16 Repeat Steps 9–12, making the turns to the left and moving the opposite foot.

17 Step onto the right foot.

18 Point the left foot forward and across.

19 Point the left foot back and to the side.

20▼ Hold the position and clap your hands to the right.

21–23 Repeat Steps 17–19 starting with the left foot.

24 Hold the position and clap your hands to the left.

25 Step onto the right foot.

26 Point the left foot forward and across and clap.

27–28 Repeat Steps 25 and 26 starting with the left foot.

Walks and Cross

29 Walk forward onto the right foot.

30 Walk forward onto the left foot.

31▲ Cross the right foot over the left.

32 Step back onto the left foot.

During the Turns to the Right and Left, ensure that you keep your feet apart and that you always track in the same direction to avoid turning back on yourself.

You are now ready to start again.

Boot Scootin' Boogie

This is one of my favourite American Country Line Dances. It is quite easy, though the Boot Scoot may seem tricky at first. Start facing the front with your weight on both feet and with the feet slightly apart ready to twist it.

Twists Moving to the Left

1▶ Standing on the heels of both feet, move the toes to the left.

2 Standing on the balls of both feet, move the heels to the left.

3–4 Repeat Steps 1 and 2.

Twists Moving to the Right

5 Standing on the balls of both feet, move the heels to the right.

6▼ Standing on the heels of both feet, move the toes to the right.

7–8 Repeat Steps 5 and 6.

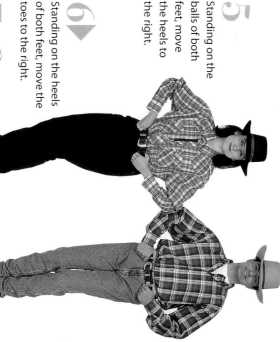

Toe Heels in Place

9
Standing on the left foot, lift the right heel and point the right toe to the floor.

10
Lower the right heel and stand on the right foot.

11
Lift the left heel and point the left toe to the floor.

12
Lower the left heel and stand on the left foot.

Kicks, Close, Point, Close

13–14
Kick the right foot forward from the knee. Repeat once.

15
Close the right foot to the left foot.

16
Point the left foot behind.

17
Close the left foot to the right foot and stand on the left foot.

Hitch

18
Standing on the left foot, raise the right knee, making a right angle at the ankle.

Triple Steps

19, 19&, 20
Move forward onto the right foot with your right side forward.
Move the left foot towards the right foot using only the ball of the foot and keeping the right side forward.
Move forward onto the right foot with your right side forward.

21, 21&, 22
Move forward onto the left foot with your left side forward.
Move the right foot towards the left foot using only the ball of the foot and keeping the left side forward.
Move forward onto the left foot with your left side forward.

Spot Turn to the Left

23
Walk forward onto the right foot, leaving the left foot behind in place.

24
Standing on the right foot, swivel a half turn (180°) to the left and transfer your weight forward onto the left foot.

Triple Steps

25–28
Dance a right foot then a left foot triple step as before.

Boot Scoots

29, 30▶
Hop forward on the left foot with the foot lightly skimming the floor and the right foot extended in front with the foot at a right angle to the leg. Repeat once.

Vine to the Right

31
Step to the side with the right foot.

32
Cross the left foot behind the right foot.

33
Step to the side again with the right foot.

Music Suggestion
Get boot scootin' to the original "Boot Scootin' Boogie" by Brooks & Dunn.

Points and Clap

34 Point the left foot forward and across.

35 Point the left foot out to the side.

36 Hold the position and clap to the right side.

Vine to the Left

37 Step to the side with the left foot.

38 Cross the right foot behind the left.

39 Step to the side with the left foot.

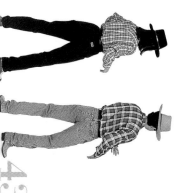

Points and Clap

40 Point the right foot forward and across.

41 Point the right foot out to the side.

42 Hold the position and clap to the left.

43 Walk forward onto the right foot, making a quarter turn to the right.

Stroll

This new move is just strolled through, keeping the steps small.

◄44 Cross the left foot behind the right foot.

45 Walk forward onto the right foot. Almost close the left foot to the right foot.

46 Almost close the left foot to the right foot.

You are now ready to start the Boot Scootin' Boogie again, but facing the wall that was on your left when you started the dance.

Houston Slide

Slightly unusually, this dance incorporates a turn to the right. Start facing the front with feet together standing on the left foot.

Taps and Slides

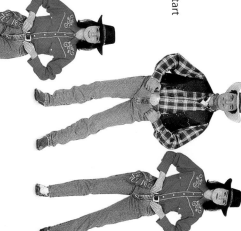

1 Tap the right toe out to the side.

2 Close the right foot to the left foot, keeping your weight on the left foot.

3 Step to the side with the right foot.

4 Slide the left foot to the right foot.

5-8 Repeat starting with the left foot.

Forward and Backwards Double and Single Taps

9, 10
Tap the right heel forward. Repeat once.

11, 12
Tap the right toe backwards. Repeat once.

13
Tap the right heel forward.

14
Tap the right toe backwards.

Step Scuffs

15
Step forward onto the right foot.

16
Standing on the right foot, swivel a quarter turn (180°) to the right and scuff the left foot.

17
Step forward onto the left foot.

18
Scuff the right foot forward.

Cowboy Reggae

19
Cross the right foot over the left foot. If you swivel a little on the left foot, you will find the move easier and more comfortable.

20
Step backwards onto the left foot.

21
Tap the right foot to the side.

22
Jump forward onto both feet to bring them together.

You are now facing the wall which was previously on your right and you are ready to start the Houston Slide again.

The Achy Breaky

So popular was the Achy Breaky Heart hit by Billy Ray Cyrus when it was first released that immediately scores of Line Dances were were devised for it. The official version was choreographed by one of America's leading Line Dance choreographers, Melanie Greenwood, and here is our interpretation of her dance. Start by facing the front and standing on the left foot.

Vine to the Right

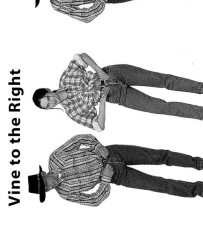

1
Step to the side with the right foot.

2
Cross the left foot behind the right foot.

3
Step to the side with the right foot.

4
Hold the position on the right foot with feet apart.

Hip Swings

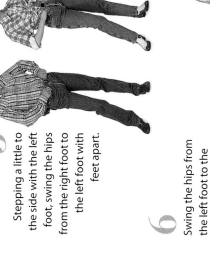

5
Stepping a little to the side with the left foot, swing the hips from the right foot to the left foot with feet apart.

6
Swing the hips from the left foot to the right foot.

7
Swing the hips from the right foot to the left foot.

8
Hold the position on the left foot.

Foot Taps Turning to the Left

9 Standing on the left foot, tap the right toe backwards.

10 Tap the right toe out to the side.

11 Swivel a quarter turn (90°) to the left and tap the right foot out to the side.

12 Swivel a half turn (180°) to the left and step backwards onto your right foot.

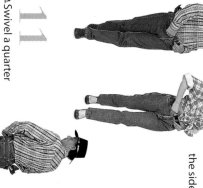

Walking Backwards to Hitch and Swing Step to the Side

13 Walk backwards onto the left foot.

14 Walk backwards onto the right foot.

15 Hitch the left foot (see the Honky Tonk Stomp).

16 Swing the left leg backwards, making a quarter turn (90°) to the left and end on the left foot with feet apart.

Walking Backwards to Stomp

17 Walk backwards onto the right foot.

18 Walk backwards onto the left foot.

19 Walk backwards onto the right foot.

20 Stomp the left foot.

21–24 Repeat Steps 5–8.

Hip Swings

Turning Stomps

25 Making a quarter turn (90°) to the right, step onto the right foot.

26 Stomp the left foot.

27 Making a half turn (180°) to the left, step onto the left foot.

28 Stomp the right foot.

Vine to the Right and Clap

29–31 Repeat Steps 1–3.

32 Close the left foot to the right foot and clap your hands.

Music Suggestion
"Achy Breaky Heart", by Billy Ray Cyrus (Phonogram).

End standing on the left foot ready to start again. You are now facing the wall which was previously on your left. The dance both starts and finishes with a Vine to the Right. Since there are two consecutive Vines to the Right, you could substitute a turn for one of them.

International Latin-American Dances

The International Latin-American dances are based in conventional dance schools which usually offer a mixture of courses and private lessons plus opportunities to enjoy the dances at regular party nights. Many schools have a programme which gradually introduces many of the dances in a single course. This is a great way to get dancing quickly. The course may also include the International Standard dances since it is customary for both styles to be featured more or less equally at each dance party. In such schools, a version of Rock 'n' Roll or Jive will usually be included as part of the Latin-American programme. The style and technique taught by qualified teachers in recognized schools will be identical worldwide. In contrast to club dancing, conventional dance schools tend to attract couples so it is worth asking a friend or partner with you at least for your first class. Once there, it's time to relax, enjoy the convivial atmosphere and get down to some serious fun!

The Cuban Family of Dances

Fans of Latin American dancing often notice a similarity between the international styles of Mambo, Rumba, Cha Cha Cha and Salsa. This is because the dances all originate from the same Cuban source, finding their roots in the Bolero-Rumba, the Danzón and the Son.

The characteristics of the Rumba produce a slow, sensuous and very beautiful dance of love. The pattern of the Cha Cha moves are similar that of the Rumba but the speed is a little quicker and the mood is much more playful and teasing.

In Salsa, which is a distillation of many Latin and Afro-Caribbean dances, turns have become an important feature, so the overall look and feel are quite different from those of the Mambo, though the dances

Mambo is one of the most exuberant of Cuban dances.

share many of the basic moves. In contrast to the Mambo, where the feel of the dance is generally based on forward and backward movements, Salsa moves have more of a side-to-side feel.

Mambo has a pattern, structure and feel which are closer to the Rumba and Cha Cha Cha, although it is a faster and more exuberant dance. The experienced Mambo dancer will use every beat of music and interpret them with four actions, comprising two steps, a movement of the foot in place and a final transfer of weight. In the international style of Mambo used in the introduction to the dance given in this book, three steps are danced over four beats of music. The steps themselves are simplified, so a "Quick" is danced to one beat and a "Slow" to two beats, following a normal pattern of "Quick Quick Slow".

There is a great technical debate in Mambo about which action occurs on which beat. Experienced dancers often argue that the transfer of weight occurs on beat one, as has become the norm in the Rumba and Cha Cha Cha, while others maintain that it occurs on the final beat. In practice, dancers with a highly developed sense of formal technique tend to dance the weight transfer on count one, while social dancers and the Latins themselves tend to dance it on count four. Since both are possible, the dancer is entitled to dance to the emphasis of the beat given by the percussionists in any given musical arrangement. For the purposes of this chapter, the rhythm is that favoured by most social dancers, where Step 1 occurs on the first beat of the bar of music. Whatever the outcome of the technical debate, no one can be wrong for getting onto the floor and enjoying dancing the Mambo.

Music and Rhythm

Mambo music is as fascinating as it is diverse. Like all Latin American dance music, the rhythm is exciting and for a dancer, the rhythm is the first concern. In Mambo, the rhythm is set by an astonishing variety of percussive instruments. These include the clave, two hardwood sticks which are tapped together to produce the basic rhythm; the guiro, which produces a rasping sound; maracas, originally hollow gourds filled with dried peas or small pebbles to make a rattle; the campana or cowbell; and a variety of drums, including the conga, tumba, bongo and timbales.

When first listening to Mambo music, it is not uncommon for the newcomer to be confused by the variety of rhythms within the umbrella of Mambo. This variety exists because Mambo marks a transition from several earlier dance rhythms into a distillation of all of them. In the same way as different chefs might produce the same dish but with variations according to each chef's preferences, so different musicians might produce one of the three different Mambo rhythms.

The first and simplest Mambo rhythm uses four basic beats, which a dancer will interpret as "Quick Quick Slow". This is the type of rhythm used in this book. The second type of rhythm tends to be faster and uses the four basic beats which are interpreted as four "Quick" counts or "Quick Quick Slow" or the two are mixed together in one dance. This rhythm has largely

become associated with Salsa. The third rhythm tends to be slower but splits beat four in half to produce three whole counts followed by two half counts. The two split beats followed by a whole beat give the familiar Cha Cha Cha rhythm. Although it may be interesting to understand what the rhythmic differences are and why they occur in the same dance, it is not necessary to delve too deeply into rhythm analysis in order to enjoy dancing the Mambo.

The tempo of Mambo music varies enormously, starting at about 32 bars per minute for Cha Cha Cha and rising to 40 for social dancing, before climaxing at a more challenging 56 bars per minute for expert dancers.

Mambo music usually has a time signature of 4/4, which means that there are four equal beats to each bar of music, though 8/8 is also possible.

This couple are preparing to dance an Underarm Turn, which can be mixed in an exotic cocktail of mambo moves.

Mambo

The Mambo enjoys a rich past, originating in the fertile mixture of Afro-Caribbean and Latin American cultures found on the island of Cuba. Cuba had always been able to boast an amazing diversity of dances and rhythms. By the 1940s, a new and exciting sound, originally led by Odilio Urfé and Arsenio Rodríguez, was beginning to emerge. A mixture of Latin with a heavy Jazz influence, the style was developed by Dámaso Pérez Prado, a Cuban band leader based in Mexico who, by 1945, had turned it into the latest dance craze. This hot new dance, the Mambo, is believed to have been named after the voodoo priests who are able to send devotees into wild, hypnotic dances. The Mambo was initially condemned by the Church in some Latin American countries and restricted by the authorities in others. But, like any forbidden fruit, the Mambo gained in popularity and flourished.

By the 1950s, spurred on by Hollywood and the amazing popularity of Pérez "Prez" Prado, the Mambo had begun to establish itself as a favourite in the USA. Prado was one of the original "Mambo Kings", along with names like Tito Puente, Israel Lopez Cachao and the legendary Mambo musician Machito, all of whom performed at the famous Palladium in New York. They were joined by probably the greatest vocal interpreter of Mambo, Benny Moré. The singer Celia Cruz also became a Latin legend, but it was Prado's hits, such as "Mambo No. 5", "Mambo No. 8", "Mambo Jambo" and "Guaglione", that really brought the music and dance to explode onto the wider world dance scene to become the enduring favourite that it is today.

Of Cuban origin, the Mambo is now enjoyed throughout the world at both social and competition levels.

The Holds

When dancing Cuban, several different holds will be used, depending on the figure being danced. Most starting figures are danced using a close contact hold.

Close Contact Hold

The man and woman are in close contact. The man places his right hand well around the woman's waist with his right forearm across the small of the woman's back. The woman places her left hand on the man's upper right arm, right shoulder or the back of his neck. The man raises his left hand to just below shoulder level with his elbow away from his body. The woman then places the middle finger of her right hand between the thumb and first finger of the man's left hand. The man closes the fingers of his left hand to take hold.

The woman is positioned slightly to the man's right, so that his left foot is outside the woman's right foot when he moves forward onto his left foot and his right foot is between the woman's feet when he moves forward onto his right foot.

Right Hand to Right Hand Hold

This hold is very similar to shaking hands except that the man holds his hand palm upwards and the woman rests her palm on it. The hold should not be tight. The hands are held at about waist height. It is important for both the man's and woman's arms to be toned, but not rigid, to allow the man to give and the woman to receive the lead. What to do with the free arm depends on the move being danced and will be dealt with later in this book.

Left Hand to Right Hand Hold

In this hold, you will be in an open position, a little apart from your partner. The man takes the woman's right hand in his left hand and the free arm is normally extended to the side at waist height.

Right Hand to Left Hand Hold

This is the same as the hold above, but the woman's left hand is held in the man's right hand.

Double Hand Hold

In this hold, the man and woman are a little apart. The man holds the woman's left hand in his right hand and her right hand in his left hand, just below shoulder height.

The close contact hold seen from the front (left) and back (above).

Basic Mambo

Even top dancers constantly return to the basic movements to rediscover the exciting simplicity of the unadorned dance. These moves perfectly characterize the Mambo's essence, and it is with these moves that we will begin. To start, take up a close contact hold. The man is standing with his weight on the right foot and the woman with her weight on the left foot.

1
COUNT – QUICK

Man Move forward onto the left foot, leaving the right foot in place.

Woman Move back onto the right foot, leaving the left foot in place.

2
COUNT – QUICK

Man Transfer your body weight back onto the right foot.

Woman Transfer your body weight forward onto the left foot.

3
COUNT – SLOW

Man Move back onto the left foot, a small step.

Woman Move forward onto the right foot, a small step.

4
COUNT – QUICK

Man Move back onto the right foot, leaving the left foot in place.

Woman Move forward onto the left foot, leaving the right foot in place.

5
COUNT – QUICK

Man Transfer your body weight forward onto the left foot.

Woman Transfer your body weight back onto the right foot.

6
COUNT – SLOW

Man Move forward onto the right foot, a small step.

Woman Move back onto the left foot, a small step.

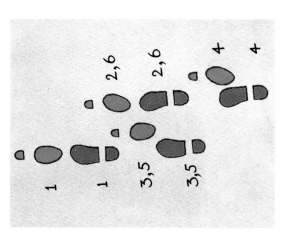

You can now repeat the Basic Mambo continuously or combine it with other moves described later in the book. Try gradually turning the Basic Mambo to the left, with no more than a quarter turn (90°) to each set of six steps.

Feet and Legs

Throughout the Mambo, a forward movement is danced by pushing the body weight forward onto the ball of the foot and then lowering the heel. This is very different from a normal walk where the heel contacts the floor first. The action is very characteristic of Afro-Caribbean Latin American dancing. On a backward movement, the knee of the moving leg straightens as the body weight moves over the hip and the heel of the foot left in place is raised slightly from the floor. This action should not be exaggerated.

Due to the speed of the Mambo, it is often not possible to transfer all of the body weight onto the stepping foot. In this case, only part of the weight is used to give a feeling of pressure through the foot taking the step. On a sideways movement, the inside edge of the ball of the moving foot should contact the floor first and then the body weight is rolled over onto a flat foot as the heel is lowered. As the body weight moves onto the foot, the heel of the foot remaining in place is allowed to lift, leaving the inside edge of the ball of that foot in contact with the floor.

La Cucuracha

In Latin American Spanish, cucuracha means "cockroach", and is the name given to a move which is popular in several of the dances originating in Cuba. This compact move is a useful one to dance when the floor is crowded or while you are deciding what your next move will be. Start in a close contact hold. The man is standing with his weight on the right foot and the woman with her weight on the left foot.

1
COUNT – QUICK

Man Move sideways onto the left foot, leaving the right foot in place.

Woman Move sideways onto the right foot, leaving the left foot in place.

2
COUNT – QUICK

Man Transfer your body weight sideways onto the right foot.

Woman Transfer your body weight sideways onto the left foot.

3
COUNT – SLOW

Man Close the left foot to the right foot.

Woman Close the right foot to the left foot.

4
COUNT – QUICK

Man Move sideways onto the right foot, leaving the left foot in place.

Woman Move sideways onto the left foot, leaving the right foot in place.

5
COUNT – QUICK

Man Transfer your body weight sideways onto the left foot.

Woman Transfer your body weight sideways onto the right foot.

6
COUNT – SLOW

Man Close the right foot to the left foot.

Woman Close the left foot to the right foot.

Style Tip
As you move to the side on Steps 1 and 4 try to keep the upper part of your body relatively still, so that the sideways movement is achieved through your body. If you find this a little tricky at first, a smaller step will help you to achieve the correct movement.

After La Cucuracha, you can repeat the move or continue into the Basic Mambo or the Dirty Mambo.

Dirty Mambo
With just two basic moves, you can already try out a new move by combining them in the Dirty Mambo. The Mambo received a great boost to its popularity when the feature film Dirty Dancing was released and this is probably how this figure got its name.

Dance Steps 1–3 of the Basic Mambo.
Dance Steps 4–6 of La Cucuracha.
Dance Steps 1–3 of La Cucuracha.
Dance Steps 4–6 of the Basic Mambo.

MAMBO: manita a   mano

Manita a Mano

Start this popular move in a double hand hold. To do this, dance a complete Basic Mambo, started as usual in close contact hold. During Steps 1–3 of the Basic Mambo, the man leads the woman to move away from him, releasing his right hand. During Steps 4–6 of the Basic Mambo, the man takes the woman's left hand in his right hand in a double hand hold. The man is now standing on the right foot and woman on the left foot ready to dance Manita a Mano.

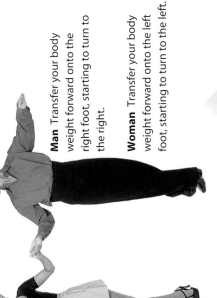

1
COUNT – QUICK

Man Using your left hand, lead the woman's right side away from you and then release hold with your left hand. Move back onto the left foot, turning a quarter turn (90°) to the left, into a side-by-side position with the woman and leaving the right foot in place.

Woman Move back onto the right foot, turning a quarter turn (90°) to the right, into a side-by-side position with the man and leaving the left foot in place.

2
COUNT – QUICK

Man Transfer your body weight forward onto the right foot, starting to turn to the right.

Woman Transfer your body weight forward onto the left foot, starting to turn to the left.

Style Tip
It is important to both the look and the feel of the Manita a Mano that, as the dancers step back into a side-by-side position, the elbows are away from the side of the body to avoid a cramped appearance.

4
COUNT – QUICK

Man Using your right hand, lead the woman's left side away from you and then release hold with your right hand. Move back onto the right foot, turning a quarter turn (90°) to the right, into a side-by-side position with the woman and leaving the left foot in place.

Woman Move back onto the left foot, turning a quarter turn (90°) to the left, into a side-by-side position with the man and leaving the right foot in place.

3
COUNT – SLOW

Man Move sideways onto the left foot to end facing the woman and resume a double hand hold.

Woman Move sideways onto the right foot to end facing the man and resume a double hand hold.

5
COUNT – QUICK

Man Transfer your body weight forward onto the left foot, starting to turn to the left.

Woman Transfer your body weight forward onto the right foot, starting to turn to the right.

6
COUNT – SLOW

Man Move sideways onto the right foot to end facing the woman and resume a double hand hold.

Woman Move sideways onto the left foot to end facing the man and resume a double hand hold.

7–9
Man & Woman Repeat Steps 1–3.

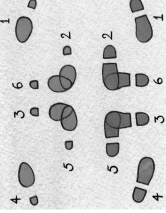

Continue into Steps 4–6 of the Basic Mambo, resuming close contact hold, or try the Underarm Spot Turn to the Right.

Underarm Spot Turn to the Right

The move gives a nice finish to a wide variety of figures. It can end in any hold and is also a great figure to use in preparing for a move which requires a change of hold. You can dance this turn after Steps 1–3 of the Basic Mambo but, for now, assume that you have just danced Manita a Mano. The man is standing on the left foot and the woman on the right foot. Both have their feet apart and are in a double hand hold. On the last step of Manita a Mano, the man should raise his left hand and release his right hand to indicate the turn. While the woman dances the Spot Turn, the man's steps are the same as Steps 4–6 of the Basic Mambo, but ending with a short side step.

1
COUNT – QUICK
Man Move back onto the right foot, leaving the left foot in place. Lead the turn by moving your raised hand to the left.

Woman On the right foot, swivel a quarter turn (90°) to the right and move forward under the man's raised hand onto the left foot, leaving the right foot in place. Once on the left foot, swivel 180° to the right to end with the left foot back. The right foot is still in place and the man is on your right.

2
COUNT – QUICK
Man Transfer your body weight forward onto the left foot.

Woman Transfer your body weight forward onto the right foot, starting to turn to the right to face the man.

3
COUNT – SLOW
Man Move sideways onto the right foot, a small step, lowering your left arm.

Woman Move sideways onto the left foot, turning to the right to face the man.

In a close contact hold, you can now continue with the Basic Mambo or La Cucuracha. In a double hand hold, you can continue with another Manita a Mano or the New York, a figure that opens up further possibilities.

The Free Arm

In Mambo, as in most Latin American dances, there are many moves in which the man and woman are holding with only one hand. By following some general guidelines about what to do with your free arm and hand, you can give your dance a superb appearance and a balanced feel.

• During a movement, the position of the free arm and hand should mirror the height and curve of the joined arm and hand. It is neater to avoid spreading the fingers.

• During a turn on the spot, the arm should be drawn out of the way across the body and then allowed to return naturally to its position mirroring the joined hand and arm.

• The free arm should never be held above shoulder height nor dropped to the side, as this not only looks bad but severely inhibits good balance.

As you develop a feel for the dance, you may wish to respond by moving the free arm in a natural, balanced and gentle way. Do not exaggerate the movements, and match not only your own movements but also those of your partner. As Mambo is one of the livelier Latin American dances, it is a good idea to keep the free arm relatively still in relation to your body. A still arm has the effect of enhancing the appearance of the leg and hip action.

New York

Many of the developments in the Mambo took place in the Hispanic barrios, or neighbourhoods, of New York, so it is entirely appropriate that this move should be named after that great melting-pot of music and dance styles. To dance the New York, start in a double hand hold, having just danced either the Basic Mambo or the Underarm Spot Turn to the Right. As a contrasting variation, you can also start the New York after Step 6 of the Manita a Mano. The man is standing on the right foot and the woman on the left foot.

1

COUNT – QUICK

Man Release hold with the right hand and draw the left hand across and forward, swivelling a quarter turn (90°) to the right on the right foot. Move forward onto the left foot, leaving the right foot in place.

Woman Release hold with the left hand and swivel a quarter turn (90°) to the left on the left foot. Move forward onto the right foot, leaving the left foot in place.

2

COUNT – QUICK

Man Transfer your body weight back onto the right foot.

Woman Transfer your body weight back onto the left foot.

3

COUNT – SLOW

Man Swivel a quarter turn (90°) to the left on the right foot and move sideways onto the left foot to face the woman.

Woman Swivel a quarter turn (90°) to the right on the left foot and move sideways onto the right foot to face the man. Resume a double hand hold.

4

COUNT – QUICK

Man Release hold with the left hand and draw the right hand across and forward, swivelling a quarter turn (90°) to the left on the left foot. Move forward onto the right foot.

Woman Release hold with the right hand and swivel a quarter turn (90°) to the right on the right foot. Move forward onto the left foot.

5

COUNT – QUICK

Man Transfer your body weight back onto the left foot.

Woman Transfer your body weight back onto the right foot.

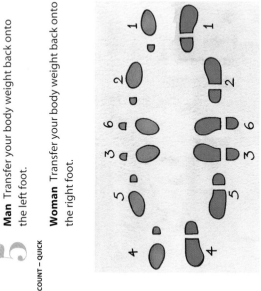

6

COUNT – SLOW

Man Swivel a quarter turn (90°) to the right on the left foot and move sideways onto the right foot to face the woman. Resume a double hand hold but do not grip.

Woman Swivel a quarter turn (90°) to the left on the right foot and move sideways onto the left foot to face the man. Resume a double hand hold.

You are now in a position to continue with the Basic Mambo, resuming a close contact hold. When you feel confident, dance Steps 1–3 again and follow straight into the Underarm Spot Turn to the Right. Another fabulous combination is to dance the six steps of the New York and then follow with Underarm Spot Turns to the Left and the Right.

Underarm Spot Turn to the Left

This is the mirror image of the Underarm Spot Turn to the Right and is not only a useful figure to have in your repertoire but also looks spectacular when combined with the Underarm Spot Turn to the Right. Start in a double hand hold. The man is standing on the right foot and the woman on the left foot. On the last step of the previous move, the man will raise his left hand and release hold with his right hand to indicate the turn.

1
COUNT – QUICK

Man Move back onto the left foot leaving the right foot in place. Lead the turn by moving your raised hand to the right.

Woman On the left foot, swivel a quarter turn (90°) to the left and move forward under the man's raised hand onto the right foot, leaving the left foot in place. Once on the right foot, swivel a half turn (180°) to the left to end with the right foot back. The left foot is still in place and the man is on your left.

2
COUNT – QUICK

Man Transfer your body weight forward onto the right foot.

Woman Transfer your body weight forward onto the left foot, starting to turn to the left towards the man.

3
COUNT – SLOW

Man Move sideways onto the left foot, a small step, lowering your hand.

Woman Move sideways onto the right foot, turning to the left to face the man.

Continue into Steps 4–6 of the Basic Mambo, taking up a close contact hold, or dance the Underarm Spot Turn to the Right.

New York Bus Stop

With a little imagination and know-how, basic moves can be combined and developed to great effect. Here is an easy variation of the New York which has a fun surprise element. To set up the move, begin by dancing the New York. You are now in double hand hold. The man is standing on the right foot and the woman on the left foot. Note the change of rhythm.

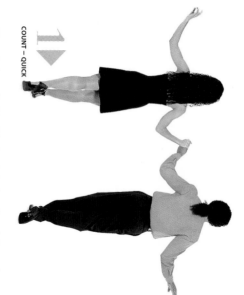

1
COUNT – QUICK

Man Release hold with the right hand and draw the left hand across and forward, swivelling a quarter turn (90°) to the right on the right foot. Move forward onto the left foot, leaving the right foot in place.

Woman Release hold with the left hand and swivel a quarter turn (90°) to the left on the left foot. Move forward onto the right foot, leaving right foot in place.

2
COUNT – QUICK

Man Transfer your weight onto the right foot.

Woman Transfer your weight back onto the left foot.

3
COUNT – QUICK

Man Swivel a quarter turn (90°) to the left on the right foot and move sideways, a small step, onto the left foot to face the woman, leaving the right foot in place. Resume a double hand hold but do not grip.

Woman Swivel a quarter turn (90°) to the right on the left foot and move sideways onto the right foot to face the man, leaving the left foot in place. Resume a double hand hold.

MAMBO: new york bus stop

5

COUNT – QUICK

Man Release hold with the right hand and draw the left hand across and forward, swivelling a quarter turn (90°) to the right on the right foot. Move forward onto the left foot, leaving the right foot in place.

Woman Release hold with the left hand and swivel a quarter turn (90°) to the left on the left foot. Move forward onto the right foot, leaving the left foot in place.

6

COUNT – QUICK

Man Transfer your body weight back onto the right foot.

Woman Transfer your body weight back onto the left foot.

4

COUNT – QUICK

Man Transfer your body weight onto the right foot.

Woman Transfer your body weight onto the left foot.

7

COUNT – SLOW

Man Swivel a quarter turn (90°) to the left on the right foot and move sideways onto the left foot to face the woman, leaving the right foot in place. Resume a double hand hold but do not grip.

Woman Swivel a quarter turn (90°) to the right on the left foot and move sideways onto the right foot to face the man, leaving the left foot in place. Resume a double hand hold.

8–14

Man & Woman Repeat Steps 1–7, in the opposite direction and using the opposite feet and hands.

El Mambo Mexicano

For ease of communication, it is often simpler to give a particular combination its own name. Let's call this one El Mambo Mexicano. This very simple but effective combination can be slipped into your programme after a little practice. It looks impressive and only you will know that it is not as complicated as it appears!

• *Underarm Spot Turn to the Right, ending in a right hand to right hand hold (maintain this hold throughout the rest of the combination)*
• *Basic Mambo*
• *Steps 1–3 of the New York*
• *Steps 4–6 of the Basic Mambo (the backward half)*
• *Steps 1–3 of the Basic Mambo (the forward half)*
• *Steps 4–6 of the New York*
• *Steps 1–3 of the Basic Mambo (the forward half)*
• *Underarm Spot Turn to the Right, resuming normal close contact hold on Step 3*

You are now in the right position to continue with the Basic Mambo or any other appropriate figure you have learned. The New York Bus Stop can be used to good effect in combination with the New York: dance a complete New York, then Steps 1–7 of the New York Bus Stop, Steps 4–6 then Steps 1–3 of the New York, and finally Steps 8–14 of the New York Bus Stop.

El Molinito

El Molinito (the "Little Windmill") is actually a combination of moves, which when put together, give a special effect. This is due mainly to the interesting use of the arms and the relative positions of the man and woman as they progress through the moves. It is easier to work through this group in sections.

Underarm Spot Turn to the Right, overturned to a side-by-side position

1

COUNT – QUICK

Man Raising your left hand to initiate the woman's turn, move back onto the right foot, leaving the left foot in place.

Woman On the right foot, swivel a quarter turn (90°) to the right and move forward under the man's raised hand onto the left foot, leaving the right foot in place. Once on the left foot, swivel a half turn (180°) to the right to end with the left foot back. The right foot is still in place and the man is on your right.

Man Transfer your body weight forward onto the left foot, continuing to turn the woman clockwise.

Woman Transfer your body weight forward onto the right foot, starting to turn to the right towards the man.

2

COUNT – QUICK

3

COUNT – SLOW

Man Close the right foot to the left foot, leading the woman to continue turning, to end with her back to you on your right side. Place the woman's right hand in your right hand and take it over her head to end with your right arm across her shoulders and your right hand holding her right hand on her right shoulder. Take hold of the woman's left hand with your left hand.

Woman Move forward onto the left foot towards the man's right side, turning to the right to face the man. On the left foot, continue to turn by swivelling a half turn (180°) to the right to end facing in the same direction as the man, on his right side.

El Molinito

4

COUNT – QUICK

Man Move forward onto the left foot, raising your right hand a little over the woman's head as she moves back.

Woman Bending forward from the waist underneath the man's arm, move back onto the right foot, retaining hold onto the right foot, and releasing hold with the left hand.

Man Move forward onto the right foot, raising your right hand and releasing hold with the left hand.

Woman Move sideways onto the right foot, retaining hold with the right hand and resuming a normal upright stance.

5

COUNT – QUICK

Man Move sideways onto the right foot, retaining hold with the right hand but releasing the left hand.

Woman Move sideways onto the left foot, retaining hold with the left hand.

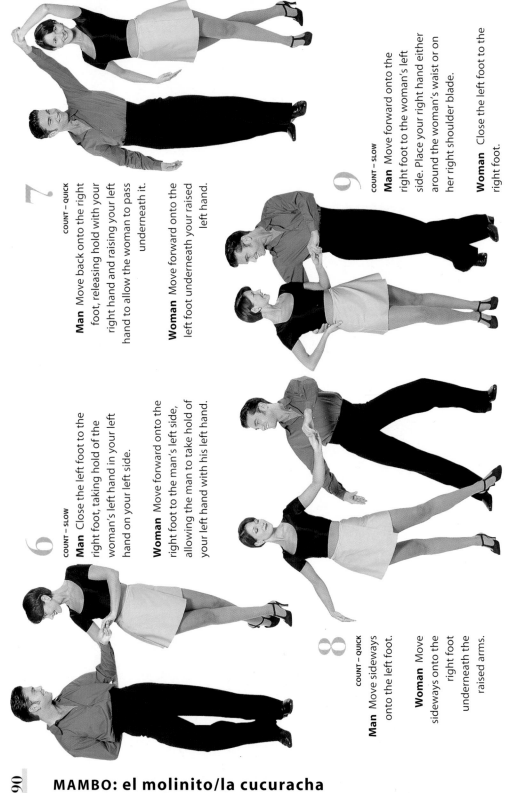

6

COUNT – SLOW

Man Close the left foot to the right foot, taking hold of the woman's left hand in your left hand on your left side.

Woman Move forward onto the right foot to the man's left side, allowing the man to take hold of your left hand with his left hand.

7

COUNT – QUICK

Man Move back onto the right foot, releasing hold with your right hand and raising your left hand to allow the woman to pass underneath it.

Woman Move forward onto the left foot underneath your raised left hand.

8

COUNT – QUICK

Man Move sideways onto the left foot.

Woman Move sideways onto the right foot underneath the raised arms.

9

COUNT – SLOW

Man Move forward onto the right foot to the woman's left side. Place your right hand either around the woman's waist or on her right shoulder blade.

Woman Close the left foot to the right foot.

La Cucuracha

10–12

COUNTS – QUICK, QUICK, SLOW

Man Dance La Cucuracha to the left.

Woman Dance La Cucuracha to the right.

10

11

12

Exit

13 ▶

COUNT – QUICK

Man Move back onto the right foot, leaving the left foot in place. Release hold with the right hand.

Woman Move forward onto the left foot, leaving the right foot in place.

14

COUNT – QUICK

Man Transfer your body weight forward onto the left foot.

Woman Move forward onto the right foot, leaving the left foot in place. On the right foot, swivel a half turn (180°) to the left to end with the right foot back.

15 ▶

COUNT – SLOW

Man Move forward onto the right foot, a small step, resuming double hand hold.

Woman Move back onto the left foot, a small step.

The Liquidizer

Don't worry. "The Liquidizer" is just a fun name for a move with a rather longer technically descriptive title. In this series of moves, the man and woman move around each other, hence the Liquidizer. This figure is not difficult but will require a little practice to ensure that the man and woman maintain a good orientation to each other. The result will be simple but spectacular. Start by dancing the first three steps of the move – these are known as El Contro Cuerpo – then change into an open position. Change to a right hand hold as you move into Step 4.

1
COUNT – QUICK

Man Move forward onto the left foot, leaving the right foot in place.

Woman Move back onto the right foot, leaving the left foot in place.

2
COUNT – QUICK

Man Transfer your body weight back onto the right foot.

Woman Transfer your body weight forward onto the left foot.

3
COUNT – SLOW

Man Turning a quarter turn (90°) to the left, move sideways onto the left foot and bring your left hand down toward your left hip.

Woman Move forward onto the right foot, starting to move across the man.

4
COUNT – QUICK

Man Move back onto the right foot, leaving the left foot in place and leading the woman to dance forward across you.

Woman Move forward onto the left foot, across the man.

5
COUNT – QUICK

Man Transfer your body weight forward onto the left foot, leaving the right foot in place and leading the woman to turn to the left.

Woman Move sideways onto the right foot, turning a 90° to the left.

6
COUNT –SLOW

Man Move forward, a small step, onto the right foot, starting to turn to the left.

Woman Continue turning and, on the right foot, make a further half turn (180°) to the left to end in a side-by-side position with the man on your right. Move back, a small step, onto the left foot.

7
COUNT – QUICK

Man Move forward onto the left foot, turning a quarter turn (90°) to the left.

Woman Move back onto the right foot.

8
COUNT – QUICK

Man Move sideways onto the right foot, turning a quarter turn (90°) to the left.

Woman Move onto the left foot, making a good step across the right foot.

9
COUNT – SLOW

Man Continue turning and, on the right foot, make a further half turn (180°) to the left and move back, a small step, onto the left foot. End in a side-by-side position with the woman on your right.

Woman Move forward, a small step, onto the right foot to end in a side-by-side position with the man on your left, starting to turn to the left.

El Lazo

The name of this part of the move means the "Loop". The man completes the figure by turning the woman in a lasso-type move into a close contact hold.

10
COUNT – QUICK

Man Move back, a small step, onto the right foot, leaving the left foot in place. Lead the woman to turn strongly to the left.

Woman Move forward onto the left foot, turning a quarter turn (90°) to the left.

11
COUNT – QUICK

Man Transfer your body weight forward onto the left foot, leading the woman to continue turning by moving your right hand to the right over her head.

Woman Move sideways onto the right foot, making a three-quarter turn to the left to end backing the man.

12
COUNT – SLOW

Man On the left foot, swivel a quarter turn (90°) to the left and move sideways onto the right foot to end facing the woman. Circle your right hand to lead the woman to turn underneath it, concluding the move by bringing your right hand back over your own head and placing the woman's right hand on your left shoulder.

Woman Move forward onto the left foot, turning to the left to face the man. Close the right foot to the left foot, without weight, underneath your body.

You can now repeat the move or continue into your choice of Basic Mambo moves by adjusting your hold.

El Mojito

During the rise of the Mambo through its adolescent years, the famous writer Ernest Hemingway spent much time in the bodegas (or bars) of Havana, imbibing, for inspiration, the rich and fruitful atmosphere of Cuba. Legend has it that the Mojito cocktail was invented in one of these bodegas. Pronounced mo – hee – to, we can apply the name to this dazzling cocktail of Mambo moves. Start in a double hand hold. The man is standing on the right foot and the woman on the left foot having danced, for example, the New York.

Half Turn to Cuddle Position

1
COUNT – QUICK

Man Move back onto the left foot, leading the woman away from you and leaving the right foot in place.

Woman Move back onto the right foot, away from the man, leaving the left foot in place.

2
COUNT – QUICK

Man Transfer your body weight forward onto the right foot. Leading the woman towards your right side, raise your left hand and start to turn her to her left by moving your left hand to the right.

Woman Transfer your body weight forward onto the left foot, starting to turn to the left.

3
COUNT – SLOW

Man Move forward, a small step, onto the left foot. Take your left hand over the woman's head and lower it to waist height into a "cuddle", with the woman ending on your right side.

Woman Move forward onto the right foot towards the man's right side, leaving the left foot in place. On the right foot, swivel a half turn (180°) to the left to end in a side-by-side position with the man on your left.

In this part of the move, the man and woman move around a circle.

4

COUNT – QUICK

Man In a Cuddle Hold, move forward onto the right foot, starting to move clockwise around a circle.

Woman In a Cuddle Hold, move back onto the left foot, starting to move clockwise around a circle.

5

COUNT – QUICK

Man Move forward onto the left foot, moving clockwise around the circle.

Woman Move back onto the right foot, moving clockwise around the circle.

6

COUNT – SLOW

Man Move forward onto the right foot, moving clockwise around the circle, and tap the left foot slightly forward without weight.

Woman Move back onto the left foot, moving clockwise around the circle, and tap the right foot slightly forward without weight.

Rolling off the Arm

7

COUNT – QUICK

Man Releasing hold with your left hand, move sideways onto the left foot, leaving the right foot in place. Lead the woman to start to roll off your right arm.

Woman Turning a quarter turn (90°) to the right, move forward onto the right foot, away from the man.

8

COUNT – QUICK

Man Partly close the right foot towards the left foot, still leading the woman to roll off your arm.

Woman Turning a further quarter turn (90°) to the right, move sideways onto the left foot, away from the man.

9

COUNT – SLOW

Man Move sideways, a small step, onto the left foot, leading the woman to finish rolling off your arm.

Woman On the left foot, pivot a half turn (180°) to the right to end facing the same way as the man and move sideways onto the right foot.

Las Quebraditas Cubanas

These are the "Split Cuban Breaks".

10

COUNT – QUICK

Man Move forward and across, a small step, to check onto the right foot, away from the woman, keeping the right foot pointing to the front.

Woman Move forward and across, a small step, to check onto the left foot, away from the man, keeping the left foot pointing to the front.

11

COUNT – QUICK

Man Transfer your body weight back onto the left foot.

Woman Transfer your body weight back onto the right foot.

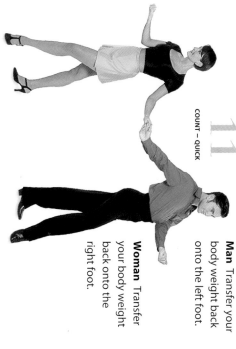

14
COUNT – QUICK

Man Transfer your body weight back onto the right foot.

Woman Transfer your body weight back onto the left foot.

15
COUNT – SLOW

Man Move sideways, a small step, onto the left foot, away from the woman.

Woman Move sideways, a small step, onto the right foot, away from the man.

13
COUNT – QUICK

Man Move forward and across, a small step, to check onto the left foot, towards the woman, keeping the left foot pointing to the front.

Woman Move forward and across, a small step, to check onto the right foot, towards the man, keeping the right foot pointing to the front.

12
COUNT – SLOW

Man Move sideways, a small step, onto the right foot, towards the woman.

Woman Move sideways, a small step, onto the left foot, towards the man.

Spot Turn

16
COUNT – QUICK

Man Release hold with your right hand. On the left foot, swivel a quarter turn (90°) to the left. Move forward onto the right foot, leaving the left foot in place. Once on the right foot, swivel a half turn (180°) to the left to end facing the woman, with the right foot back.

Woman On the right foot, swivel a quarter turn (90°) to the right and move forward onto the left foot, leaving the right foot in place. Once on the left foot, swivel a half turn (180°) to the right to end with the left foot back.

18
COUNT – SLOW

Man Move forward onto the right foot, resuming hold.

Woman Move forward onto the left foot, resuming hold.

Continue with your choice of hot Mambo moves.

17
COUNT – QUICK

Man Transfer your body weight forward onto the left foot.

Woman Transfer your body weight forward onto the right foot.

MAMBO: el mojito

Los Giros Locos

Here is a short but impressive move, which starts with a turn one way and then the other, hence the name, which means "the Crazy Turns". Start in a double hand hold. The man is standing on the right foot and the woman on the left foot. If you prefer, you can build a variation into the figure in Steps 7–9.

1
COUNT – QUICK

Man Move back onto the left foot, leaving the right foot in place and leading the woman away from you.

Woman Move back onto the right foot, away from the man, leaving the left foot in place.

2
COUNT – QUICK

Man Transfer your body weight onto the left foot. Take your left hand over the woman's head and lower it to shoulder height into a Cuddle Position, with the woman ending on your right side and your right hand around her waist.

Woman Move forward onto the right foot, towards the man's right side, leaving the left foot in place. On the right foot, swivel approximately a half turn (180°) to the left to end in a side-by-side position with the man on your left.

3
COUNT – SLOW

Man Move forward, your body weight onto the right foot. Leading the woman towards your right side, raise your left hand and start to turn the woman to her left by moving your left hand to the right.

Woman Transfer your body weight forward onto the left foot, starting to turn to the left.

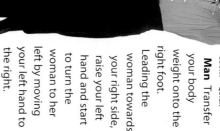

4
COUNT – QUICK

Man Move back onto the right foot, leaving the left foot in place and turning approximately a quarter turn (90°) to the right to create space for the woman. Lead the woman to dance a turn to the right in place with a firm pull of your right hand, while moving your left hand over her head.

Woman Transfer your body weight onto the left foot, swivelling strongly in place, a half turn (180°) to the right.

5
COUNT – QUICK

Man Transfer your body weight forward onto the left foot, starting to turn to the left. Lower your left hand to waist height and raise your right hand ready to pass underneath it.

Woman Move forward onto the right foot, turning to the right and moving around the back of the man.

6
COUNT – SLOW

Man Move sideways and across onto the right foot, passing your right hand over your head and ending with both hands at waist height.

Woman Move sideways onto the left foot, ending on the man's left side.

MAMBO: los giros locos

Changing Sides – *Once you have danced Steps 7–9, you can repeat them in the opposite direction using the opposite foot, then again in the original direction and with the original foot, in which case you are dancing the Beach Blanket.*

9

COUNT – SLOW

Man Move sideways onto the left foot, across the woman.

Woman Move sideways onto the right foot, across and behind the man, ending on his right side a little behind him.

12

COUNT – SLOW

Man Move forward onto the right foot.

Woman Move back onto the left foot.

Continue with your favourite Mambo move.

8

COUNT – QUICK

Man Transfer your body weight forward onto the right foot.

Woman Transfer your body weight back onto the left foot.

11

COUNT – QUICK

Man Transfer your body weight forward onto the left foot, still leading the woman forward. End by leading the woman to swivel sharply to her left to face you.

Woman Move forward onto the right foot, leaving the left foot in place. On the right foot, swivel to the left to face the man.

7

COUNT – QUICK

Man Move back, a small step, onto the left foot, leaving the right foot in place.

Woman Move forward, a small step, onto the right foot, leaving the left foot in place.

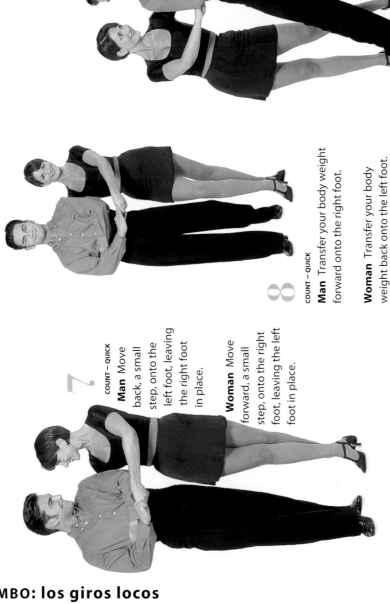

Exit

10

COUNT – QUICK

Man Release hold with your right hand and move back onto the right foot, leaving the left foot in place and leading the woman forward with your left hand.

Woman Move forward onto the left foot.

Rumba

The slow, pulsating rhythm and romantic music of the Rumba have contributed greatly to its ageless and universal appeal. The dance itself exudes the strength and confidence of an archetypal male Latin lover, sensuous and seductive, whose passion tempts his partner to become lost in the intensity and innuendo of the rhythm. But, in Rumba, the woman does not yield so readily. She displays her own will by remaining coy, teasing and toying with the man as she repeatedly lures him and then rejects his advances in this intimate courtship. If Tango is the dance of passion, Rumba is the unquestionable dance of love. There are few more profoundly beautiful moments in dancing than when taking up a hold and feeling the pure intensity of even the Basic Rumba; moving with carefully restrained power to the raw rhythm and romantic but simple strains echoing back to the Guajira, and the timeless truths of a man and a woman facing fate in a dance.

The "international" style Rumba owes an inestimable debt to the Cuban "Guajira" – an earlier folklore dance, the name of which points to its rural origin. Perhaps the best known Guajira music is the internationally popular tune "Guantánamera", composed by Joseíto Fernandez, which has since become a Rumba classic. In the Cuban tradition, the verb "rumbiar" simply means to dance and "Rumba" is a generic term which can refer to a variety of dances or even a

Music and Rhythm

The tempo or speed of Rumba music is a slow, smouldering 26–27 bars per minute, though the authentic Rumba is still often played at between 22–34 bars per minute, perhaps to reflect appropriately the mood of the lyrics. The music's 4/4 time signature means that each bar of music has four equal beats but it is the fourth beat of the bar that the Latin percussionist will accentuate.

Timing

In Forward and Backward Rumba moves, the experienced dancer will use the first half of the beat to place the foot into position while remaining still in the body. The dancer then uses the second half of the beat to transfer the body weight onto the foot.

In sideways-moving steps where two beats are used, the dancer will place the foot in position using the first half of the beat and then effect a slower and more deliberate transfer of the body weight onto the foot, using the remaining half beat and the next full beat.

Many first-time Rumberos find the timing difficult to master in the beginning, as they are told by their teacher to try to dance on Beat 2. This

refers to the fact that the forward and backward steps, which are often associated with starting a dance, are danced on Beat 2. Some teachers, however, recommend starting on the accentuated fourth beat by placing the foot into position, and then using the remainder of the fourth beat and the whole of Beat 1 to transfer the body weight onto the foot. A forward or backward step on the second beat then follows naturally.

Alternatively, many beginners simplify the start of the dance by choosing to make a preparatory side step on Beat 1, which eases them into taking the following forward or backward step on Beat 2. While learning the pattern of the moves, beginners may also find it useful to think of the timing as "Quick, Quick" for forward and backward steps and "Slow" for the side steps. Later, when they are more accustomed to the characteristics of the move, they can then concentrate on making their timing slicker. Interestingly, while great weight is placed by the august bodies of the international dance community on the correct interpretation of the rhythm as described above, the Latins themselves generally seem happy dancing the Rumba by beginning on the more easily understandable count of "one."

"dance party". In the Spanish-speaking world, the Rumba to which we now refer is often known as the "Bolero-Rumba". The "Square Rumba", an even more compact close-hold style than the current form, first came to prominence in the early 1930s. By the late 1940s, as the style developed in Europe and the USA, the perhaps somewhat-inaccurately called "Cuban Rumba" was beginning to emerge, with more figures danced in open hold, enabling a more dynamic approach and greater fluency in the dance.

By the 1990s, the international-style Rumba reached new heights as it found expression in the unparalleled showmanship of 13-times World Professional Latin-American Dance Champions from Britain, Donnie Burns and Gaynor Fairweather and their formidable successors from Germany, Hans Galke and Bianca Schreiber. Yet, to those people who still live their lives to dance their dance in the bars of Havana and in the villages of provincial Cuba, it must seem strange that the only thing they recognize of their own dance is its name. Now though, more people are visiting Cuba and the Caribbean and more and more people are being touched by the honest and modest simplicity of what Latin-American dancing is all about – a man, a woman, the music and what follows naturally.

The Rumba Action

The "action" means the type of movement used when taking a step. The enticing hip action of the Rumba is often talked about in a state of mild excitement but disaster strikes when those trying to emulate a hip action merely end up wiggling about and looking faintly ridiculous. It is therefore important to understand how a good Rumba Action is generated – and it is not with the hips! A good hip-action is simply the result of a good foot, ankle, knee and leg action, after which the hips generally take care of themselves. Let us have a look at that action in the Forward and Backward Walks.

Forward and Backward Walks

When taking a Forward Walk, the move will be initiated by a slight forward poise. The foot is then peeled heel first and moved forward with the toe still in contact with the floor. When the foot has reached the desired position, first the toe, then the ball of the foot start to feel pressure through them as they lower and begin to take the body weight. The dancer should try to use the foot and ankle to offer some resistance to the body weight and control the rate at which the body weight moves onto the foot. Avoid lowering onto the foot abruptly as the heel is finally lowered to complete the step. At the end of the step, the new standing leg will be straight while the leg without weight will remain taut. It is normal for the leg without weight to have turned out slightly as a result of taking the step.

When taking a Backward Walk, many of the same characteristics will still apply. First the foot is placed into position and then the body-weight transferred. As the body-weight moves onto the foot taking the step, the leg will straighten and it is normal – as for the forward step – for the foot and leg taking the backward step to turn out slightly. At the end of the backward step, the heel of the front foot will be released slightly from the floor.

It is the characteristics of this type of action that result unconsciously in a good hip action. It is intrinsic to most styles of Latin-American dancing that, when a step is taken, the other foot remains in place on the floor so that only one foot moves position on one step.

Forward Walk

Backward Walk

The action used for a sideways move is again similar to the Forward or Backward Walk but the speed of the body-weight transfer from one foot to the other is slower, as it is taken over two beats.

Some believe that the the historical roots of the Rumba saw Afro-Cuban slaves originally dancing an early form of the dance with their ankles shackled together. The resulting small steps – once caused by hardship – have now become an intrinsic part of Rumba style. It is essential that the dancer should always endeavour to keep the steps small and compact.

The action of a side step involves placing the foot in position (left) then transferring the body weight onto that foot (right) over two beats of music.

Footwork

Footwork means the part or parts of the foot used during a step. In Rumba, the basic footwork is Ball-Flat. In those moves where the footwork alters, the modification is highlighted in the appropriate description of the move.

The Rumba is a dance that occupies only a small area of the dance floor throughout the dance. It does not move around in an exaggerated manner. At all times, the dancers should be aware of other couples on the floor and should avoid dancing any moves that may impede other dancers. Remember, the Rumba is a dance of love and you can tell a lot about a person by how he or she dances!

Basic Rumba

There is no better way to start feeling the Rumba than with the basic move. Even experienced dancers love to dance the basic move and frequently include it in between more adventurous figures to bring them back to the inherent beauty of the basic Rumba. Please note that it is not unusual for moves in Rumba to end with the feet apart. Take up a close contact hold. Check your poise. The man is standing on his right foot with his feet together and the woman her left foot, feet together. Now begin . . . and be aware of the slow, precise and deliberate feel of the moves.

Forward Basic Rumba

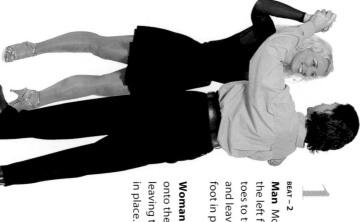

1
BEAT – 2

Man Move forward onto the left foot allowing the toes to turn out slightly and leaving the right foot in place.

Woman Move back onto the right foot leaving the left foot in place.

2
BEAT – 3

Man Transfer weight back onto the right foot leaving the left foot in place.

Woman Transfer weight forward onto the left foot allowing the toes to turn out slightly and leaving the right foot in place.

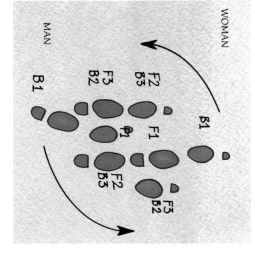

3
BEAT – 4 – 1

Man Place the inside edge of the ball of the left foot to the side as you turn a little to the left and roll your weight onto the left foot.

Woman Place the inside edge of the ball of the right foot to the side as you turn a little to the left and roll your weight onto the right foot.

Backward Basic Rumba

1

BEAT – 2

Man Move back onto the right foot, leaving the left foot in place.

Woman Move forward onto the left foot, allowing the toes to turn out slightly and leaving the right foot in place.

2

BEAT – 3

Man Transfer your weight forward onto the left foot, allowing the toes to turn out slightly and leaving the right foot in place.

Woman Transfer your weight back onto the right foot, leaving the left foot in place.

3

BEAT – 4 – 1

Man Place the inside edge of the ball of the right foot to the side as you turn a little to the left and roll your weight onto the right foot.

Woman Place the inside edge of the ball of the left foot to the side as you turn a little to the left and roll your weight onto the left foot.

The intensity of the Rumba is evoked by the eye contact between the man and the woman and enhanced by the stillness of the upper body. This stillness also emphasizes the strong but sensuous leg and foot action which is so attractive in the basic movements.

The Basic Rumba turns gradually a quarter turn (90°) anticlockwise (counter-clockwise) over six steps. You can repeat the Basic Rumba – Forward and Backward – continuously.

El Viraje – The Switch Turn

The man may choose to dance a greater amount of turn and increase it from a quarter turn (90°) over the Forward and Backward Basics to a half turn (180°). This is best done in a close contact hold because the woman is on the outside of the turn and has further to travel than the man who is on the inside of the turn. See the section on Cumbia and Vallenato for the step descriptions.

The Fan

The Fan is one of the most popular moves in the international-style Rumba. It is not only a very effective move in itself but it leads the dancers to a new type of position to which it gives its name – Fan Position. It is from Fan Position that a variety of new moves can be danced. Start by dancing the Forward Basic Rumba.

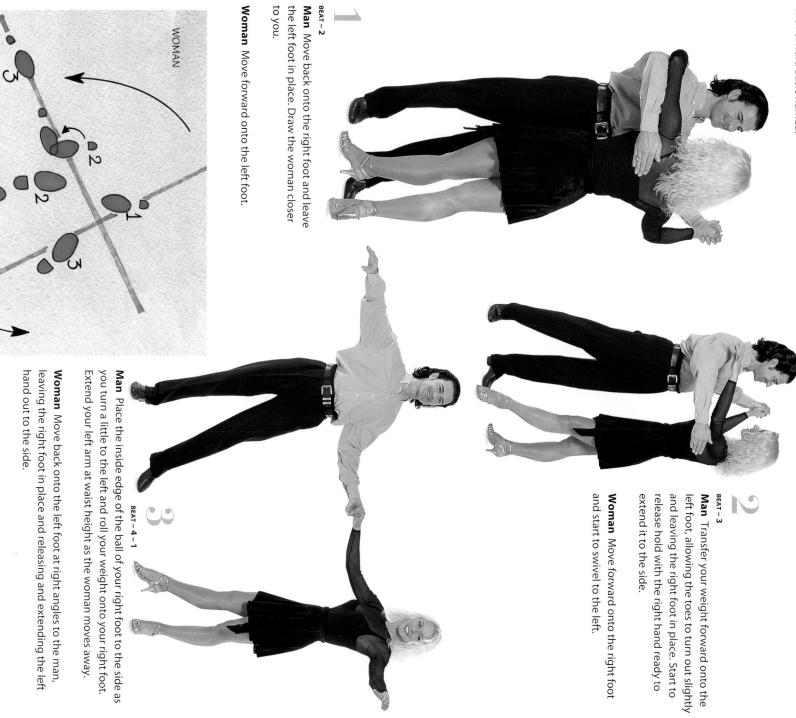

1
BEAT – 2

Man Move back onto the right foot and leave the left foot in place. Draw the woman closer to you.

Woman Move forward onto the left foot.

2
BEAT – 3

Man Transfer your weight forward onto the left foot, allowing the toes to turn out slightly and leaving the right foot in place. Start to release hold with the right hand ready to extend it to the side.

Woman Move forward onto the right foot and start to swivel to the left.

3
BEAT – 4 – 1

Man Place the inside edge of the ball of your right foot to the side as you turn a little to the left and roll your weight onto your right foot. Extend your left arm at waist height as the woman moves away.

Woman Move back onto the left foot at right angles to the man, leaving the right foot in place and releasing and extending the left hand out to the side.

This position where the woman is in an open hold at right angles to the man is known as the Fan Position. Now continue with either the Hockeystick or an Alemana Turn.

The Hockeystick

The classic figure with which to follow the Fan is the Hockeystick, so called because the pattern of the move resembles the shape of a hockeystick. Start in Fan Position.

1
BEAT – 2

Man Move forward onto the left foot, allowing the toes to turn out slightly and leaving the right foot in place.

Woman Close the right foot to the left foot to end standing on the right foot.

2
BEAT – 3

Man Transfer your weight back onto the right foot, leaving the left foot in place. Start to draw the woman towards you.

Woman Walk forward onto the left foot.

3
BEAT – 4 – 1

Man Close the left foot to the right foot and transfer your weight onto the left foot, adjusting the hand hold on Step 3 to lead the Hockeystick ending.

Woman Walk forward onto the right foot.

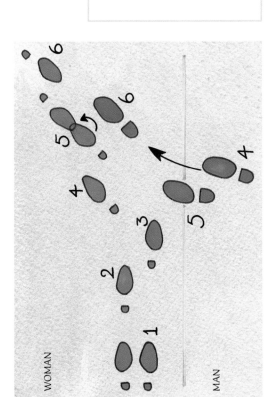

Adjusting the Hand Hold and Arms during the Hockeystick

The man will start the move with the palm of his left hand uppermost as he draws the woman towards him on Step 2. On Step 3, he will raise his left arm to indicate the turn and, at the same time, rotate his hand first towards him and then towards the woman to resume a palm-to-palm hold, thumb down. Over Steps 4–5, the woman will draw in her left hand across her upper body, then allow it to naturally extend out to the side again on Step 6.

BEAT – 4

Man Move back onto the right foot, leaving the left foot in place and turn a little to the right. Lead the woman across you taking your hand above her head.

Woman Walk forward onto the left foot, starting to turn left across the man.

BEAT – 5

Man Transfer your weight forward onto the left foot, leaving the right foot in place. Lead the woman to dance forward away from you. When she has taken her step, lower your left hand to waist height.

Woman Walk forward onto the right foot, continuing to turn left, and move away from the man. Then swivel to left in place.

BEAT – 6

Man Move forward onto the right foot in open facing position.

Woman Move back onto the left foot to end facing the man.

You can now continue by resuming the close hold as you dance into the Basic Rumba. A very stylish option is to modify the ending of the Hockeystick into the Spiral Cross.

The Spiral Cross

On Step 5, the man can lead the woman to increase her turn. The woman will allow her feet to cross while remaining in place. This is called a Spiral Cross. The man and woman will then both move forward on Step 6 to end almost in a side-by-side position. Continue with the New York as shown in the Mambo section but, of course, danced in Rumba time.

Mambo Moves in Rumba

Since both Mambo and Rumba share a common origin, both also share many moves which can be enjoyed in either dance. Moves already described in the Mambo section which can also be used in Rumba include:

- Manita a Mano
- The Underarm Spot Turns to Right or Left
- The New York
- El Molinito
- The Liquidizer
- El Mojito

It is important to remember that the moves must be adaptable to the style and rhythm of the dance. It is for this reason that Los Giros Locos would not be danced in Rumba, though they could easily be danced in Salsa; likewise, the New York Bus Stop would not be danced in Rumba, but works very well when adapted to the Cha Cha Cha.

The Alemana Turn

A basic but nonetheless popular turn for the woman is the Alemana Turn. Literally, it means the German Turn and refers back to a much earlier era of courtly dancing. The "Alemand" of square dancing and the "Dosey-Doe" or "Dos-à-dos" (literally "back-to-back") also stem from that period. In Rumba, the Alemana Turn is a simple turn for the woman consisting of three forward walks made under the man's raised arm. The couple dance Steps 1–3 of the Hockeystick, then the following:

1

BEAT – 2

Man Having raised the left arm on the previous step, move back onto the right foot, leading the woman in front of you and circling the left hand clockwise as the woman turns.

Woman Move the left foot forward and across the body, then turn right to end on the left foot with a straight left leg.

2

BEAT – 3

Man Transfer the body weight forward onto the left foot, circling the left hand clockwise.

Woman Move forward onto the right foot and continue the turn by swivelling to the right.

3

BEAT – 4 – 1

Man Take a small step side onto the right foot. Bring the woman to close hold.

Woman Move forward onto the left foot to end facing the man in close hold.

Continue with the Basic Rumba or with the Opening Out to Right and Left.

Opening Out to Right and Left

The simplest moves can often be the most effective. Here is one such move. Start in close hold and, as you dance the move, allow it to flow naturally from the preceding figure.

The Man's Movements

The man will dance a Cucuracha to the Left and Right (see Mambo section) in Rumba time, extending the hand to the side to which he is stepping and placing the other hand on the woman's upper back. On Steps 3 and 6, the man will guide the woman by holding her with both hands. Close hold will be resumed on Step 6.

BEAT – 2

1

Woman Swivel on the left foot, turning to right and moving back onto the right foot. Allow the right arm to extend naturally.

BEAT – 3

2

Woman Transfer your weight forward onto the left foot.

BEAT – 4 – 1

3

Woman Move forward across the man onto your right foot and turn left to end squarely facing him. Place your right hand on the man's upper arm or shoulder.

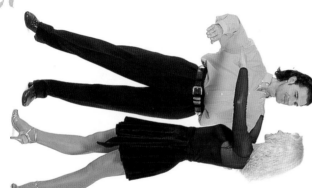

BEAT – 2

4

Woman Swivel on the right foot, turning to left and moving back onto the left foot. Allow the left arm to extend back onto the left foot. Allow the left arm to extend naturally.

BEAT – 3

5

Woman Transfer your weight forward onto the right foot.

BEAT – 4 – 1

6

Woman Move forward across the man onto your left foot, and turn right to end squarely facing him. Resume close hold.

Continue with the Basic Rumba or repeat Steps 1–3, resume close hold and continue with a Backward Basic.

Making your Rumba Ravishing

There are many ways to make simple moves sizzle. Here are some favourites.

The Double Fan

Dance a Fan, then Steps 1–3 of the Hockeystick over counts 2, 3, 4, but without the man raising his left arm. On Beat 1, the man points his right foot to the side and leads the woman to swivel a half turn (180°) to right, to end facing in the opposite direction. Continue into a second Fan.

The Fan and Switch

Dance a Fan, then Steps 1–3 of the Hockeystick over counts 2, 3, 4, raising the arm as normal. On Beat 1, the man brings the left hand down smartly over the woman's head, leading her to turn left in place, while he lunges sideways to left. The woman flexes her right knee and, leaving her feet in place, swivels a half turn (180°) to left. Her left leg is extended and straight, knees together. To continue into a second Fan, the man dances a side-close-side movement to right.

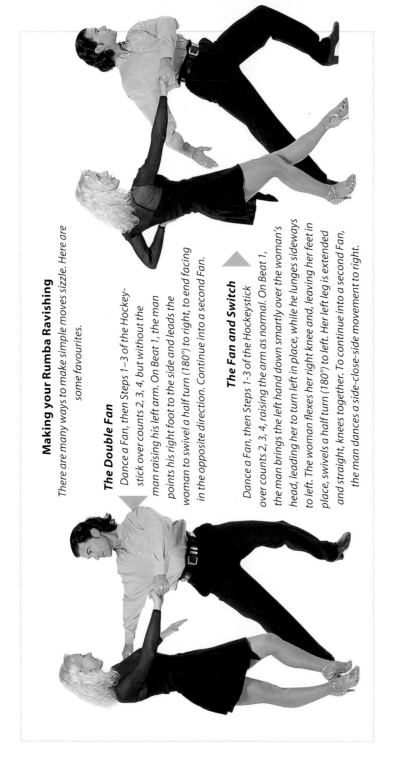

The Aïda

This is a delightful but very easy move. Start by dancing Steps 1–3 of Manita a Mano as described in the Mambo section but with a Rumba timing. Remember to use a Rumba Action and avoid allowing the toes of the front foot to release when walking backwards.

The Fallaway

4 BEAT – 2

Man Walk back on the right foot, starting to turn right.

Woman Walk back on the left foot, starting to turn left.

5 BEAT – 3

Man Walk back on the left foot, continuing to turn right.

Woman Walk back on the right foot, continuing to turn left.

6 BEAT – 4 – 1

Man Walk back on the right foot, ending in a side-by-side position.

Woman Walk back on the left foot, ending in a side-by-side position.

Option One from the Aïda – Cucurachas

Turning to face each other, the man dances a Cucuracha to Left and Right, and the woman a Cucuracha to Right and Left, followed by the Basic Rumba.

Option Two from the Aïda – The Cuban Rocks

BEAT – 2

1

Man Rock forward onto the left foot.

Woman Rock forward onto the right foot.

BEAT – 3

2

Man Rock back onto the right foot.

Woman Rock back onto the left foot.

Option One from the Cuban Rocks – The Basic Exit

BEAT – 2

1

Man Rock back onto the right foot.

Woman Rock back onto the left foot.

BEAT – 3

2

Man Rock forward onto the left foot, starting to turn left.

Woman Rock forward onto the right foot, starting to turn right.

BEAT – 4 – 1

3

Man Rock forward onto the right foot, turning left to end facing the woman.

Woman Rock forward onto the left foot, turning to right to end facing the man.

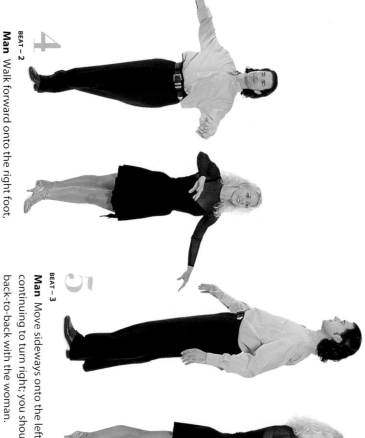

To follow the Cuban Rocks, there are a number of graded options – starting with the easiest.

Continue with the Basic Rumba.

Option Two from the Cuban Rocks – The Open Turn

The man and woman dance an open turn where the feet remain apart. It is vital that each dancer takes each step moving along a straight line and parallel with their partner. Release hold on the last step of the Cuban Rocks.

BEAT – 2

4

Man Walk forward onto the right foot, starting to turn right.

Woman Walk forward onto the left foot, starting to turn left.

BEAT – 3

5

Man Move sideways onto the left foot, continuing to turn right; you should now be back-to-back with the woman.

Woman Move sideways onto the right foot, continuing to turn left; you should now be back-to-back with the man.

BEAT – 4 – 1

6

Man Move sideways onto the right foot, continuing to turn right to complete a three-quarter turn (270°) to the right, to end facing the woman.

Woman Move sideways onto the left foot, continuing to turn left, to complete a three-quarter (270°) turn to the left, facing the man.

Continue with the Basic Rumba.

Option Three from the Cuban Rocks – The Spot Turns

The man dances a Spot Turn to Left and the woman a Spot Turn to Right, so the dancers will initially turn inwards towards each other. Both the man and woman start the turn on the last of the Cuban Rocks, when they release hold.

1

BEAT – 2

Man Swivelling on the left foot to the left, move onto the right foot forward and across yourself, to end facing in the opposite direction to the Cuban Rocks. Then, swivelling in place, continue to turn left to complete a full turn.

Woman Swivelling on the right foot to the right, move onto the left foot forward and across yourself, to end facing in the opposite direction to the Cuban Rocks. Then, swivelling in place, continue to turn right to complete a full turn.

2

BEAT – 3

Man Transfer the body weight forward onto the left foot, continuing to turn left.

Woman Transfer the body weight forward onto the right foot, continuing to turn right.

3

BEAT – 4 – 1

Man Move sideways onto the right foot, to end facing the woman.

Woman Move sideways onto the left foot, to end facing the man.

Continue with the Basic Rumba, or dance the Spot Turns in the opposite direction and follow them with a Backward Basic Rumba.

The Open Hip Twist

The Open Hip Twist is one of those moves that both the men and the women love to dance, but don't be misled by the figure's name. It is a useful move because it starts in Open Facing Position. The man's left hand is extended towards the woman, palm uppermost. She rests her right hand in his left hand. The man should always hold but not grip the woman's hand. The man is standing on his right foot and the woman is standing on her left foot.

1

BEAT – 2

Man Move forward onto the left foot, leaving the right foot in place.

Woman Move back onto the right foot, leaving the left foot in place.

2

BEAT – 3

Man Transfer the body weight back onto the right foot.

Woman Transfer the body weight forward onto the left foot.

◀3a

BEAT – 4

Man Close the left foot back to the right foot without weight. Bring the left hand back towards the left hip.

Woman Walk forward onto the right foot.

3b ▲

BEAT – 1

Man Transfer weight onto the left foot. Move the left hand slightly forward to lead the woman to swivel to the right.

Woman On the right foot, swivel ¼ turn to right. Bring the left hand up and across the upper body.

4

BEAT – 2

Man Move back onto the right foot, leaving the left foot in place.

Woman Walk forward onto the left foot.

5

BEAT – 3

Man Transfer the body weight forward onto the left foot, allowing the left arm to extend as the woman moves away.

Woman Walk forward onto the right foot and, leaving the feet in place, swivel ½ turn to the left.

6

BEAT – 4 – 1

Man Move sideways onto the right foot.

Woman Walk back onto the left foot in Fan Position, allowing the arm to extend naturally.

The arm extends naturally by unfolding in a sequence of shoulder before elbow before wrist before fingers. Continue with any move, starting in Fan Position.

La Elenita

Here is a super example of how quite basic moves can be combined to give an exquisite cocktail of sensuous interplay between the man and the woman.

The Alemana Turn

Previously, you have danced the Alemana Turn from Fan Position. This time, start in Open Facing Position. The man is holding the woman's right hand in his left. From this position, dance the Alemana Turn. Finish in a double hand hold. The man ends on his right foot, feet apart, and the woman on her left foot, with her feet apart.

The Elenita Turn

Here, the man and the woman are in double hand hold. The woman performs a sensuously slow turn on the spot while the man remains motionless.

1

BEAT – 2

Man Move forward and across yourself onto the left foot, turning a little to the right. Lower the right hand to waist height and raise the left arm, leading the woman to turn into your right arm.

Woman Move forward and across yourself onto the right foot, leaving the left foot in place and making a quarter turn (90°) to the left.

2

BEAT – 3

Man Hold the position while leading the woman to continue turning slowly to the left, in place.

Woman Still on the right foot and leaving both feet in place, start to swivel slowly to the left.

3

BEAT – 4 – 1

Man Hold the position while lowering your left hand to waist height, still leading the woman to turn slowly to the left.

Woman Still on the right foot and leaving both feet in place, continue to swivel slowly to the left, to end with the man on your left side.

Changing Sides

The couple now change sides to prepare for the next move.

1
BEAT – 2

Man Releasing hold with the right hand, move back onto the right foot, starting to turn left.

Woman Move forward onto the left foot, starting to turn left.

2
BEAT – 3

Man Move sideways onto the left foot, continuing to turn left.

Woman Move sideways onto the right foot, continuing to turn left.

3
BEAT – 4 – 1

Man Move forward onto the right foot, outside the woman's right side, completing a quarter turn (90°) to the left. Place your right hand, thumb down, on the woman's right hip.

Woman Move back onto the left foot, completing a quarter turn (90°) to the left.

The couple are now positioned a little apart, almost right side to right side.

Three Circling Walks with Open Hip Twist Ending

The dancers now circle each other around a central point. On the third step, the man leads the woman to conclude the move with an Open Hip Twist.

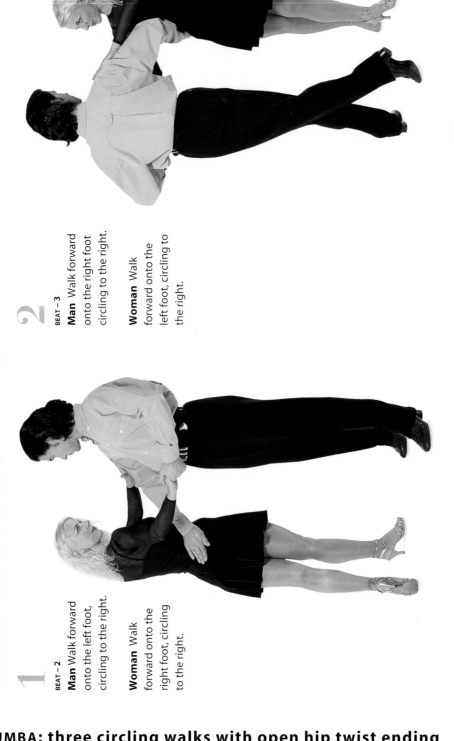

1
BEAT – 2

Man Walk forward onto the left foot, circling to the right.

Woman Walk forward onto the right foot, circling to the right.

2
BEAT – 3

Man Walk forward onto the right foot circling to the right.

Woman Walk forward onto the left foot, circling to the right.

3a
BEAT – 4

Man Walk forward onto the left foot, circling to the right.

Woman Walk forward onto the right foot, circling to the right.

3b
BEAT – 1

Man On the left foot, swivel slightly to the right, moving the left hand slightly forward to lead the woman to swivel to right. Release the right hand and move it back out of the way.

Woman On the right foot, swivel to the right to end at right angles to the man.

Continue with Steps 4–6 of the Open Hip Twist.

RUMBA: three circling walks with open hip twist ending

The Fencing Line

The fencing line is a dramatic figure.

Earlier we saw how many of the most fashionable figures start from the Fan Position. The Fencing Line is one such figure which can be used to great effect. Start in Fan Position.

The entry into the Fencing Line is similar to that for the Double Fan, but with less turn for the woman. Dance Steps 1–3 of the Hockeystick over counts 2, 3, 4, but without the man raising his left arm. On Beat 1, the man points his right foot to the side, leading the woman to swivel a quarter turn (90°) to the right, to end facing the man.

BEAT – 2
1

Man Move forward and across onto the right foot with a small step, flexing both knees and keeping them together. Stay facing square to the woman. Lead the Fencing Line by rotating the left hand, palm downwards.

Woman Move forward and across onto the left foot with a small step, flexing both knees and keeping them together. Stay facing square to the man.

BEAT – 3
2

Man Transfer the body weight back onto the left foot, resuming normal height.

Woman Transfer the body weight back onto the right foot, resuming normal height.

BEAT – 4 – 1
3

Man Move sideways onto the right foot.

Woman Move sideways onto the left foot.

Continue with the Basic Rumba or any move which starts in Open Facing Position, or with the Rumba Hip Rolls.

Topical Tip

Avoid "dipping" too much: a slight flexing of the knees gives a greater visual effect than is felt by the dancers. On Step 1, the dancers add extra style when the man looks well to his left and the woman well to her right.

The Rumba Hip Rolls

This move should be approached carefully in order to produce the appropriate action and evoke the sensuous nature of the dance. The couple begin facing each other, no hold, feet apart. The man is standing on his right foot and the woman on her left foot.

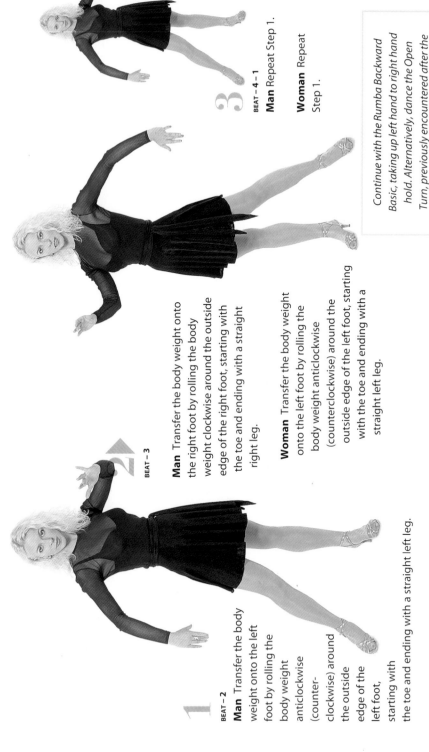

1

BEAT – 2

Man Transfer the body weight onto the left foot by rolling the body weight anticlockwise (counter-clockwise) around the outside edge of the left foot, starting with the toe and ending with a straight left leg.

Woman Transfer the body weight onto the right foot by rolling the body weight clockwise around the outside edge of the right foot, starting with the toe and ending with a straight right leg.

2

BEAT – 3

Man Transfer the body weight onto the right foot by rolling the body weight clockwise around the outside edge of the right foot, starting with the toe and ending with a straight right leg.

Woman Transfer the body weight onto the left foot by rolling the body weight anticlockwise (counterclockwise) around the outside edge of the left foot, starting with the toe and ending with a straight left leg.

3

BEAT – 4 – 1

Man Repeat Step 1.

Woman Repeat Step 1.

Continue with the Rumba Backward Basic, taking up left hand to right hand hold. Alternatively, dance the Open Turn, previously encountered after the Cuban Rocks, but this time increase the amount of turn in Step 1 to compensate for the different starting position.

More Tips for Hips

Hip rolls can be danced not only when the feet are side by side, but when one foot is in front of the other, using a similar action. Selective use of the hip roll can add panache and spice up some of the basic moves with which you are now familiar. If the hip rolls are danced to a rhythm of 2, & 3, 4, 1 the move will leave you on the same foot as when you interrupted the basic figure, allowing you to continue the move as normal.

Try dancing a Fan or Open Hip Twist. Once in Fan Position, dance the hip rolls using the 2,&3,4,1 rhythm and then continue as normal into your next move.

You can add the 2,&3,4,1, hip roll into your Hockeystick by dancing it between steps 4 and 5. It is especially seductive when you dance the hip rolls facing your partner.

El Paseo

In this teasingly playful figure, the man and woman alternate spot swivel turns. Think of the move as travelling along a single line. Start in Open Facing Position and release hold.

1–3
BEAT – 2, 3, 4 – 1

Woman Dance a Backward Basic Rumba stepping forward on 3.

1
BEAT – 2

Man Move forward onto the left foot, leaving the right foot in place.

2
BEAT – 3

Man On the left foot, swivel a half turn (180°) to the right and transfer the body weight forward onto the right foot, ending with your back to the woman.

3
BEAT – 4 – 1

Man Move forward onto the left foot, still with your back to the woman.

4
BEAT – 2

Man On the left foot, swivel half turn (180°) to the right and move back onto the right foot, leaving the left foot in place. End facing the woman.

Woman Move forward onto the left foot, leaving the right foot in place.

5
BEAT – 3

Man Transfer the body weight forward onto the left foot, leaving the right foot in place.

Woman On the left foot, swivel a half turn (180°) to the right and transfer the body weight forward onto the right foot, ending with your back to the man.

6

BEAT – 4 – 1

Man Move forward onto the right foot.

Woman Move forward onto the left foot, still with your back to the man.

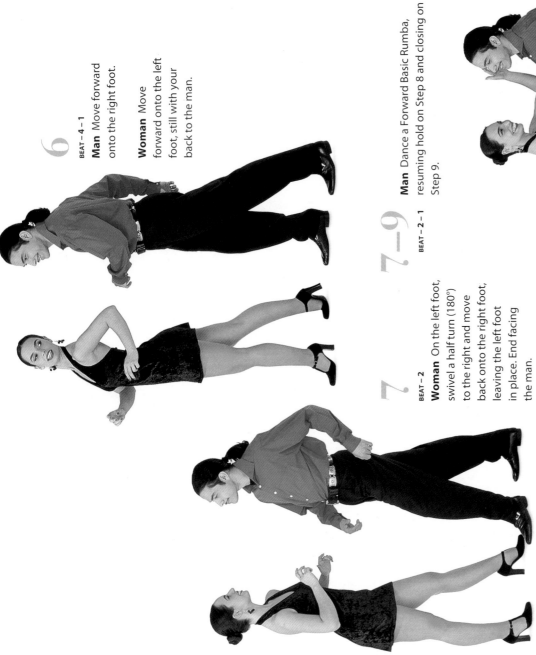

7

BEAT – 2

Woman On the left foot, swivel a half turn (180°) to the right and move back onto the right foot, leaving the left foot in place. End facing the man.

7–9

BEAT – 2 – 1

Man Dance a Forward Basic Rumba, resuming hold on Step 8 and closing on Step 9.

8

BEAT – 3

Woman Transfer the body weight forward onto the left foot and resume hold.

9

BEAT – 4 – 1

Woman Close the right foot to the left foot.

Continue with the Basic Rumba, or with your choice of appropriate move.

Music Suggestions

There are many beautiful Rumbas but the most evocative are those performed by authentic Latin-American bands. Some groups such as Los Paraguayos have become internationally acclaimed. Classic Bolero-Rumbas include "Solamente Una Vez", "Amor", "Besame Mucho" and "Te Quiero Dijiste". Eydie Gormé has also produced a variety of deliciously sensuous Rumbas including the wonderful "Cuando Vuelvo a Tu Lado". The Spaniard, Juan Luis Guerra, offers "Bachata Rosa" and "Burbujas de Amor" and the Spanish group, Pequeña Compañia, has a great value album of non-stop excellent Rumbas. A host of other less well-known groups offer much, much more.

Cha Cha Cha

The Cha Cha Cha is another of the Cuban family of dances and is one of the most popular of the social Latin-American dances. The patterns of many of the Cha Cha Cha moves, therefore, have a striking similarity to those of the Rumba or international-style Mambo, but with one major difference – the Cha Cha Cha! The name itself derives from the splitting of the fourth beat of the music to give it that unmistakable and catchy Cha Cha Cha rhythm.

The dance was originally simply a variant of the Mambo and Rumba but, in 1948, Enrique Jorrín was responsible for combining two Cuban rhythms: the *danzón*, from which the Mambo had originated, and the *montuno*. The effect was something spectacularly different and exciting. His new composition, *"Engañadora"*, which means "The Cheat", was recorded in 1953 and achieved huge popularity. The dancers just kept on demanding more and more. The catchy nature of the Cha Cha music was easily translated into almost any format, ranging

from small combos to Big Bands, and it was not too long before almost every dance musician was playing Cha Cha Cha.

The character of the dance, like the music, is vibrant, flamboyant, playful and effervesces with a unique sense of fun to which dancers the world over can relate and enjoy.

Music and Rhythm

The time signature, like that of the Mambo and Rumba, is 4/4 but the fourth beat of the bar is split into two to give the characteristic 2, 3, 4 & 1 rhythm of the Cha Cha Cha. The first beat is accentuated. The tempo is slightly faster than that of the Rumba, and is currently set at 30 bars per minute for examinations and competitions, though the additional steps needed to dance the Cha Cha Cha rhythm make the dance sometimes seem quite a lot faster.

Timing

The split fourth beat of the Cha Cha Cha music and the first beat of the following bar of music are interpreted by dancers in a move called the Cha Cha Cha Chassé. To make the steps of the Cha Cha Cha Chassé coincide with the Cha Cha Cha rhythm of the music, the dancers will take the forward and backward steps of the Basic Move on the second beat of the bar. Many dancers simplify the start of the dance by making a side step on Beat 1 (effectively the last step of the Cha Cha Cha Chassé), which is then easily followed by the forward or backward step on Beat 2.

The moves and technique described in the Cha Cha Cha section of this book are a simplified version of the technique which is recognized internationally. This has evolved over many years as the result of eminent exponents standardizing the stylized method into a format

now used worldwide. While this "international" style is acceptable everywhere in the world, it should be acknowledged that the development of the "international" style from its original form has removed a high level of authenticity from the more raw and basic style of the dance's originators. Latins will therefore tend to dance the Cha Cha Cha on Beat 1, to remain in a very close contact hold throughout the entire dance, and are not averse to dancing forward walks with a heel. If the dancers are enjoying their dance, who should judge what is right or wrong but the dancers themselves?

However, the "international" style and technique do bring with them a greater sophistication. The flexibility to introduce new moves and combinations which invest the dance with a freshness and vigour are welcomed by dancers who may want to continue enjoying the dance over many years. A standard technique also considerably aids communication. This is true not only on a day-to-day level between dancers, but also from generation to generation, as the distillation of the best and most economical way of achieving a certain sought-after style is passed on from master to pupil and from dancer to dancer.

The Cha Cha Cha Action

The "Action" means the type of movement used when taking a step. While the "international" style action used for both Cha Cha Cha and Mambo are based on the beautiful, classic Rumba action, the speed of the Cha Cha Cha prevents the dancer from performing it as fully as in the Rumba. This results in a number of minor technical differences which need not concern the social dancer who has already developed a good Rumba action.

Footwork

Footwork means the part or parts of the foot used during a step. In Cha Cha Cha, the basic footwork is Ball-Flat. In those moves where the footwork alters, the modification is highlighted in the appropriate description of the move.

Getting Started

The Cha Cha Cha is a dance which occupies a small area of the dance floor throughout the dance. It does not move around the room and it is not good style for the dancers to take large steps or to move around in an exaggerated manner. At all times, the dancers should be aware of other couples on the floor and should avoid dancing any moves which impede other dancers. Now it's time to stand up, assume a good posture, take up hold and get dancing.

Basic Cha Cha Cha

The Cha Cha Cha will, at first, seem quite fast so it is important to take small steps, especially on the Cha Cha Cha, and to ensure that the move is compact and hardly travels. Start in close hold. Many dancers find it easier to start in time with the music by dancing a preparatory side step on Beat 1. The man does this with his right foot and the woman with her left foot. Then continue into the Basic Cha Cha Cha.

1
BEAT – 2

Man Move forward onto the left foot, allowing the toes to turn out slightly and leaving the right foot in place.

Woman Move back onto the right foot, leaving the left foot in place.

2
BEAT – 3

Man Transfer your weight back onto the right foot, leaving the left foot in place.

Woman Transfer your weight forward onto the left foot, leaving the right foot in place.

3
BEAT – 4

Man Move sideways onto the left foot.

Woman Move sideways onto the right foot.

4
BEAT – &

Man Move the right foot sideways towards the left foot.

Woman Move the left foot sideways towards the right foot.

5
BEAT – 1

Man Move sideways onto the left foot.

Woman Move sideways onto the right foot.

6
BEAT – 2

Man Move back onto the right foot, leaving the left foot in place.

Woman Move forward onto the left foot, allowing the toes to turn out slightly and leaving the right foot in place.

Steps 3–5 and 8–10 are Cha Cha Cha Chassés.

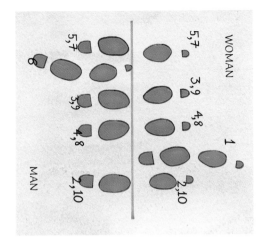

WOMAN

5,7 3,9 4,8 1

6 5,9 4,8 2,10

MAN

BEAT – 7

Man Transfer your weight forward onto the left foot, leaving the right foot in place.

Woman Transfer your weight back onto the right foot, leaving the left foot in place.

BEAT – 10

Man Move sideways onto the right foot.

Woman Move sideways onto the left foot.

BEAT – 8

Man Move sideways onto the right foot.

Woman Move sideways onto the left foot.

BEAT – 9

Man Move the left foot sideways towards the right foot.

Woman Move the right foot sideways towards the left foot.

BEAT – &

Man Move the left foot sideways towards the right foot.

Woman Move the right foot sideways towards the left foot.

Translating Moves from other Dances

You will note how similar the pattern of the Basic Cha Cha Cha is to the pattern of the Basic Rumba. This is because the Cha Cha Cha was originally a syncopated version of the Rumba. It is therefore relatively easy to translate some of the simpler moves from the Rumba and Mambo into Cha Cha Cha by syncopating each third step in the Rumba or Mambo into a Cha Cha Cha with a timing of 4 & 1. Remember too that the forward or backward steps which occur on Beat 1 in the Mambo would occur on Beat 2 in the Cha Cha Cha or Rumba.

Mambo Moves in the Cha Cha Cha

• Manita a Mano • The New York • The Underarm Spot Turns to Right and Left • The New York Bus Stop • El Molinito • The Liquidizer • El Mojito

Rumba Moves in the Cha Cha Cha

• The Fan • The Hockeystick • The Alemana Turn • El Paseo

Sideways-moving Cha Cha Chassés should be danced square to your partner and kept compact. When translating a move, it will be necessary to know how to dance a Forward and Backward Cha Cha Chassé.

The Forward and Backward Cha Cha Cha Chassé

Both the man and woman will be required to dance the Forward and Backward Cha Cha Cha Chassés. When the man dances the Forward Cha Cha Cha Chassé the woman dances the Backward Cha Cha Cha Chassé and vice versa.

The Forward Cha Cha Cha Chassé

1
BEAT – 4

Man and Woman Move forward onto the right foot, bringing the right side of the body forward with the foot, and straighten the right leg.

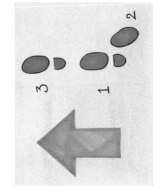

2
BEAT – &

Man and Woman Turn the toes of the left foot outward and bring them to the heel of the right foot, allowing both knees to flex. The heel does not lower.

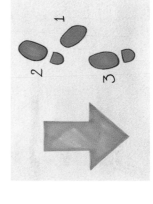

3
BEAT – 1

Man and Woman Move forward onto the right foot, bringing the right side of the body forward with the foot and straightening the legs.

The Backward Cha Cha Cha Chassé

1
BEAT – 4

Man and Woman Move back onto the toes only of the left foot, turning the toes outward and bringing the left side of the body back with the left foot. Straighten the left leg. The left heel does not lower.

2
BEAT – &

Man and Woman Bring the right foot back with the right heel next to the left toe, allowing both knees to flex.

3
BEAT – 1

Man and Woman Move back onto the left foot, bringing the left side of the body back with the left foot. Straighten the legs.

The Fan

You are already familiar with the Fan as a move in the Rumba. Let's now see how it looks in the Cha Cha. Start by dancing the Forward Basic Cha Cha, then continue as follows.

1
BEAT – 2

Man Move back onto the right foot, leaving the left foot in place, lowering the left arm and leading the woman to dance forward outside your left side.

Woman Walk forward onto the left foot outside the man's left side.

2
BEAT – 3

Man Transfer the body weight forward onto the left foot, releasing hold with the right hand.

Woman Walk forward onto the right foot and start to swivel to the left.

3–5
BEAT – 4 – 1

Man Dance a Cha Cha Cha Chassé to the right, extending the left arm at waist height as the woman moves away from you.

Woman Dance a Backward Cha Cha Cha Chassé at right angles to the man to end in Fan Position.

The whole move may rotate a little anticlockwise (counterclockwise). Continue with The Hockeystick or Alemana Turn.

The Hockeystick

The Hockeystick is every bit as popular in this dance as in the Rumba, so let's check it out in the Cha Cha. Start in Fan Position. The man is standing on his right foot, feet apart. The woman is standing on her left foot, which is behind the right foot.

1–5
BEAT – 2 –1

Man Dance a Forward Basic Cha Cha Cha, keeping the Chassé compact and drawing the woman towards you. On Step 5, raise the left arm to lead the woman's turn to the left.

1
BEAT – 2

Woman Close the right foot to the left foot, leaving the left foot in place, to end standing on your right foot.

2
BEAT – 3

Woman Walk forward onto the left foot moving towards the man.

Adjusting the HandHold and Arms During the Hockeystick

The man will start the move with the palm of his left hand uppermost as he draws the woman towards him. On Step 5, he will raise his left arm to indicate the turn and, at the same time, rotate his hand first towards him and then towards the woman to resume a palm-to-palm hold, thumb down. Over Steps 4–5, the woman will draw her left hand in across her upper body and then allow it to naturally extend out to the side again on Step 8.

3–5
BEAT – 4 – 1

Woman Dance a Forward Cha Cha Cha Chassé.

6
BEAT – 2

Man Move back onto the right foot, leaving the left foot in place, and turn a little to the right. Lead the woman across you, taking your hand above her head.

Woman Walk forward onto the left foot, starting to turn left across the man.

7
BEAT – 3

Man Transfer the weight forward onto the left foot, leaving the right foot in place. Lead the woman to dance forward away from you. When she has taken her step, lower the left hand to waist height.

Woman Walk forward onto the right foot, continuing to turn left, moving away from the man. Then swivel to the left, in place, to face the man.

8–10
BEAT – 4 – 1

Man Dance a Forward Cha Cha Cha Chassé, ending in Open Facing Position.

Woman Dance a Backward Cha Cha Cha Chassé, ending in Open Facing Position.

Changing Hands

It is always better to try to change hands in a smooth and natural way. A good place to change from a left-hand to right-hand to a right-hand to right-hand hold is at the end of the Hockeystick, when the man's left hand lowers.

The Peek-a-Boo

This is a simple, fun figure which starts in Open Facing Position, with a right-hand to right-hand hold. Note the slightly unusual start for the man.

1
BEAT – 2

Man Move back onto the left foot, leaving the right foot in place.

Woman Move back onto the right foot, leaving the left foot in place.

2
BEAT – 3

Man Transfer the body weight forward onto the right foot.

Woman Transfer the body weight forward onto the left foot.

3–5
BEAT – 4 – 1

Man Making a quarter turn (90°) to the right, dance a Cha Cha Cha Chassé to the left, leading the woman to turn left across and in front of you, then release hold.

Woman Making a quarter turn (90°) to the left, dance a Cha Cha Cha Chassé to the right, across and in front of the man, releasing hold.

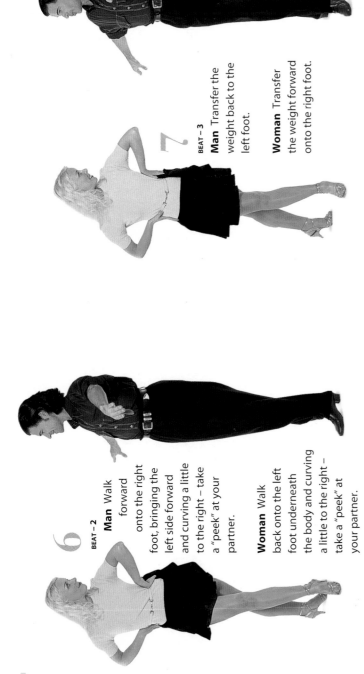

6

BEAT – 2

Man Walk forward onto the right foot, bringing the left side forward and curving a little to the right – take a "peek" at your partner.

Woman Walk back onto the left foot underneath the body and curving a little to the right – take a "peek" at your partner.

7

BEAT – 3

Man Transfer the weight back to the left foot.

Woman Transfer the weight forward onto the right foot.

8–10

BEAT – 4 – 1

Man Dance a Cha Cha Cha Chassé to the right, across and behind the woman.

Woman Dance a Cha Cha Cha Chassé to the left, across and in front of the man.

11

BEAT – 2

Man Walk forward onto the left foot, bringing the right side forward and curving a little to the left – take a "peek" at your partner.

Woman Walk back onto the right foot underneath the body and curving a little to the left – take a "peek" at your partner.

12

BEAT – 3

Man Transfer the weight back to the right foot.

Woman Transfer the weight forward onto the left foot.

13–15

BEAT – 4 – 1

Man Dance a Cha Cha Cha Chassé to the left, moving across and behind the woman.

Woman Dance a Cha Cha Cha Chassé to the right, across and in front of the man.

16–20

BEAT – 2 – 1

Man Dance Steps 6–10 of the Hockeystick, resuming an appropriate hold for your next figure.

Woman Dance Steps 6–10 of the Hockeystick, resuming an appropriate hold for your next figure.

CHA CHA CHA: the peek-a-boo

The New York Overspill

The New York is a standard figure for Mambo, Rumba and Cha Cha Cha and is fully described in the Mambo section. When translating a move from Mambo to Cha Cha Cha, remember that every third step in the Mambo section. When translating a move from Mambo to Cha Cha Cha, step 1 of the move will be on count 2. In this way, the New York and New York Chassé and that, in Cha Cha Cha, step successfully translated into this dance from the Mambo.

Now let's look at another New York fun variation – the New York Overspill. This is best danced as part of a short routine of New York fun variation – the New York Overspill. This is of the New York in Cha Cha Cha and then continue as follows.

BEAT – 1

1

Man Release hold with the left hand and draw the right hand across and forward, swivelling a quarter turn (90°) to the left on the left foot. Move forward onto the right foot, leaving the left foot in place.

Woman Release hold with the right hand and swivel a quarter turn (90°) to the right on the right foot. Move forward onto the left foot, leaving the right foot in place.

BEAT – 2

2

Man Move forward onto the left foot, straightening the left leg and bending slightly forward at the waist.

Woman Move forward onto the right foot, straightening the right leg and bending slightly forward at the waist.

BEAT – 3

3

Man Move back onto the right foot.

Woman Move back onto the left foot.

BEAT – &

4

Man Move back onto the left foot.

Woman Move back onto the right foot.

BEAT – 4

5

Man Move sideways onto the right foot. Making a quarter turn (90°) to the right to face the woman, resuming normal posture and changing to a left-hand to right-hand hold.

Woman Move sideways onto the left foot. Making a quarter turn (90°) to the left to face the man, resuming normal posture and changing to a right-hand to left-hand hold.

BEAT – 5

Continue with the Basic Cha Cha Cha or, of course, with the New York!

More Fun with New Yorks

The New York may be a basic figure, but you will really be able to have a lot of fun using some exciting variations.

The New York Rondé

This uses a standard timing but a far-from-standard method of dancing the move. Note that Steps 3–5 replace the standard Cha Cha Chassé. Start as for a standard New York.

Man Draw the left hand across and forward, swivelling a quarter turn (90°) to the right on the right foot. Move forward onto left foot.

Woman Swivel a quarter turn (90°) to left on the left foot. Move forward onto right foot.

2

BEAT – 3

Man "Drop" the body weight back onto the right foot, flexing the right knee and allowing the left foot to swing slightly off the floor, around behind the right foot. The foot swing, or rondé, allows you to swivel to the left on the right foot.

Woman "Drop" the body weight back onto the left foot, flexing the left knee and allowing the right foot to swing slightly off the floor around behind the left foot. The foot swing, or rondé, allows you to swivel to the right on the left foot.

3

BEAT – 4

Man Cross the left foot behind the right foot, turning the left toes outward and flexing both knees.

Woman Cross the right foot behind the left foot, turning the right toes outward and flexing both knees.

The Syncopated New York

In the Syncopated New York, the dancers deviate momentarily from the dance's normal rhythm in a surprise syncopation which adds great panache. To dance the Syncopated New York, simply dance the Mambo New York but to a rhythm of 2 & 3, 4 & 1 which can be thought of as a double Cha Cha rhythm. Note that, in the Syncopated New York, the normal Cha Cha Chassé steps are eliminated. To cope with this faster interpretation, the legs and arms will need to be toned and strong.

The man will turn a quarter turn (90°) to the right and the woman to the left as they step forward, the man onto his left and the woman her right foot on count 2. On the "&" count, the couple simply transfer their weight back onto the other foot before turning to face each other as they step to the side on count 3. The move is then repeated but in the opposite direction. The hold and arm positions are as shown in the Mambo section and the couple will feel pressure through the joined arms as they dance through the Syncopated New York.

See the Mambo section for a more detailed and illustrated analysis.

BEAT – 4

Man Place the right foot to the side, small step.

Woman Place the left foot to the side, small step.

BEAT – 5

Man Move sideways onto the left foot, facing the woman, knees straight.

Woman Move sideways onto the right foot, facing the man, knees straight.

It is possible to dance the same move in the opposite direction with the man using the woman's steps and vice versa. However, that is too ostentatious, and too many "highlight" moves crowded together never look good. It is far better to continue with something simple, such as Steps 6–10 of a standard Cha Cha Cha New York or Steps 2–5 of the Side Steps described in the Merengue section to a timing of 2, 3, 4, 1 and without hold. Then continue with Steps 6–10 of the standard Cha Cha Cha New York. If you are in exuberant mood, pop in the New York Party Popper.

The New York Party Popper

Like the rest of the New York moves, this can go either to the right or left depending on which foot the move is started on. Here, we will assume that you have just danced the New York Rondé. The man and woman are in open facing position with feet apart. The man is standing on his left foot and the woman on her right. The man takes hold with his right hand and releases hold with his left as normal. Now it's time to pop!

BEAT – &

Man Hop on the right foot or slip it back underneath the body.

Woman Hop on the left foot or slip it back underneath the body.

BEAT – 2

Man Draw the right hand across and forward, swivelling a quarter turn (90°) to the left on the left foot. Move forward onto the right foot, relaxing the right knee and allowing the body to overturn slightly.

Woman Swivel a quarter turn (90°) to the right on the right foot. Move forward onto the left foot, relaxing the left knee and allowing the body to overturn slightly.

BEAT – 3

Man Move back onto the left foot and recover the body shape.

Woman Move back onto the right foot and recover the body shape.

BEAT – 4 & 1

Man Draw the right hand back to its original position. On the left foot, swivel a quarter turn (90°) to right and dance the Cha Cha Cha Chassé to right. Take hold with left hand then release hold with the right hand. End facing the woman.

Woman On the right foot, swivel a quarter turn (90°) to left and dance the Cha Cha Cha Chassé to left. End facing the man.

Continue with your preferred move or try the Zig Zag.

CHA CHA CHA: the zig zag

The Zig Zag

The Zig Zag is a simple and straightforward move, but is particularly useful if your area of the floor is becoming crowded and you want to move a little way into clear space. It is a good figure to dance having completed a full New York, and you can easily take up a double hand hold during the final Cha Cha Cha Chassé. Note the rhythm change which drops the Cha Cha Cha timing. Start in open facing position with a double hand hold, feet apart. The man is standing on his right foot and the woman on her left foot.

1

BEAT – 2

Man Move forward onto the left foot, making a one-eighth turn (45°) to the right.

Woman Move back onto the right foot by making a one-eighth turn (45°) to the right.

2

BEAT – 3

Man Move sideways onto the right foot, making a one-eighth turn (45°) to the left to come square with the woman.

Woman Move sideways onto the left foot, making a one-eighth turn (45°) to the left to come square with the man.

3

BEAT – 4

Man Move back onto the left foot, making ⅛ turn to left.

Woman Move forward onto the right foot, making ⅛ turn to left.

4

BEAT – 1

Man Move sideways onto the right foot, making a one-eighth turn (45°) to the right to come square with the woman.

Woman Move sideways onto the left foot, making a one-eighth turn (45°) to the right to come square with the man.

Style Tip

A slight inclination of the body towards your partner enhances the look of the move and will enable the man and the woman to work off each other. However, you should never lean on your partner.

The Zig Zag may be repeated if necessary. Continue with a New York, your choice of the New York variations or dance Spot Turns (Right for the man and Left for the woman).

Spot Turns

A Spot Turn is simply the name given to a turn which takes place on the spot. This type of turn can be made either to the right or to the left and by either the man or the woman. Typically, if the man and the woman both dance a Spot Turn simultaneously, they will make their turns in opposite directions.

Spot Turn to Right

Start with the feet apart, standing on the right foot, no hold.

1
BEAT – 2
Man and Woman
Place the left foot forward and across, then turn onto the left foot.

2
BEAT – 3
Man and Woman
Transfer the body weight forward onto the right foot, still turning to the right.

3–5
BEAT – 4 – 1
Man and Woman
Dance a Cha Cha Cha Chassé moving to the left – left-right-left – completing a full turn to the right.

Spot Turn to Left

1
BEAT – 2
Man and Woman
Place the right foot forward and across, then turn onto the right foot.

2
BEAT – 3
Man and Woman
Transfer the body weight forward onto the left foot, still turning to left.

3–5
BEAT – 4 – 1
Man and Woman
Dance a Cha Cha Cha Chassé moving to the right (right-left-right) completing a full turn to the left.

Continue with any appropriate figure.

The Alemana Turn and the Turkish Towel

This move combines two classic Cha Cha figures. You have already encountered the Alemana Turn in the Rumba. The Turkish Towel is so called because the man appears to be using the woman as a towel to dry his back! Don't be put off by the apparent length of this combination. We will break it down into sections which we can build up gradually, practising each section before moving on to the next. Start in Fan Position.

The Alemana Turn

1
BEAT – 2

Woman Close the right foot back to the left foot to end feet together.

2
BEAT – 3

Woman Walk forward onto the left foot.

3–5
BEAT – 4 – 1

Woman Dance a forward Cha Cha Cha Chassé, turning to the right on Step 5.

6
BEAT – 2

Man Move back onto the right foot, leaving the left foot in place and circling the left hand clockwise as the woman turns.

Woman Move the left foot forward and across the body, then turn right to end on the left foot.

7
BEAT – 3

Man Transfer the body weight forward onto the left foot starting to turn left. Take the woman's right hand in your right hand at shoulder height.

Woman Move forward onto the right foot, continuing the turn by swivelling to the right.

1–5
BEAT – 2 – 1

Man Dance a complete Forward Basic Cha Cha Cha, keeping the Cha Cha Cha Chassé on the spot. Draw the woman towards you as you dance the Cha Cha Cha Chassé and raise your left arm, palm uppermost. The woman should now be in front of your left side.

The Turkish Towel

8–10
BEAT – 4 – 1
Man Dance a Cha Cha Cha Chassé turning to left. Start with the right foot moving to the side across and in front of the woman. On Step 9, take the woman's left hand in yours at shoulder height.

Woman Continue turning right to complete a half turn (180°) and dance a Cha Cha Cha Chassé, moving left across and behind the man.

11 ▶
BEAT – 2
Man Move back onto the left foot, leaving the right foot in place.

Woman Move forward onto the right foot, leaving the left foot in place.

◀12
BEAT – 3
Man Transfer the body weight forward onto the right foot.

Woman Transfer the body weight back onto the left foot.

13–15
BEAT – 4 – 1
Man Dance a Cha Cha Cha Chassé, moving left across and in front of the woman.

Woman Dance a Cha Cha Cha Chassé, moving right across and behind the man.

16
BEAT – 2
Man Move back onto the right foot, leaving the left foot in place.

Woman Move forward onto the left foot, leaving the right foot in place.

17
BEAT – 3
Man Transfer the body weight forward onto the left foot.

Woman Transfer the body weight back onto the right foot.

18–20
BEAT – 4 – 1
Man Dance a Cha Cha Cha Chassé, moving right across and in front of the woman.

Woman Dance a Cha Cha Cha Chassé, moving left across and behind the man.

21–25
BEAT – 2 – 1
Man Repeat Steps 11–15, releasing hold with your left hand on Step 25.

Woman Repeat Steps 11–15, ending on the man's right side.

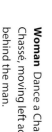

The Hockeystick Ending

26 BEAT – 2

Man Move back onto the right foot, leading the woman forward with your right hand at waist height.

Woman Walk forward onto the left foot.

27 BEAT – 3

Man Transfer the body weight forward onto the left foot, leading the woman to turn left towards you at the end of the step.

Woman Walk forward onto the right foot, then, on the right foot, swivel a half turn (180°) to the left to end facing the man.

28–30 BEAT – 4 – 1

Man Dance a forward Cha Cha Cha Chassé, bringing the woman in line with you, and then release hold to resume a left-hand to right-hand hold.

Woman Dance a backward Cha Cha Cha Chassé, moving in line with the man.

Turkish-Towel Tip

As the couple pass in front and behind each other, they will find it more comfortable to turn slightly towards each other so that, on the forward and backward steps, they can make eye contact with their partners – just to ensure they are enjoying themselves, of course.

Continue with your preferred move.

Lado a Lado

The Latin-American dances offer a myriad of moves in which the man and woman dance opposite each other and where they weave intricate moves around each other. But the Cha Cha Cha offers the chance to dance some stunning steps in a new orientation – side by side, or lado a lado. In such moves, the man and woman both dance the same steps. In order to do this, either the man or the woman must change from the normal opposite foot to their partner onto the same foot and, at the end of the move, back again. This is not as difficult as it sounds. Let's see how. Start in open facing position, feet apart. As usual, the man is standing on his right foot and the woman on her left foot. Stand not too far apart. (Practice will help you gauge just how far in order to make the move comfortable to dance.)

Moving into Lado a Lado Position

1-5 BEAT – 2,3, 4 & 1

Man The man dances a standard Forward Basic Cha Cha releasing hold to allow the woman to turn on 3-4.

1 BEAT – 2

Woman Move back onto the right foot, leaving the left foot in place.

2 BEAT – 3

Woman Transfer the body weight forward onto the left foot.

New York or New York Party Popper

The man and woman and now dance Steps 5–10 of the man's steps for the Cha Cha Cha New York, or Steps 1–6 of the man's steps for the New York Party Popper, but making a half turn (180°) to the right over the Cha Cha Cha Chassé to end with the woman in front and the man behind, both on the right foot. The rhythm for Steps 1–5 is the same for the man and woman: 2, 3, 4 & 1 (New York) or 2 & 3, 4 & 1 (Party Popper). Here illustrated is the New York.

BEAT – 3-4

Woman
Move forward onto the right foot next to the man's right side. On the right foot, swivel a half turn (180°) to the left to end facing the same direction as the man.

BEAT – 5

Woman Move sideways onto the left foot.

You are now in a side-by-side position, with both the man and the woman standing on the left foot, feet apart, and ready for the next move.

BEAT – 1-2

1

Man and Woman
On the left foot, swivel a quarter turn (90°) to the left and move forward onto the right foot leaving the left foot in place.

BEAT – 3

2

Man and Woman
Transfer the body weight back onto the left foot.

BEAT – 4

3

Man and Woman
On the left foot, swivel a quarter turn (90°) to the right and move sideways onto the right foot.

BEAT – 4 &

Woman
Move forward onto the right foot next to the man's right side. On the right foot, swivel a half turn (180°) to the left to end facing the same direction as the man.

BEAT – &
Man and Woman
Move the left foot sideways towards the right foot. End standing on the left foot.

5

BEAT – 1
Man and Woman
Move sideways onto the right foot.

Tandem Points

2

BEAT – 4 – 1
Man and Woman Point the right foot back but remain standing on the right foot. Allow the body to counter-balance the pointing leg.

1

BEAT – 2 – 3
Man and Woman Point the left foot forward but remain standing on the right foot. Allow the body to counter-balance the pointing leg.

CHA CHA CHA: new york or new york party popper/tandem points

Tandem Points

The man and woman now dance Steps 1–5 of the man's steps for the Cha Cha Cha New York, or Steps 1–6 of the woman's steps for the New York Party Popper, but making a half turn (180°) to the left over the Cha Cha Cha Chassé, to end on the left foot. Beat – 2, 3, 4 & 1 (New York) or 2 & 3, 4 & 1 (Party Popper).

1
BEAT – 2 – 3

Man and Woman Point the right foot forward but remain standing on the left foot. Allow the body to counter-balance the pointing leg.

2
BEAT – 4 – 1

Man and Woman Point the right foot back but remain standing on the left foot. Allow the body to counter-balance the pointing leg.

Now repeat the first section of the New York or New York Party Popper, but making only a quarter turn (90°) to the right over the Cha Cha Chassé, to end on the right foot, feet apart, side-by-side.

New York or New York Party Popper in the opposite direction

The man and woman now dance in the opposite direction

Option One

1
BEAT – 2

Man Move back onto the left foot.

&
BEAT – &

Man Close the right foot to the left foot.

2
BEAT – 3

Man Move forward onto the left foot.

3
BEAT – 4 & 1 OR 4–1

Man Dance a Forward Cha Cha Chassé.

The Exit

The woman now dances the Hockeystick Ending which we used to conclude the Turkish Towel, but the man must dance a foot change to revert to the normal opposite foot to the woman. He can do this in one of two ways.

Option Two

1–3
BEAT – 2 & 3

Man Dance a Forward Cha Cha Chassé, starting with the left foot.

4–6
BEAT – 4 & 1

Man Dance a Forward Cha Cha Cha Chassé, starting with the right foot.

The couple will use the last move to reposition themselves ready to resume hold and continue into their next move.

Music Suggestions

Normally I would prefer Latin bands for Latin music, but the Cha Cha Chas by the international dance orchestra of Ross Mitchell are especially good, with a clear rhythm and an excellent sound – his versions of "The Shoop Shoop Song" and "Pata-Pata" are strongly recommended. Los Paraguayos are always good for both listening and dancing. For authentic Cha Cha Cha, Rumba and Salsa, try Venezuelan artist Oscar d'Leon.

Paso Doble

The Paso Doble rather uninspiringly means "two-step". Yet this dance, in which the man represents the matador and the woman his cape in the drama of a Spanish bull-fight, has inspired an enduring passion, not only in its homelands of France and Spain but throughout the world. Though most often associated with Spain, many of the more popular figures have French names, underlining the fact that the Paso Doble is one of France's standard dances. The Paso Doble shares with the Viennese Waltz an image of requiring a high level of technical ability. This is due to most people having only seen either dance performed in televised competitions. However, it is the equally delightful but simplified social

version of the Paso Doble which is enjoyed, irrespective of age or ability, throughout Spain, France, Latin-America and in dance clubs all over the world.

Music and Rhythm

The music, while quite inspiring, has a simple 1–2–1–2 march rhythm which is easy enough for the first-time dancer to follow. There are few rhythm changes in the steps and the dance can easily be enjoyed by everyone. The tempo or speed of the dance is a brisk but not difficult 60 bars per minute.

Some of the terms used in Paso Doble are used in the Standard Partner Dance section, where full explanations are given.

Style Tip

In this section, I have tried to impart the sense of passion which characterizes the Paso Doble's story. However, most social dancers in the Latin countries have a less dramatic and more jovial approach to their enjoyment of Paso Doble. The dance does not therefore need to be ostentatious or showy to be enjoyed. After all, it's your dance and you should enjoy it in your own way.

Basic Paso Doble – "Sur Place"

One of the basic Paso Doble moves is called "Sur Place", which is French for "on the spot". Take up a close hold but remain a little apart. Lift the arms a little higher than before. Correct poise gives great style to even the basic Paso Doble, so stand up with your feet together and, without leaning on your partner, bring your body weight slightly forward until your heels are just about to leave the floor. To dance "Sur Place", the man will be facing the wall. He will start with his right foot and the woman with her left foot. Dance eight mark-time steps on the spot, keeping the legs relatively straight, and using only the balls of the feet. The "Sur Place" move can also be rotated on the spot to left or right.

WOMAN	2, 4, 6, 8	1, 2, 3, 4
MAN	2, 4, 6, 8	1, 2, 3, 4

Recommended Music

The Spanish Gypsy Dance, which is also known as España Cani, has become the universal anthem of the Paso Doble. Among many other excellent Paso Dobles are "En El Mundo" and "El Gato Montes". Authentic Paso Doble music played by Spanish, French or Latin-American bands will tend to be slower than the internationally agreed tempo for competitions. "Y Viva España" was a fun international commercial hit in the mid-seventies.

The Separation

The Separation is a standard move in Paso Doble. It is a characteristic move by the man, in which he stamps his foot in a gesture reminiscent of the matador attracting the attention of the bull. The gesture is known as the "Appel", which is French for "call". In the Separation, the man moves the woman (the cape) away from him and then draws her slowly back to him as if trying to lure the bull to charge. As usual, the man is standing on his left foot, feet together, and the woman is positioned opposite correspondingly.

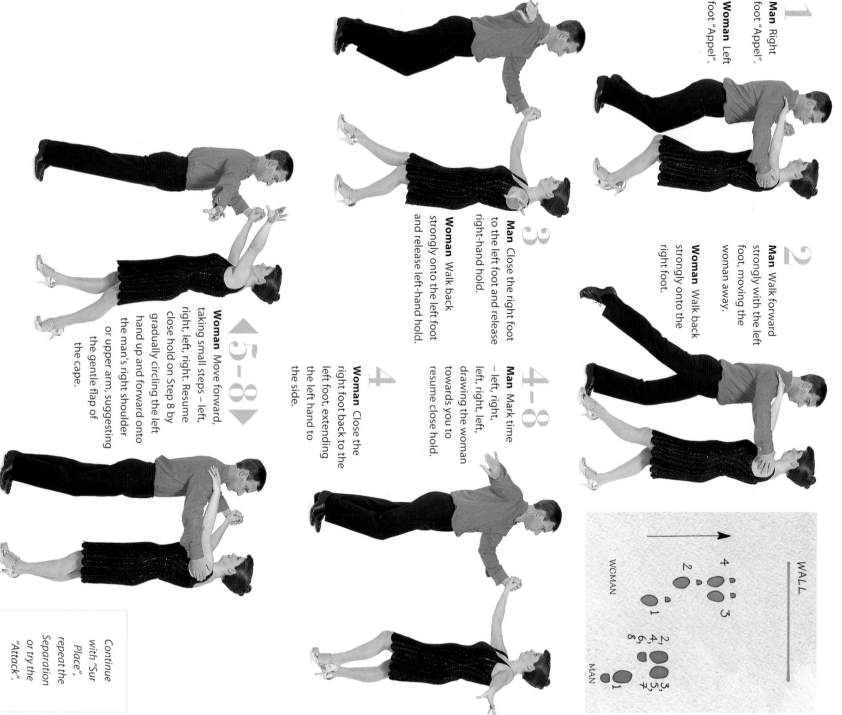

1

Man Right foot "Appel".

Woman Left foot "Appel".

2

Man Walk forward strongly with the left foot, moving the woman away.

Woman Walk back strongly onto the right foot.

3

Man Close the right foot to the left foot and release right-hand hold.

Woman Walk back strongly onto the left foot and release left-hand hold.

4

Man Mark time – left, right, left, right, left, drawing the woman towards you to resume close hold.

Woman Close the right foot back to the left foot, extending the left hand to the side.

4–8

5–8

Woman Move forward, taking small steps – left, right, left, right. Resume close hold on Step 8 by gradually circling the left hand up and forward onto the man's right shoulder or upper arm, suggesting the gentle flap of the cape.

Continue with "Sur Place", repeat the Separation or try the "Attack".

The Attack

The Separation worked. The bull has been provoked into an attack and charges towards the matador. The matador holds his ground until the last moment, then he makes his move.

The swish of the cape as the bull passes beneath it is caught in the motion of the couple's joined hands as they circle outwards and down during Steps 2–4, to end close to the waist. And now a moment for the matador to regain composure as the couple perform four "Sur Place" steps, turning half a turn (180°) to the left, ending with the man facing the centre line of the room, completing the count of eight.

1
Man Right foot "Appel".

Woman Left foot "Appel".

2
Man Walk forward strongly onto the left foot.

Woman Walk back strongly onto the right foot.

3
Man Side step to the right.

Woman Side step to the left.

4
Man Close the left foot to the right foot.

Woman Close the right foot to the left foot.

Elevations to Right

In a display of proud defiance, the matador arrogantly struts his mastery as he takes up a new position to face and taunt the bull. The man is now facing the centre line of the room and is standing on his left foot. The woman is standing on her right foot.

1
Man Place the right foot to the side, raising the left hand above head height and allowing the left arm to curve in a continuation of the body line, curving slightly to the right. Switch the head to look right and down. Legs are relatively straight and dance the move on the toes.

Woman Place the left foot to the side, toes mirroring those of the man.

The effect is of four counts of "high" Chassés, followed by four counts of "low" Chassés.

2
Man Close the left foot to the right foot, maintaining the same body position.

Woman Close the right foot to the left foot, toes mirroring those of the man.

3–4
Man Repeat Steps 1–2.

Woman Repeat Steps 1–2, mirroring the man.

5–8
Man Repeat Steps 1–4, extending left hand down and looking down towards the left hand. The body is curved slightly to the left. The knees are relaxed and the feet are flat.

Woman Repeat Steps 1–4, feet flat, mirroring the man.

Continue with the Attack, turning the four "Sur Place" movements a half turn (180°) to the left, to end with the man facing the wall. Then you can start again or, in a triumphal gesture, dance the "Huit".

The Huit

"Huit" is simply the count of "Eight" used for this triumphal exhibition of the matador as he sweeps his cape to and fro, perhaps mesmerising the bull, or perhaps goading it into an attack which may result in the final coup de grâce. The man is facing the wall, feet together, standing on his left foot. The woman is standing on her right foot, feet together.

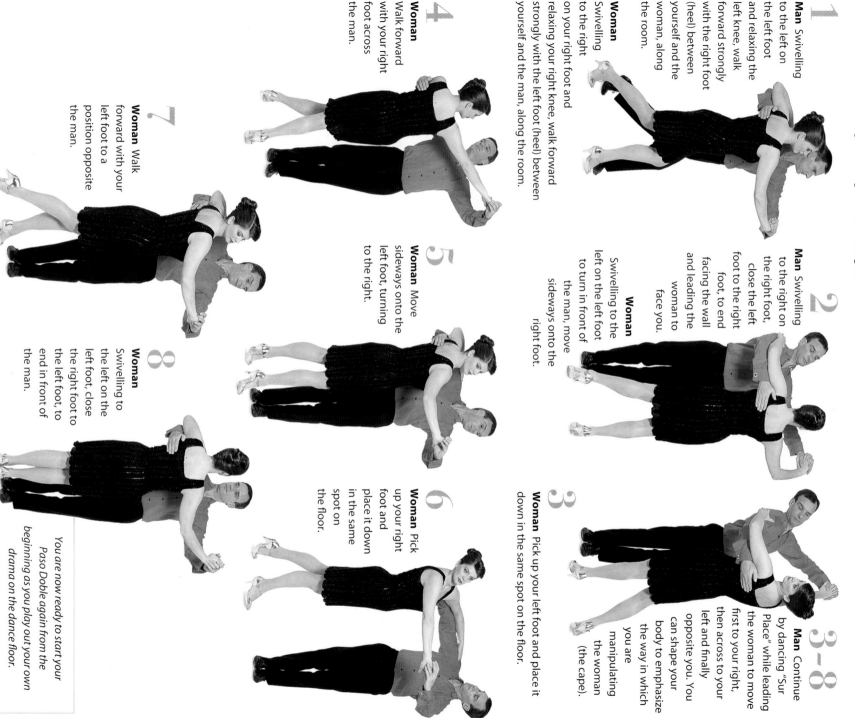

1

Man Swivelling to the left on the left foot and relaxing the left knee, walk forward strongly with the right foot (heel) between yourself and the woman, along the room.

Woman Swivelling to the right on your right foot and relaxing your right knee, walk forward strongly with the left foot (heel) between yourself and the man, along the room.

2

Man Swivelling to the right on the right foot, close the left foot to the right foot, to end facing the wall and leading the woman to face you.

Woman Swivelling to the left on the left foot to turn in front of the man, move sideways onto the right foot.

3-8

Man Continue by dancing "Sur Place" while leading the woman to move first to your right, then across to your left and finally opposite you. You can shape your body to emphasize the way in which you are manipulating the woman (the cape).

3

Woman Pick up your left foot and place it down in the same spot on the floor.

4

Woman Walk forward with your right foot across the man.

5

Woman Move sideways onto the left foot, turning to the right.

6

Woman Pick up your right foot and place it down in the same spot on the floor.

7

Woman Walk forward with your left foot to a position opposite the man.

8

Woman Swivelling to the left on the left foot, close the right foot to the left foot, to end in front of the man.

You are now ready to start your Paso Doble again from the beginning as you play out your own drama on the dance floor.

Open Promenade to Open Counter Promenade

In this move, the matador may be imagined strutting around the arena, acknowledging the applause and cheers of the crowd. In this move, Open Promenade and Open Counter Promenade positions are used. Open Promenade Position is similar to the Promenade Position explained in the Standard Partner Dance section, but the couple are apart, holding only left-hand to right-hand. Open Counter Promenade Position is the opposite position, though the hold remains the same. Start in close hold. The man faces the wall. He is standing on his left foot, the woman on her right.

1

Man Right-foot "Appel". Release hold with the right hand, bringing the elbow back and extending the lower arm vertically towards the floor. Extend the left hand a little to the left, turning the bottom of the wrist outwards to lead the woman.

Woman Left-foot "Appel", releasing hold with the left hand and matching the man's right-arm position.

2

Man Move sideways onto the left foot in Open Promenade Position.

Woman Move sideways onto the right foot in Open Promenade Position.

3

Man Walk forward and across onto the right foot in Open Promenade Position, starting to move across the woman.

Woman Walk forward and across onto the left foot in Open Promenade Position.

4

Man Move sideways onto the left foot, backing down the room, turning strongly to the right.

Woman Walk forward down the room onto the right foot.

5

Man Move sideways onto the right foot, turning right to end in Open Counter Promenade Position.

Woman Move to the side down the room onto the left foot in Open Counter Promenade Position.

The Spanish Line

The matador feeds on the crowd's applause and encourages the people to shout "Olé!" as he strikes a pose – The Spanish Line. There are several Flamenco-style moves which have come to typify everyone's preconception of Paso Doble. The Spanish Line is one such figure and, while it may be a little stereotyped if danced conservatively, it can be very effective and a lot of fun. Continue straight from the Open Promenade to Open Counter Promenade.

1
Man Walk forward onto the right foot.

Woman Walk forward onto the left foot.

2
Man Move sideways onto the left foot, down the room, turning to the right and releasing hold.

Woman Move sideways onto the right foot, down the room, turning to the left and releasing hold.

3
Man Move back onto the right foot, turning the toes out and completing a half turn (180°) to the right, to end facing against the flow.

Woman Move back onto the left foot, turning the toes out and completing a half turn (180°) to the left, to end facing against the flow.

6
Man Walk forward and across onto the left foot, down the room in Open Counter Promenade Position.

Woman Walk forward and across onto the right foot, down the room in Open Counter Promenade Position.

7
Man Walk forward onto the right foot, down the room.

Woman Move sideways onto the left foot, backing down the room, turning strongly to the right.

8
Man Walk forward onto the left foot, down the room in Open Promenade Position.

Woman Walk forward onto the right foot, down the room in Open Promenade Position.

Dance straight into the Spanish Line or into the Promenade Close.

4 ▶

Man Keeping the right knee straight, point the toes of the left foot to the floor and, raising the left heel high off the floor, place them slightly across the right foot without weight. The left arm is curved across but not too close to the chest, and the right arm continues the curve behind the lower back. This is the Spanish Line.

Woman Keeping the left knee straight, point the toes of the right foot to the floor and, raising the right heel high off the floor, place them slightly across the left foot without weight. The right arm is curved across but not too close to the chest, and the left arm continues the curve behind the lower back. This is the Spanish Line.

Style Tip

Some dancers prefer to raise the back arm on Steps 4 and 8, but you should be aware that this tends to make the couple look smaller and is perhaps a little too ostentatious for social dancing. If the Flamenco Taps are danced then the arms should not be raised.

5–8

Man Dance 1–4 of the woman's steps, moving in the opposite direction against the flow, and ending facing down the room.

Woman Dance 1–4 of the man's steps, moving in the opposite direction against the flow, and ending facing down the room.

Continue with the Promenade Close.

The Promenade Close

The couple resolve the Spanish Line by dancing the Promenade Close.

1

Man Walk forward and across onto the right foot, down the room, in Open Promenade Position without hold.

Woman Walk forward and across onto the left foot, down the room, in Open Promenade Position without hold.

2

Man On the right foot, swivel to face the wall. Close the left foot to the right foot and resume a close hold.

Woman On the left foot, swivel to face the man. Close the right foot to the left foot and resume a close hold.

The Flamenco Taps

The Flamenco Taps can be danced after Step 4 or Step 8 of the Spanish Line. The figure is danced on the spot and the Spanish Line arm positions are held the same.

Man after Step 4 (or Woman after Step 8) of the Spanish Line

1
Stand on the left foot.

2
Pointing the toes of the right foot to the floor and raising the heel high off the floor, tap the right foot twice behind the left foot.

3–4
Dance 3–4 of the man's steps of the Spanish Line.

The normal format for dancing the Flamenco Taps is to dance the following:

Steps 1–4 of The Spanish Line – Flamenco Taps – Steps 5–8 of The Spanish Line – Flamenco Taps – The Promenade Close.

Man after Step 8 (or Woman after Step 4) of the Spanish Line

1
Stand on the right foot.

2
Pointing the toes of the left foot to the floor and raising the heel high off the floor, tap the left foot twice behind the right foot.

3–4
Dance 3–4 of the woman's steps of the Spanish Line.

1   **2**   **3**   **4**

3
Man Move sideways onto the right foot against the flow, facing the wall.

Woman Move sideways onto the left foot against the flow.

4
Man Close the left foot to the right foot.

Woman Close the right foot to the left foot.

It is now a good idea to dance four "Sur Place" movements to complete the count of eight before starting your Paso Doble again from the beginning.

Samba

The Portuguese explorers who first sailed along the coast of South America one January morning discovered the beauty of a series of bays with golden beaches, fed by a fresh river running through lush tropical peaks. When they named that idyllic spot "January River", or Rio de Janeiro in Portuguese, they could hardly have imagined what the future had in store. Portuguese colonists soon settled and, as agriculture prospered, slaves were brought from the Portuguese-controlled areas of south-west Africa to work in the plantations of Bahia, in the north-east of what would later become Brazil. Samba began to develop in the Bahia region as a response to the strong percussive rhythms of a type of drums called "Batuque", which the slaves had brought with them from Africa. The hypnotic beat of the drum enabled the early Samba dancers to escape for a while from their everyday troubles and dance barefoot, a tradition still upheld today in the Samba de Roda. In the language of those slaves, the word for dance was "Semba", a word that was destined to pass into the folklore of Brazil as the proud name of the national dance.

Now the Samba is the dance of celebration and joy at the Carnival held in Rio each February. The Carnival Samba dancers vie with each other as to who can wear the most enormous and fabulous headdresses which make all but the most basic foot movements impossible. This kind of Samba is very different from the more stylized international version. In Rio, the Samba is danced solo whereas the international Samba is a dance for couples. To a rhythm of "Quick, Quick, Slow &", the Rio dancers perform fast three-step weight changes with a slight knee lift, the sections of which are led with alternate feet. The women are adept at showing off their hip movements while the men's action is less exaggerated. Meanwhile, the head is kept perfectly still to avoid toppling the magnificent edifice it is supporting. The Samba as a dance for couples is also popular in Brazil and a slower version, called the Pagode (pronounced pa-go-day), is enjoyed for social purposes.

The Maxixe (pronounced ma-shee-shay) was the first version of the Samba to become known outside Brazil and gained some popularity in Europe, although that dwindled during the First World War. By the late 1930s, however, the catchy, carefree, fun-loving Samba was enthralling dancers in the USA and during the late 1930s and 1940s, both Rio and its Samba were capturing the imagination of the masses through the medium of cinema. Carmen Miranda featured in many Hollywood films, forging the popular archetypal images of Brazil and the Samba. Fred Astaire and Ginger Rogers further popularized the idea of Rio as an exotic, romantic and sophisticated backdrop to the dance in the motion picture *Flying Down to Rio* and the Samba flourished around the world.

When the popularity of a dance transports it beyond the boundaries of its own traditional and cultural context, it is natural that it will develop in a more international style. If such changes take place within the original character and spirit of the dance, then the result can enrich the dance, making it more varied and internationally appealing. Although inappropriate fad styles are sometimes applied to the Samba, as in the disco look given to the dance in the 1970s or the sharp, staccato feel of the 1990s, these tend not to stand the test of time and fade in favour of an approach which embraces the dance's original character.

For many social dancers, their local Latin American club, restaurant or bar is the place to relax, meet friends and dance the Samba. At these clubs, the music tends to be more authentically Brazilian, with dance moves taking on a more spontaneous and improvisational style. This book, though, will describe simplified versions of standard figures in the international style of Samba which is quite different from the Samba danced by Carnival-goers in Rio. It is taught by officially recognized dance teachers throughout the world and not only ensures compatibility of moves between dancers from different countries, but also provides a logical, structured and easily understandable approach to learning the Samba.

Smart, casual clothes are best for dancing the Samba. Women should wear short dresses for ease of movement, as well as shoes with a heel. Men should choose shoes with a good sole – rubber-soled shoes are not suitable.

The dramatic, energetic Samba is danced by couples not only in Brazil, but all over the world.

On the Floor

In the International Standard Dances, such as the Waltz and Quickstep, couples move around the dance floor in an overall anticlockwise direction. In some internationally standardized Latin American dances, such as the Mambo, Cha Cha Cha or the Rumba, couples generally do not progress around the floor but dance occupying only a small area of the floor. In the Samba, however, some moves remain relatively stationary, while others progress around the room. To learn the pattern of the figures and to move comfortably around the floor, with consideration for the other dancers, you will first need to become accustomed to orientating yourself in the room.

Going with the Flow

Assuming that the room is rectangular, the man stands facing the wall and the woman stands backing the wall. To progress with the flow of floor traffic as it moves anticlockwise around the room, the man moves to his left and the woman to her right. The line of flow runs around the floor, parallel with the wall.

Floorcraft adds to your dancing pleasure.

The Centre Line

With the couple still in the same position, the room's centre line runs parallel to the wall, behind the man and in front of the woman.

Cornering

In the Samba, you may choose to dance a particular figure to help you move from one wall to the next. But mostly, you will simply curve the figures as necessary when you reach a corner of the room. Care should be taken not to distort the figures too much and make them difficult or uncomfortable to dance. Once you have negotiated the corner, you will need to re-orientate yourself along the new wall.

Basic Floorcraft

While you are dancing around the floor, you should try to be aware of other dancers and their likely direction of travel. The ability to avoid problems is a great asset to a dancer and ways of doing this are highlighted later in the book. There are, however, a few general rules which are worth mentioning at this point.

- *It makes sense for more experienced dancers to give way to less experienced dancers.*
- *Whoever can see a potential problem should take avoiding action. This is usually the couple who are further back in the flow of floor traffic.*
- *Less experienced dancers and dancers who progress more slowly around the floor should follow a path near to the wall so as not to impede more experienced and quicker dancers.*
- *Never dance across the centre line of the room into the oncoming flow of floor traffic.*

With practice, the ability to avoid problems will itself become an enjoyable feature of your dancing.

Music and Rhythm

The euphoric excitement of the Carnival effervesces through the surging rhythms and vivacious melodies of the Samba to bring a party atmosphere to any occasion. The speed, or tempo, of the Samba can vary quite dramatically from 48–52 bars per minute for social dancing, up to 58 bars per minute for very fast Brazilian Sambas. The variety of percussive instruments available to musicians in the Samba's native Brazil has led to a multiplicity of rhythms, each of which echoes the dance's origins in south-west Africa and has its own special accent and feel. The time signature of the Samba is generally 2/4, which means that the rhythm has two counts to one bar of music with a value of four beats (i.e. two beats to each count), or 4/4, which means four counts to one bar. The Samba moves and figures have different rhythms and you will become accustomed to these with time.

For the purposes of this book, we will assume that the time signature is 2/4. If you are finding this difficult to understand, don't worry. Many of the fantastic Brazilian musicians have no technical knowledge of the rhythms they are producing yet can still make music which is pure South American magic. It is not necessary to think consciously about the beat values while you are dancing, although an *Enjoy the beat of the Samba.*

appreciation of the nature of the rhythms will inevitably help you to understand the figures.

Each step of the figures in the book will be given a count. Using the 2/4 time signature, the value of each count will be one of the following:

Slow = 1 beat or Quick = 1/2 beat. The beat will frequently be split to provide exciting rhythmic combinations. The split beats are conventionally described as: & = 1/2 beat or a = 1/4 beat.

When the beat is split, the smaller, quicker fraction of the beat is taken from the preceding beat. In the count of 1 a 2, the "a" count is taken from the preceding "1" count, so that the "1" count is only 3/4 of a beat and not a whole beat.

Examples:

Count	Beat value
1 a 2	3/4 1/4 1
Slow a Slow	3/4 1/4 1
1 a 2 a 3 a 4	3/4 1/4 3/4 1/4 3/4 1/4 1
Slow a Slow	3/4 1/4 3/4 1/4 3/4 1/4 1
a Slow a Slow	1/4 3/4 1/4 3/4 1/4 3/4 1/4 1
Slow Quick Quick	1 1/2 1/2
Quick Quick Slow	1/2 1/2 1

When the music has a 4/4 time signature, the beat values given above are doubled.

The Dance Floor

Consideration for other dancers is vital dance-floor etiquette.

As the dance floor is primarily for the benefit of the dancers, it should not be used as a thoroughfare. Always walk around the edge of the floor and never across it – the sudden emergence of a bystander trying to dodge dancing couples can cause chaos and disruption. When taking to the floor, you should try to avoid causing any problems for the dancers who are already on the dance floor. Given that the man will normally start the dance facing the outside of the room, it is a natural mistake for him to walk on to the floor backwards with his attention focused on his partner, rather than on the other dancers. As he will not easily be able to avoid dancers in this position, it is far better to approach the floor and assess the flow of floor traffic before taking up a starting position with due consideration to the other dancers. A little common sense is all that is needed and it makes the experience of dancing much more pleasant for everyone. When leaving the floor, especially during a dance, the same consideration should be shown.

Which Foot to Start with and Why

Some dance schools advocate starting the dance with a move called the Natural Basic Movement which starts with the man moving his right foot forward, or the Reverse Basic Movement in which the man moves his left foot forward. Either are in theory correct. However, if the man can move forward with either foot but without a turn, it is impossible for the woman to tell which foot he intends to use. For this reason, the best start to the dance is to use the Side Basic Samba or a Samba Whisk (see further on in this section) in which the man begins by moving sideways and, as a result, is able much more easily to communicate his intention to his partner.

The Hold

The close hold, seen from two angles.

In different Samba figures, different holds will be used which give variety to the shape and feel of the dance. These various holds will be described as you progress through the figures in the book. At the start of the dance, it is sensible for the man to choose a simple hold which offers him the best contact with the woman in order to lead her into their first move. Most social dancers therefore start in a close hold.

Close Hold

The man and woman stand a little apart and square to each other. The man's right hand cups the woman's left shoulder-blade while she rests her left hand lightly on his right upper arm or shoulder, so that her arm follows the same curve as the man's. With his left elbow at the same height as his right elbow, the man raises his left hand to just below eye level and takes the woman's right hand. His left arm should be curved gently forward so that his hand is on a line running between the couple. The man takes hold by presenting his left hand to the woman as if he were a policeman stopping traffic. His thumb should extend naturally to the side. The woman then hooks her middle finger on to the man's hand between his thumb and fingers, palm to palm. She lowers her second and fourth fingers over her middle finger and then lowers her little finger. She wraps her thumb around the base of the man's thumb and the man closes his fingers around the woman's hand. The woman's right arm matches the curve of the man's left. To minimize the possibility of treading on each other's feet during forward and backward movements in close hold, the woman should stand slightly to the man's right so that the line of his shirt buttons is opposite her right shoulder. Despite the name "Close Hold", the couple do not have any abdominal contact.

Basic Samba

While you are still beginning to accustom yourself to the speed, rhythm and action of the Samba, it is a good idea to start the dance with an easy move. Start in Close Hold, with the man facing the wall and the woman facing the centre line of the room. Your feet should be together, the man standing with his weight on the left foot and the woman with her weight on the right foot.

Side Basic Samba to the Right

1
COUNT – SLOW
Man Move sideways on to the right foot.

Woman Move sideways on to the left foot.

2
COUNT – a
Man Close the left foot to the right foot.

Woman Close the right foot to the left foot.

3
COUNT – SLOW
Man Transfer your body weight on to the right foot.

Woman Transfer your body weight on to the left foot.

Rhythm Tip
As you dance the Side Basic Samba, you might like to reinforce the rhythm by saying to yourself, "Step, Change feet".

Side Basic Samba to the Left

1
COUNT – SLOW
Man Move sideways on to the left foot.

Woman Move sideways on to the right foot.

2
COUNT – a
Man Close the right foot to the left foot.

Woman Close the left foot to the right foot.

3
COUNT – SLOW
Man Transfer your body weight on to the left foot.

Woman Transfer your body weight on to the right foot.

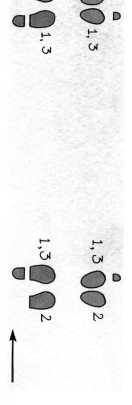

Samba Action

Once you have learned the simple pattern of the Side Basic Samba, you will want to practise it a few times continuously. As you do this, you can start to introduce the all-important Samba Action which gives the dance its unique feel.

1

Man and Woman
Start with both knees a little flexed. As you start the move to the side, straighten the knees. As you put your weight on to the moving foot, lower from the ball of the foot on to the flat foot and flex knees to end the first count.

2

Man and Woman As you dance Step 2, straighten the knees a little but do not lower the heel on to the floor.

3

Man and Woman Relax down (ball–flat) again into Step 3.

> *This action is known as the "Samba Bounce Action" but you must be careful not to exaggerate it: it should be a gentle, rhythmic action felt through the knees and ankles. The Samba Bounce Action will be used in some of the other figures in the book.*

Samba Whisk

The Samba Whisk is a very useful basic figure which uses the Samba Bounce Action to full advantage. Start in close hold with the man facing the wall and the woman facing the centre line of the room. The man is standing with his weight on the left foot and the woman with her weight on the right foot.

Samba Whisk to the Right

1

COUNT – SLOW

Man Move sideways on to the right foot (ball–flat).

Woman Move sideways on to the left foot (ball–flat).

2

COUNT – a

Man Cross the left foot behind the right foot with the toes of the left foot just behind the heel of the right foot and turned out a little. Flex both knees. Allow the right heel to lift momentarily from the floor as you stand on the toes of the left foot.

Woman Cross the right foot behind the left foot, with the toes of the right foot just behind the heel of the left foot and turned out a little. Flex both knees. Allow the left heel to lift momentarily from the floor as you stand on the toes of the right foot.

3

COUNT – SLOW

Man Lower your body weight on to the right foot (ball–flat).

Woman Lower your body weight on to the left foot (ball–flat).

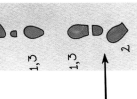

Samba Whisk to the Left

1

COUNT – SLOW

Man Move sideways on to the left foot (ball–flat).

Woman Move sideways on to the right foot (ball–flat).

2

COUNT – a

Man Cross the right foot behind the left foot, with the toes of the right foot just behind the heel of the left foot and turned out a little. Flex both knees. Allow the left heel to lift momentarily from the floor as you stand on the toes of the right foot.

Woman Cross the left foot behind the right foot, with the toes of the left foot just behind the heel of the right foot and turned out a little. Flex both knees. Allow the right heel to lift momentarily from the floor as you stand on the toes of the left foot.

3

COUNT – SLOW

Man Lower your body weight on to the left foot (ball–flat).

Woman Lower your body weight on to the right foot (ball–flat).

Footwork:

Footwork refers to the part of the foot used in contact with the floor during a step. Dancers often note footwork using abbreviations.

B = ball of the foot
F = flat foot
T = toe

In the Samba Whisk, the footwork is therefore: 1.BF, 2.T, 3.BF.

Samba Walks in Promenade Position

So far, you have been dancing the Side Basic Samba and the Samba Whisk in a stationary position. The Samba Walks will allow you to move steadily forwards with the flow along the room. The Samba Walks are danced in Promenade Position, so you will need to modify the Samba Whisk to end in the correct starting position for this figure. First dance a Samba Whisk to the Right, then a Samba Whisk to the Left and then another to the Right. On the final Samba Whisk to the Right, the man turns a quarter turn (90°) to his left anticlockwise (counterclockwise) and the woman a quarter turn (90°) to her right – clockwise – to end facing with the flow in Promenade Position. The man is standing with his weight on his right foot and the woman with her weight on the left foot.

Left Foot Samba Walk

1

COUNT – SLOW

Man Move forward a small step, on to the left foot, moving with the flow and ending with your right foot. Allow the right knee to close towards the left knee.

Woman Move forward a small step, on to the right foot, moving with the flow and ending with your hips over your foot. Allow the left knee to close towards the right knee.

2

COUNT – a

Man Extend the right foot back (part weight).

Woman Extend the left foot back (part weight).

Style Tip

A little Samba Bounce Action is used on the Samba Walks, so you should feel a slight rocking movement as you dance this figure.

Footwork:

1.BF, 2.B (inside edge), 3. F

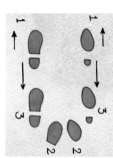

Right Foot Samba Walk

1
COUNT – SLOW

Man Move forward a small step, on to the right foot, moving with the flow and ending with your hips over your foot. Allow the left knee to close towards the right knee.

Woman Move forward a small step, on to the left foot, moving with the flow and ending with your hips over your foot. Allow the right knee to close towards the left knee.

2
COUNT – a

Man Extend the left foot back (part weight).

Woman Extend the right foot back (part weight).

3
COUNT – SLOW

Man Slip the right foot back underneath your body.

Woman Slip the left foot back underneath your body.

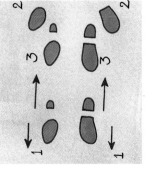

Footwork
1. BF, 2. B (inside edge), 3. F

3
COUNT – SLOW

Man Slip the left foot back underneath your body.

Woman Slip the right foot back underneath your body.

Now repeat the Samba Walk. This time the man starts with his right foot and the woman with her left.

You can now repeat the Samba Walks in Promenade Position, starting them with alternate feet.

Basic Samba: Short Routine

With the moves you have already learned, you can now dance a short basic routine.

- *Samba Whisk to the Right, Left and Right, ending in Promenade Position*
- *Left Foot Samba Walk, Right Foot Samba Walk*
- *Left Foot Samba Walk, Right Foot Samba Walk*
- *Samba Whisk to the Left, turned 90° to the right or clockwise for the man, to end facing the wall, and 90° to the left anticlockwise (counterclockwise) for the woman, to end facing the centre line*
- *Start again from the beginning*

Side Samba Walk

Some Samba figures are joined together by inserting a linking move. The Side Samba Walk is a modified version of the figure you have just learned and will enable you to progress into the next classic Samba figure – the Volta. Start having just danced a Left Foot Samba Walk in Promenade Position. The man is now standing on the left foot and the woman on the right foot. The couple is in Promenade Position, facing with the flow. A slight Samba Bounce Action is used in this figure.

1
COUNT – SLOW

Man Move forward a small step, on to the right foot, moving with the flow and ending with your hips over your foot. Allow the left knee to close towards the right knee.

Woman Move forward a small step, on to the left foot, moving with the flow and ending with your hips over your foot. Allow the right knee to close towards the left knee.

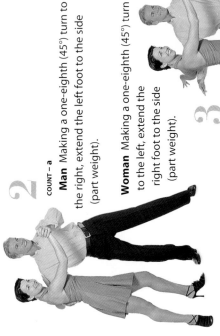

2
COUNT – a

Man Making a one-eighth (45°) turn to the right, extend the left foot to the side (part weight).

Woman Making a one-eighth (45°) turn to the left, extend the right foot to the side (part weight).

3
COUNT – SLOW

Man Slip the right foot to the left underneath your body. You have ended in Open Promenade Position.

Woman Slip the left foot to the right underneath your body. You have ended in Open Promenade Position.

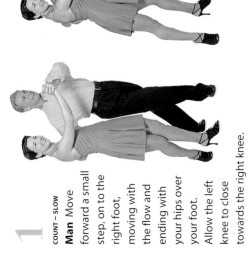

Footwork
1. BF, 2. B (inside edge), 3. F

Continue with the Travelling Volta or the Bota Fogos in Shadow Position.

Travelling Voltas

The Volta is a Samba move which is so full of vibrant rhythm and colour it has become a classic figure in the Samba repertoire. The Volta's popularity has led it to be adapted to be danced in a wide variety of interesting and enjoyable ways. In this version, the man's and woman's paths cross over each other as they progress along the floor in the Travelling Volta. This move extends the "Slow a Slow" rhythm across two bars of music and is conventionally counted as "1 a 2 a 3 a 4". Start having just danced the Side Samba Walk. The man is standing on the right foot and the woman on the left foot in Open Promenade Position. The man is holding the woman's right hand in his left. The Samba Bounce Action is used throughout this figure and the body weight is focused over the front foot.

Travelling Volta to the Right

Man Dance a gentle curve first towards the wall, then to the left to end facing the centre line of the room. The left and right feet will travel the path of the figure in parallel lines. At the start of the move, lift the left hand to allow the woman to pass under your arm and in front of you. When the woman has passed, you can return the hand to its normal position. Start with the left foot, which will remain in front.

Woman Dance a gentle curve first towards the centre line, then to the right to end facing the wall. The right and left feet will travel the path of the figure in parallel lines. During the move, the man will raise your hand to allow you to pass under his arm and in front of him. Start with the right foot, which will remain in front.

1
COUNT – SLOW – 1
Man Move the left foot across, in front of the right foot and along the curve (Latin Cross).

Woman Move the right foot across, in front of the left foot and along the curve (Latin Cross).

2
COUNT – a
Man Move the right foot sideways, a short step along the curve (part weight).

Woman Move the left foot sideways along the curve (part weight).

3
COUNT – SLOW – 2
Man Move the left foot across, in front of the right foot and along the curve (Latin Cross).

Woman Move the right foot across, in front of the left foot and along the curve (Latin Cross).

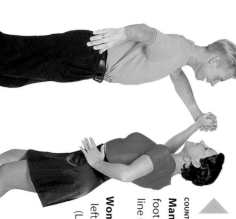

4
COUNT – a
Man Move the right foot sideways a short step along the curve (part weight).

Woman Move the left foot sideways a short step along the curve (part weight).

5
COUNT – SLOW – 3
Man Repeat Step 3.

Woman Repeat Step 3.

6
COUNT – a
Man Repeat Step 4 (part weight).

Woman Repeat Step 4 (part weight).

7
COUNT – SLOW – 4
Man Move the left foot across, in front of the right foot and along the curve to end facing the centre line (Latin Cross).

Woman Move the right foot across, in front of the left foot and along the curve to end facing the wall (Latin Cross).

You can now continue with the Travelling Volta to the Left.

Footwork:
1. BF, 2. T, 3. BF, 4. T, 5. BF, 6. T, 7. BF

SAMBA: travelling voltas

Travelling Volta to the Left

Man Dance a gentle curve first towards the centre line, then to the right to end facing the wall. The right and left feet will travel the path of the figure in parallel lines. At the start of the move, lift the left hand to allow the woman to pass under your arm and in front of you. When the woman has passed, you can return the hand to its normal position. Start with the right foot, which will remain in front, and focus your body weight over this foot.

Woman Dance a gentle curve first towards the wall, then to the left to end facing the centre line. The left and right feet will travel the path of the figure in parallel lines. During the move, the man will raise your hand to allow you to pass under his arm and in front of him. Start with the left foot, which will remain in front, and focus your body weight over this foot.

1
COUNT – SLOW - 1

Man Move the right foot across, in front of the left foot, and along the curve (Latin Cross).

Woman Move the left foot across, in front of the right foot, and along the curve (Latin Cross).

2
COUNT – a

Man Move the left foot sideways a short step along the curve (part weight).

Woman Move the right foot sideways a short step along the curve (part weight).

3
COUNT – SLOW - 2

Man Move the right foot across, in front of the left foot and along the curve (Latin Cross).

Woman Move the left foot across, in front of the right foot and along the curve (Latin Cross).

4
COUNT – a

Man Move the left foot sideways a short step along the curve (part weight).

Woman Move the right foot sideways a short step along the curve (part weight).

5
COUNT – SLOW - 3

Man Move the right foot across, in front of the left foot and along the curve (Latin Cross).

Woman Move the left foot across, in front of the right foot and along the curve (Latin Cross).

6
COUNT – a

Man Move the left foot sideways a short step along the curve (part weight).

Woman Move the right foot sideways a short step along the curve (part weight).

7
COUNT – SLOW - 4

Man Move the right foot across, in front of the left foot and along the curve to end facing the wall (Latin Cross).

Woman Move the left foot across, in front of the right foot and along the curve to end facing the centre line (Latin Cross).

Footwork
1. BF, 2. T, 3. BF, 4. T, 5. BF, 6. T, 7. BF

Action Tip
For both the man and the woman, it is important that the body weight is held forward over the front foot during the Travelling Voltas, with only sufficient weight moving over the back foot to allow the front foot to progress. The lowering (ball–flat) on to the front foot and the rising (toe) on to the back foot should not be exaggerated and you should not feel more than a suggestion of up and down movement through the Samba Bounce Action. The body should remain upright and over your front foot. Small steps are not only more comfortable but much more stylish.

Having danced the Travelling Voltas to the Left and to the Right, you are now in a position to continue back into your routine, starting with the Samba Whisk to the Left.

What to Do with the Free Arm

In the Samba, there are many moves requiring a hold with only one hand. By following some general guidelines about what to do with your free arm and hand, you can give your dance a superb appearance and a balanced feel.

• In social dancing, the free arm should never be held above shoulder height. There is no good reason to do so and it makes the dancer look shorter.

• The free arm should never be dropped to the side as this severely inhibits good balance.

• In a travelling move, the position of the free hand and arm should mirror the height and curve of the joined hand and arm. The fingers of the free hand can be held either all together with the thumb extended or with the third and fourth fingers lowered slightly to give a more "Latin" look.

• During a turn on the spot, the arm should be drawn out of the way across the body and then allowed to return naturally to its position mirroring the joined hand and arm.

• As you develop a feel for the dance, you may wish to respond by moving the free arm in a natural, balanced and gentle way.

• Do not exaggerate the movements and match not only your own movements but also those of your partner.

• It is a good idea to keep the free arm relatively still in relation to your body. A still arm enhances the appearance of the leg and hip action. For more guidance, refer to the photographs accompanying the figures throughout the section.

Leg and Hip Action

Much is talked about the Samba hip action, yet an appropriate hip action is really only the by-product of a good leg, knee and ankle action. The Samba Bounce Action has already been described in detail, and "Action Tips" accompany the figures which use a different type of action.

Bota Fogos in Shadow Position

Bota Fogo (pronounced boat-a-foe-go) is a neighbourhood in the beautiful city of Rio de Janeiro and it was after this part of the city that your next figure was named. The Bota Fogos, like the Voltas, have become a classic figure essential to the character of the Samba. You can now insert the Bota Fogos in Shadow Position between the Side Samba Walk and the Travelling Volta to the Right. During the Bota Fogos, the man retains hold with the left hand while the woman dances her Bota Fogos across and in front of him. A slight Samba Bounce Action is used throughout. This figure progresses slightly with the flow.

1

COUNT – SLOW

Man Move forward on to the left foot, moving right behind the woman.

Woman Move forward on to the right foot, moving in front of the man.

2

COUNT – a

Man Starting to turn to the left, move sideways on to the right foot (part weight).

Woman Starting to turn to the right, move sideways on to the left foot (part weight).

3

COUNT – SLOW

Man Step in place with the left foot, completing a quarter (90°) turn to the left.

Woman Step in place with the right foot, completing a quarter (90°) turn to the right.

4

COUNT – SLOW

Man Move forward on to the right foot, moving left behind the woman.

Woman Move forward on to the left foot, moving in front of the man.

Footwork

1. BF, 2. inside edge of toe, 3. BF, 4. BF, 5. inside edge of toe, 6. BF, 7. BF, 8. inside edge of toe, 9. BF

Style Tip

If you have danced the Bota Fogos after the Side Samba Walk, you can now continue your routine by dancing the Travelling Volta to the Right.

5
COUNT – a

Man Starting to turn to the right, move sideways on to the left foot (part weight).

Woman Starting to turn to the left, move sideways on to the right foot (part weight).

6
COUNT – SLOW

Man Step in place with the right foot, completing a quarter (90°) turn to the right.

Woman Step in place with the left foot, completing a quarter (90°) turn to the left.

7–9
COUNT – SLOW a SLOW

Man & Woman Repeat Steps 1–3.

Possible Combinations

• Side Samba Walk, Bota Fogos, Travelling Volta to the Right.

• Travelling Volta to the Right, Bota Fogos (4–6, then 1–3), Travelling Volta to the Left.

Experimentation is half the fun of putting together your own routine, so have a go and enjoy it.

This figure can also be danced between the Travelling Volta to the Right and the Travelling Volta to the Left. In this case, start the Bota Fogos in Promenade Position at Step 4: dance Steps 4–6 and 1–3, then continue into the Travelling Volta to the Left.

Kick Change

Once you have danced the Travelling Volta to the Right, you can insert a fun figure into your Samba. The man is facing the centre line and is standing on the left foot which is crossed over the right foot. The woman is facing the wall and is standing on the right foot which is crossed over the left foot. The man retains a left hand to right hand hold with the woman.

1
COUNT – SLOW

Man Move forward on to the right foot slightly to the left.

Woman Move forward on to the left foot slightly to the right.

2
COUNT – SLOW

Man Swaying a little to the left, kick the left foot forward from the knee.

Woman Swaying a little to the right, kick the right foot forward from the knee.

3
COUNT – SLOW

Man Move back on to the left foot.

Woman Move back on to the right foot.

Footwork:
1. BF, 2. Kick, 3. BF, 4. B, 5. BF

Samba Side Steps

Many Samba moves really come alive when you relax and enjoy the rhythm. The Samba Side Steps can be inserted into your programme after the Travelling Volta to the Left and before continuing into the Samba Whisk to the Left. The figure moves sideways along the room with the flow.

The man starts by taking a double hand hold, with his palms facing the woman and hands at shoulder height. The man is standing on the right foot facing the wall and the woman on the left foot facing the centre line.

Style Tip

It adds a stylish flair to this figure for the couple to touch free hands on Step 2, the kick. If, however, you find this move a little tricky at first, you can try substituting a simple tap behind with the right foot for the man and the left foot for the woman for Steps 4–5. The tap will have a count of Slow.

COUNT – a

Man Place the right foot behind the left foot (part weight).

Woman Place the left foot behind the right foot (part weight).

5
COUNT – SLOW

Man Step in place with the left foot.

Woman Step in place with the right foot.

Review of Samba Routine

- Samba Whisk to the Right, Left and Right, ending in Promenade Position
- Left Foot Samba Walk, Right Foot Samba Walk, Left Foot Samba Walk
- Side Samba Walk
- Bota Fogos in Shadow Position
- Travelling Volta to the Right
- Kick Change, Kick Change
- Bota Fogos, Steps 4–6, 1–3 (optional)
- Travelling Volta to the Left
- Samba Whisk to the Left
- Start again

Many dancers like to repeat this move before continuing into the Travelling Volta to the Left.

1
COUNT – SLOW

Man Move sideways on to the left foot.

Woman Move sideways on to the right foot.

2
COUNT – SLOW

Man Close the right foot to the left foot.

Woman Close the left foot to the right foot.

3
COUNT – QUICK

Man Move sideways on to the left foot.

Woman Move sideways on to the right foot.

Style Tip

The Samba Side Steps use a "Merengue" (pronounced may-ren-gay) action. This dance is typified by delaying the transfer of weight on to the foot you are moving until the other foot moves.

1 Place the foot in position with a little pressure on to the floor but do not transfer your weight just yet.

2 Transfer your weight on to the foot just moved and straighten the knee. Make the next step but without putting any weight on to the foot and holding the heel clear of the floor. Straighten the knee of the standing leg, allowing the other knee to move a little across the standing knee. Use this action throughout the Samba Side Steps except Step 10.

4
COUNT – QUICK

Man Close the right foot to the left foot.

Woman Close the left foot to the right foot.

5
COUNT – SLOW

Man & Woman Repeat Step 1 of Samba Side Step.

6–9
COUNT – SLOW, SLOW, QUICK, QUICK

Repeat Steps 2–5.

10
COUNT – SLOW

Repeat Step 2.

The Samba Strut

The Samba Strut is a Latin-American Sequence Dance, performed to faster Samba music and synchronized with the musical phrase. The couples are arranged in a circle around the room. The men are on the inside of the circle facing outwards, and the women are on the outside facing the centre. The dancers start in a double hand hold.

1
Man Move the left foot to the side.

Woman Move the right foot to the side.

◀2
Man Close the right foot to the left foot.

Woman Close the left foot to the right foot.

3
Man Move the left foot to the side.

Woman Move the right foot to the side.

4▲
Man Touch the right foot to the side without weight.

Woman Touch the left foot to the side without weight.

5
Man Move the right foot to the side.

Woman Move the left foot to the side.

7
Man Move the right foot to the side.

Woman Move the left foot to the side.

6
Man Close the left foot to the right foot.

Woman Close right foot to left foot.

8
Man Touch the left foot to the side without weight.

Woman Touch the right foot to the side without weight.

9–16▲
Man Repeat Steps 1–8, releasing the right-hand hold, raising the left arm under which the woman will turn and taking up a Promenade hold on Step 16.

◀9
Woman Release the left-hand hold. Place the right foot forward, turning right under the man's raised arm.

10▲
Woman Move the left foot to the side, with your back to the man.

11
Woman Move the right foot to the side, facing the man.

12▲
Woman Touch the left foot to the side without weight.

13
Woman Move the left foot forward, turning left under the man's raised arm.

14
Woman Move the right foot to the side, with your back to the man.

15
Woman Move the left foot to the side, facing the man.

16
Woman Touch the right foot to side, without weight, ending in Promenade Position.

17–28
Man and Woman The couple, now in Promenade position, dance a Left Foot Samba Walk and a Right Foot Samba Walk, then repeat them. These are described fully earlier in the Samba section.

29–32
Man Release hold. Repeat Steps 1–4 towards the centre. Clap on Step 32.

Woman Release hold. Repeat Steps 1–4 towards the wall. Clap on Step 32.

33–36
Man Repeat Steps 5–8, gradually turning to face outwards and resume starting hold.

Woman Repeat Steps 5–8, gradually turning to face inwards, and resume starting hold.

The MC might decide to make the dance progressive. This means that either the man or the woman, whichever is customary at the particular dance club, will move forward to the next partner over steps 33–36.

Jive *from Lindy Hop to Rock 'n' Roll*

Dance styles have always followed musical trends and none more so than the dance which was to become Rock 'n' Roll. While we tend to think of the Rock 'n' Roll phenomenon as beginning in the 1950s, the dance actually started emerging more than two decades earlier in the USA. During the early 1920s, there had been a veritable zoo of animal dances, the best known of which was probably the Turkey Trot. These were in addition to other dance crazes, such as the Charleston and Black Bottom, whose wild moves got wilder as the music got faster. Other dances and styles developed from these and the Texas Tommy or Breakaway, in which the couple moved apart and came back together, emerged during the 1920s.

The Lindy Hop and Jitterbug

By the end of the decade, this style was extremely popular.

In 1927, when Charles Lindbergh piloted the Spirit of St Louis solo across the Atlantic, the newspaper headlines declaring this event were adopted as the new name for the dance, the Lindy Hop. As the dance continued to develop into the 1930s, it found a home in the Harlem Savoy Ballroom, where it grew up with the great Swing bands of the era. The line-up of orchestras who played at the Harlem Savoy sounds like a Who's Who of Swing, Benny Goodman, Cab Calloway, Tommy Dorsey, Louis Armstrong, Count Basie and Duke Ellington all performed at the Savoy. The bands inspired the dancers and the dancers inspired the bands in an upward-reaching spiral towards new heights of dance and musical expression.

When Benny Goodman gave a concert at the Paramount Theatre, New York, in 1937, teenagers went wild and poured into the aisles to "jitterbug", as the newspapers called the dance. The craze swept across America. Variations in technique led to styles such as Boogie-woogie and Swing Boogie, with "Jive" gradually emerging as the generic term that covered Lindy Hop, Jitterbug and Boogie-woogie dances. Whichever term was used in the 1940s, the music was Swing.

Dance Styles – Lindy Hop to Rock 'n' Roll

After the Second World War, bands got smaller and the music changed. By the 1950s, the music was no longer as smooth and polished as Swing but it had huge popular appeal; this music was Rock 'n' Roll. With the change in music came a change in the dancers' interpretation of the music. The heavier beat engendered a more two-dimensional jive with a "choppier" feel. By the end of the 1950s, jive had already reached the ballrooms and dance schools but in a different style.

The basis of all the dances from the Lindy Hop, through Boogie-woogie to Rock 'n' Roll is virtually the same: a six-beat musical rhythm (though the Lindy Hop also used an eight-beat rhythm). In the basic dance, the dancers take two steps which rock or swing sideways, then a step backwards and a replace step. The step backwards and replace movement remained fairly standard, as it gave the dances their rhythmic point of reference. However, the sideways rock or swing steps underwent many changes of style.

In Boogie-woogie, a tap is often added to make the sequence: tap, step, tap, step, step back, replace. The steps are danced well down into the knees.

In Rock 'n' Roll competitions, the Boogie taps became flicks in the sequence: flick, step, flick, step, step back, replace. This style has become quite extreme in dance competitions, with routines of dazzling acrobatic moves interspersed with the more basic dance moves. While it is very impressive, this performance style owes more to acrobatic prowess than to the notion of a man and woman coming together to dance. Most dancers prefer to dance to good music for their own enjoyment, which is the focus of this section, leaving the performance hybrid of Rock 'n' Roll to others.

The figures or moves introduced in this book are described without flicks or taps, with a basic style reminiscent of Lindy Hop. When you have practised and are confident with the basic steps, you can add the Rock 'n' Roll flicks or the Boogie taps if you prefer. Rock 'n' Roll is danced more upright because of the flicking action, while the Boogie style calls for very flexed knees.

Above: The Lindy Hop originated in the late 1920s after Charles Lindburgh's transatlantic flight. It developed and gained in popularity throughout the 1930s and 1940s.

Right: The spirit of fifties Rock 'n' Roll is as popular as ever in specialist clubs and classes.

Music Suggestions

As you learn the basic moves and begin to concentrate on perfecting your style, you will want to dance to the appropriate music. For Boogie-woogie fans, it would be hard to find better than "The Calloway Boogie" recorded in New York in 1940 by Cab Calloway and still available on the Giants of Jazz label or "Hamp's Boogie-Woogie" by Lionel Hampton & His Septet" available on the Living Traditions label. Louis Jordan's classic "Choo Choo Ch'Boogie" is on the Giants of Jazz label. Other artists to look out for are Count Basie, Memphis Slim, Joe Turner, Pete Johnson, Albert Ammons, Milt Buckner, Jay McShann and Sammy Price.

For Lindy Hoppers, swing is the thing and among many greats are "Posin'" by Jimmie Lunceford and Duke Ellington's "Let's Get Together". Glenn Miller's fabulous "In the Mood" and "Tippin' In" by Erskine Hawkins are steady ones especially good for practice. These are all available on the Living Traditions label. Look for music by these artists plus Cab Calloway, Benny Goodman, Lionel Hampton, Count Basie and Artie Shaw on the Living Traditions and Giants of Jazz labels.

Rock 'n' Rollers will get moving to music of the 1950s. "Cincinatti Fireball" by Johnny Burnette (Liberty Records), is a good number and a good one to start with. "See You Later Alligator" and "Shake, Rattle and Roll" by Bill Haley and His Comets (MCA) are two Rock 'n' Roll classics with steady tempos that are good for practice. When you have a little more confidence, "Tutti Frutti" by Little Richard (Specialty Records) starts with a medium tempo but picks up the pace. Most music of the 1950s with a steady 4/4 beat and a tempo ranging from 36-48 bars per minute will be suitable.

Getting Started

Initially, the most important thing is to get to grips with the rhythm. This is vital because, even when you know the moves, you will have to synchronize with each other to make the steps work and your cue is the rhythm. First, listen to some music, whether swing or Rock 'n' Roll is your preference. Swing and Rock 'n' Roll music has four beats to each bar of music. To start with, listen to the drum or rhythm line rather than to the melody. The drum provides the beat and you will notice that the drummer emphasizes beats 1 and 3 in each bar. You do not need to understand musical bars, just to be able to hear the all-important beat. A "quick" count equals one beat of music, while a "slow" count equals two beats. In a few figures, such as the Arm Breaker, two steps are danced to one beat of music. These are indicated by an "&" count, and are danced "quick, and" in the space of one beat.

The man and woman's roles are quite clearly defined. The man's job is generally to stay put, while the woman moves more around the floor. The roles of each can be summed up as follows:

The Man's Role:

• To keep the couple synchronized with the music and with each other. The woman must synchronize with the man, even if he is off-time with the music. This role is particularly important as an aid to the woman when she has completed a spin or turn and needs a point of reference to continue the dance in time with the music.

• To decide which figures to dance and in which order, leading the woman to dance them. Your main responsibility is to make your own moves clear and decisive to avoid confusing your partner. The lead should be clear and firm rather than strong and aggressive. The idea is to communicate the move to the woman rather than force her to dance it.

• To provide a point of orientation for the woman. While you stay mainly in place and the woman dances towards, around and away from you, it is easy for her to become disorientated. On completion of each move, she will be looking to orientate herself on your position before starting the next move. The man's steps are generally less difficult than the woman's, allowing you to "manage" the dance.

The Woman's Role:

• To be aware of the man's intentions as communicated by his lead and not to anticipate or guess moves. If you anticipate a move by committing your body weight in a certain direction too early, the man will have to revise his intentions, although he is in the worst position to do so. The resulting moves can be very awkward and clumsy.

• To check constantly that your rhythm is synchronized with that of the man and that you are orientating yourself in relation to him, particularly as a move ends. Check your rhythm on each "back, replace" step. If you are not synchronized with the man, don't try to slow down or speed up your next move to compensate. Just stop briefly and start again.

Couples should keep themselves from getting carried away by the music at the cost of getting the steps and rhythm wrong. More concentration is required in the learning stage but it will be amply rewarded when swinging from one figure to another becomes second nature to you. On the "back, replace" step, you should mostly be opposite your partner or sometimes side by side. Whichever it is, make sure that you are clearly in this position. If you are not and your partner decides to continue with a move requiring a strong lead, you may find your own body weight and impetus working against you, which can sometimes result in injuries such as a sprained wrist or jarred shoulder. Rock 'n' Roll and Jive are not in themselves dangerous dances but common sense should prevail.

The Basic Hold

There are a number of holds in Rock 'n' Roll dancing. The hold will depend on the preceding move, the current move and the following move. The transition from one type of hold to another should be quite natural. Tips on how to achieve this are given in the text as each change of hold is required.

To start the dance, face your partner with your feet slightly apart. The man stands with his weight on the right foot and the woman with her weight on the left foot. The man slips his right hand around the woman's waist, without drawing her too close to him. The woman rests her left hand comfortably on the man's upper right arm. Her right hand is held in the man's left hand, palm to palm and with her fingers between his fingers and thumb, her thumb curled around his thumb.

Use the basic hold to start off the dance, although you may use other holds as the dance progresses.

Basic Jive

In this introduction to jive, the descriptions of the figures or moves will use the basic steps without flicks or taps. Later, when you have practised, you can add the Rock 'n' Roll flicks or the Boogie taps as preferred. In this basic move, it is essential that the knees remain quite flexed. Steps 3 and 4 are known as the "back, replace" steps and will be referred to often.

2
COUNT – SLOW

Woman Rock to the side onto the left foot, taking a small step and leaving the right foot in place.

Man Rock to the side onto the right foot, taking a small step and leaving the left foot in place.

3
COUNT – QUICK

Man Rock onto the left foot, moving it under the body and placing the left toe behind the right heel. Lift the right foot just off the floor.

Woman Rock onto the right foot, moving it under the body and placing the right toe behind the left heel. Lift the left foot just off the floor.

4
COUNT – QUICK

Man Transfer your body weight forward onto the right foot.

Woman Transfer your body weight forward onto the left foot.

1
COUNT – SLOW

Man Rock to the side onto the left foot, taking a small step and leaving the right foot in place.

Woman Rock to the side onto the right foot, taking a small step and leaving the left foot in place.

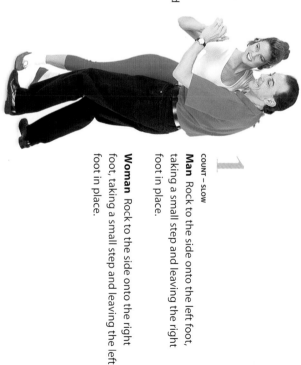

Style Tips

On Steps 1 and 2, you might like to sway a little in the direction of the step to improve the feeling. (For the man, this will also give a nice indication to the woman to move.) Do not use heels on any steps. Try to keep the feet under the body during the moves to avoid creating excessive movement and making the dance difficult. Small steps are far more controlled than large ones.

Styling your Jive

The basic rock-rock-step-replace action of the Jive can be modified to suit your preferred style of Jive.

For the Lindy Hop and Jitterbug, incline the upper body slightly forward, moving the centre of the body weight further back in the seat. Dance the step, replace, by sliding the feet more in contact with the floor. Dance the rock, rock, steps as described.

For Boogie-woogie, assume the same posture as for Lindy Hop but with more flexing of the knees. On the rock to the left, the right toe will tap towards the left foot and, on the rock to the right, the left toe will tap towards the right foot.

For competition Rock 'n' Roll, assume an upright stance. On the rock to the left, the right foot will be flicked forward with a loose ankle and, on the rock to the right, the left foot will be flicked forward with a loose ankel. For informal social dancing, the flick is optional.

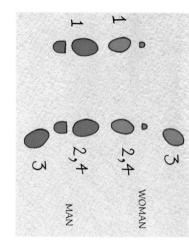

```
        1    2,4   3      WOMAN
        1    2,4   3      MAN
```

Repeat the Basic Jive as many times as you want as a useful way of practising dancing to the rhythm. The Basic Jive can also be turned gently in an anti-clockwise (counterclockwise) direction during Steps 1 and 2. At least four Basic Jives should be used to turn a full circle.

Throwaway

Experienced dancers will not use a set programme or routine, but before you get to that stage, it is useful to put together a practice programme. The Throwaway can be introduced immediately after the Basic Jive. The man dances the Basic Jive, turning on Steps 1 and 2 and leading the woman into an open position. Steps 3 and 4 remain the same.

1

COUNT – SLOW

Man Rock to the side onto the left foot, taking a small step and starting to turn to the left. Lead the woman to start to turn by bringing your left hand down to the left hip.

Woman Rock forward onto the right foot, towards the man's left side.

2

COUNT – SLOW

Man Rock to the side onto the right foot, taking a small step and completing a quarter turn (90°) to the left. Lead the woman into an open position by moving your left hand forward at waist height.

Woman Turn on the right foot to face the man and rock backwards onto the left foot away from the man into an open position.

3–4

COUNT – QUICK, QUICK

Man Dance Steps 3 and 4 of the Basic Jive (the back, replace steps).

Woman Dance Steps 3 and 4 of the Basic Jive.

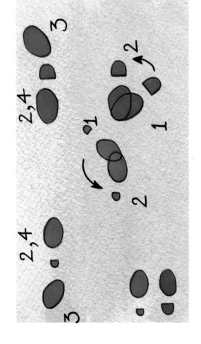

The Link

From this position, dance the Basic Jive by moving towards your partner on the rock steps and resuming hold – this is called The Link. Alternatively, try the Underarm Turn to the Right.

Underarm Turn to the Right

This very popular figure features a turn to the right. The couple have danced the by now familiar rhythm of the Basic Jive and have just finished the back, replace steps. They are standing in an open position with a left hand to right hand hold. The man is standing on the right foot and the woman on the left foot.

COUNT – SLOW

Man Rock to the side onto the left foot, lifting the left arm to lead the woman to turn underneath.

Woman Turn underneath the man's left arm. Rock forward onto the right foot, starting to turn to the right.

COUNT – SLOW

Man Rock to the side onto the right foot, making a quarter turn (90°) to the left and returning the left hand to waist height.

Woman Rock to the side and back onto the left foot, continuing to turn to the right underneath the man's arm.

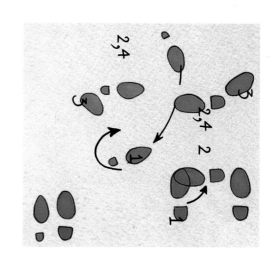

3–4

COUNT – QUICK, QUICK

Man Dance Steps 3 and 4 of the Basic Jive.

Woman Dance Steps 3 and 4 of the Basic Jive continuing the turn to end facing the man.

Comb

This figure has come to typify the Rock 'n' Roll style, despite the fact that it was already used 20 years before the Rock 'n' Roll era in the Lindy Hop. Teddy Boys were renowned for the care they took over their hair which involved frequent combing, hence the name of this classic figure. As usual, the couple have danced the back, replace steps. The man is now standing on the right foot and the woman on the left foot. The couple are in a right hand to right hand hold ready to dance the Comb.

Practice Programme

You can now continue with a Link and the Basic Jive. The programme can be danced in the sequence: Rock Basic (dance several times, including a rotation to the left, if desired), Throwaway, Underarm Turn to the Right, Link, Basic Jive.

1

COUNT – SLOW

Man Rock to the side onto the left foot towards the woman, lifting the right hands over your head as if combing your hair…

Woman Rock forward onto the right foot towards the man, allowing him to raise your right hand over his head…

Man …End with the right hand at your right shoulder.

Woman …It is comfortable to turn slightly to the left to a side-by-side position.

2

COUNT – SLOW

Man Rock to the side onto the right foot away from the woman, releasing the right hand and allowing the woman's right hand to slip down your arm to your left hand, where you resume hold.

Woman Rock backwards onto the left foot, sliding the right hand down the man's left arm to resume hand hold.

3–4

COUNTS – QUICK, QUICK

Man Dance the usual back, replace steps, resuming an open facing position.

Woman Dance the usual back, replace steps, resuming an open facing position. End standing on the left foot.

When practising, follow the Comb with a Link and resume your practice programme. If you want to start exploring other options, try following the Comb with the Underarm Turn to the Right.

Style Tip

While it is typical of 1950s-style Rock 'n' Roll for the man to lean back a little on Steps 1 and 2 of this move, the freer and more expressive style of Lindy Hop promoted much more personal interpretation, even allowing the man's upper body to incline much more forward during this move.

Basic Turns

It is practical to intersperse basic turns between figures. There are a variety of turns which can be danced from either the basic hold or the open position.

Change of Place Right to Left

To dance the Change of Place Right to Left, start in the basic hold. Dance a Rock Basic and finish with the man on the right foot and the woman on the left foot, ready to go into this turn.

1

COUNT – SLOW

Man Rock to the side onto the left foot, raising the left arm to lead the woman to dance under your arm to the right. It is sometimes helpful to use the right hand to confirm to the woman that she is about to dance under your arm.

Woman Rock forward onto the right foot, starting to turn to the right.

2

COUNT – SLOW

Man Rock to the side onto the right foot, making a quarter turn (90°) to the left. End by lowering the left arm to waist height.

Woman Turning to the right under the man's arm, rock backwards onto the left foot to face the man.

Dance the back, replace steps, then continue with the Underarm Turn to the Right or dance the next figure.

Change of Place Left to Right

This figure retraces the path of the Change of Place Right to Left.

1

COUNT – SLOW

Man Rock to the side onto the left foot, raising the left arm to lead the woman across to your right.

Woman Rock forward onto the right foot, moving towards your left of the man.

2

COUNT – SLOW

Man Rock to the side onto the right foot, making a quarter turn to the right. End by lowering the left arm to a basic hold.

Woman Standing on the right foot, turn left under the man's arm to face him and rock to the side onto the left foot.

3–4

COUNT – QUICK, QUICK

Man Dance the back, replace steps, facing the woman in a basic hold.

Woman Dance the back, replace steps, facing the man in a basic hold.

Continue with a Link.

Change of Hands behind the Back

This stylish figure is not at all difficult if the guidelines are followed. Start as usual when you have just danced the standard back, replace steps and are in an open position.

1

COUNT – SLOW

Man Rock forward onto the left foot and place the woman's right hand into your right hand.

Woman Rock forward onto the right foot, aiming slightly towards the left of the man.

2

COUNT – SLOW

Man Rock to the side onto the right foot, making a quarter turn to the left. Placing both hands behind your back, transfer the woman's right hand into your left hand. End with your back to the woman.

Woman Rock to the side onto the left foot, making a quarter turn to the right. End facing the man's back.

Changing Hands

It is the man's job to change hands when required by the next figure. The Change of Place Right to Left and Left to Right can both be concluded with either of the man's hands. If a turn under the arm has taken place, you should complete the change of hands at the end of the downward arm movement. Never let go of the woman's hand until you have placed it into your other hand.

3–4

COUNT – QUICK, QUICK

Man Dance the back, replace steps, making a quarter turn to the left to end facing the woman in an open position.

Woman Dance the back, replace steps, making a quarter turn to the right to end facing the man in an open position.

Bringing Your Jive Alive

Now that you are familiar with some of the classic Jive and Rock 'n' Roll figures, you can concentrate on perfecting that style.

Suggested Programme

1 Basic Jive

2 Throwaway

3 Underarm Turn to the Right, ending in a right hand to right hand hold

4 Comb

5 Change of Hands behind the Back

6 Change of Place Left to Right

7 Link

- Generally keep the steps small. Remember that the objective is not to move around the floor.

- The man should try to avoid concentrating on what his partner is doing and should never follow her. Don't look at each other's feet. In many dances, when the woman steps backwards, the man steps forward. This is not the case in Jive, so it is far better to concentrate on your own steps and moves.

- Don't under any circumstances fudge the moves. Be accurate and clear.

- Maintain a steady rhythm and stick to it. The man should not, for example, hesitate to allow extra time for the woman to complete a turn.

- Don't be tempted to take short cuts. Women in particular must avoid turning too early. Learn the moves properly and you will quickly get them working for you instead of you working at them.

- Keep the movements compact. Avoid getting too far away from your partner, as this will make the dance uncomfortable and you may lose contact with each other.

Leading

You will already have picked up many useful and practical tips on leading through dancing the figures you have learned so far. Here are some further points to help you.

- In the open position, the man's hand should be palm uppermost with the woman's fingers held lightly between the man's palm and thumb.

- The man should always raise his arm high enough for the woman to turn beneath it comfortably, without having to duck.

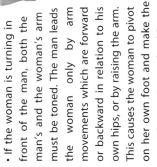

- If the woman is turning in front of the man, both the man's and the woman's arm must be toned. The man leads the woman only by arm movements which are forward or backward in relation to his own hips, or by raising the arm. This causes the woman to pivot on her own foot and make the turn. The man's arm should never be extended with a view to pulling or pushing the woman.

- When the man leads the woman to turn or spin under his arm to the right using his right hand, the palm of the hand should first be rolled through 270° in the woman's hand until the two hands are again palm to palm. The back of the man's right hand will now be facing his body. If the right arm is now extended to a point above the woman's head and then lowered behind her head, she will automatically be led to turn. The man should decide how quickly to lower his arm in order to be in time with the rhythm of the music. The speed of lowering the arm has a direct effect on the speed of the woman's turn or spin.

Chicken Walks and Jump

Now it's time to have more fun with another figure that has withstood the test of time. The Chicken Walks originated with the Lindy Hop and were used throughout the Jitterbug years before becoming a favourite with Rock 'n' Rollers. Lindy Hoppers favour a style where the man is inclined forward from the waist during the actual Lindy Chicken Walks in contrast to the more upright Rock 'n' Roll stance. The figure starts with an Overturned Throwaway.

Overturned Throwaway

1-2
COUNT – SLOW, SLOW
Man Dance Steps 1 and 2 of the standard Throwaway. At the end of Step 2, firmly bring the left arm back a little to turn the woman to face you.

1
COUNT – SLOW
Woman Rock forward onto the right foot, towards the man's left side.

2
COUNT – SLOW
Woman Standing on the right foot, turn to face away from the man and rock forward onto the left foot into an open position. Do not fully extend your arm or take too big a step. Standing on the left foot, swivel to the right to face the man with knees together, the left knee flexed and the right knee extended straight forward with the right foot turned out a little.

> You should now feel tension through the arms and as if you and your partner are pulling away from each other slightly.

Chicken Walks

1
COUNT – SLOW
Man Close the left foot to the right foot.

Woman Transfer your body weight forward onto the right foot. With knees together, point the left foot straight forward and turn it out slightly.

2
COUNT – SLOW
Man Take a small step backwards onto the right foot.

Woman Transfer your body weight forward onto the left foot. With knees together, point the right foot forward and turn it out slightly.

Style Tip
The action of the Chicken Walks is very important in order to get the classic look and feel. While taking a step backwards with the right foot, the right toe is placed against the left heel. The heel is only lowered when you transfer your body weight to allow the left foot to move backwards on the next step. The same action is used when taking a step backwards onto the left foot.

4

COUNT – QUICK

Man Take a small step backwards onto the right foot.

5–6

COUNT – QUICK, QUICK

Man Repeat Steps 3 and 4.

Continue with a Jive Basic or Throwaway or another Overturned Throwaway leading into the Chicken Walks. The first rock to follow the Jump will be a transfer of your body weight as the foot is already in position.

3

COUNT – QUICK

Man Take a small step backwards onto the left foot.

3–6

COUNT – QUICK, QUICK, QUICK, QUICK

Woman Repeat Steps 1 and 2 twice.

Jump

1

COUNT – QUICK

Man and Woman Jump forward towards your partner, landing on both feet, with feet apart and knees very flexed.

2

COUNT – QUICK

Man and Woman Pause.

Arm Breaker

This is the move that everyone wants to be able to do. In Jive, it is called the Apache Spin and, in the Lindy Hop, it is the Texas Tommy. In Rock 'n' Roll, the name of this advanced figure gives warning of the need to practise it slowly at first, while you gradually get used to the timing and feel of the move. When danced at full speed, the Arm Breaker is quite spectacular. Start in an open position with the woman's right hand in the man's left. Having just danced the standard back, replace steps, the man is standing on the right foot and the woman on the left foot. During the whole figure, you should make at least a half turn to the right.

1

COUNT – SLOW

Man Rock forward onto the left foot, starting to turn to the right and leading the woman towards your right side. Then, still holding the woman's right hand in your left, place both hands behind her back at waist level.

Woman Rock forward onto the right foot, towards the man's right side.

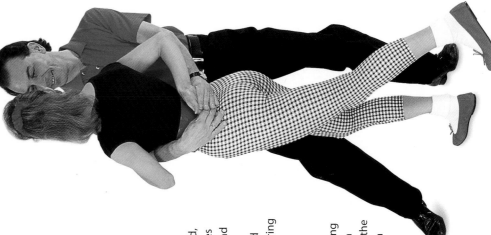

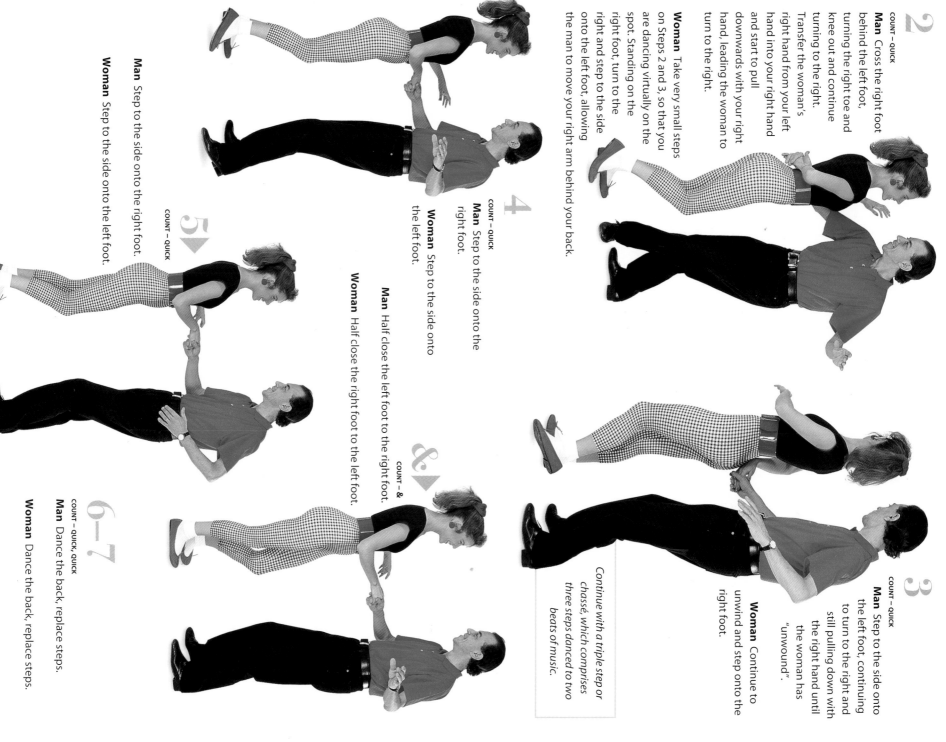

COUNT – QUICK

2

Man Cross the right foot behind the left foot, turning the right toe and knee out and continue turning to the right. Transfer the woman's right hand from your left hand into your right hand and start to pull downwards with your right hand, leading the woman to turn to the right.

Woman Take very small steps on Steps 2 and 3, so that you are dancing virtually on the spot. Standing on the right foot, turn to the right and step to the side onto the left foot, allowing the man to move your right arm behind your back.

COUNT – QUICK

3

Man Step to the side onto the left foot, continuing to turn to the right and still pulling down with the right hand until the woman has "unwound".

Woman Continue to unwind and step onto the right foot.

Continue with a triple step or chassé, which comprises three steps danced to two beats of music.

COUNT – QUICK

4

Man Step to the side to the right foot.

Woman Step to the side onto the left foot.

Man Step to the side onto the left foot.

Woman Step to the side onto the left foot.

COUNT – &

&

Man Half close the left foot to the right foot.

Woman Half close the right foot to the left foot.

COUNT – QUICK

5

Man Step to the side onto the right foot.

Woman Step to the side onto the left foot.

COUNT – QUICK, QUICK

6–7

Man Dance the back, replace steps.

Woman Dance the back, replace steps.

Arm Breaker with Triple Spin

An even flashier, but more advanced finish is for the woman to dance a Triple Spin while the man dances the Triple Step or Chassé. Dance the figure as described previously, with the following modifications:

1–3

COUNT – SLOW, QUICK, QUICK

Dance up to Step 3 of the Arm Breaker. At the end of this step, the man will raise the right arm above the woman's head.

4

COUNT – QUICK

Man Lower the right arm, leading the woman to spin a half (180°) turn.

Woman Spin a half turn (180°) to end facing the man.

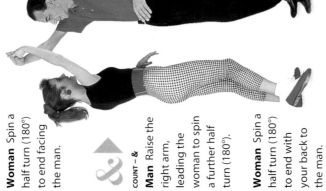

&

COUNT – &

Man Raise the right arm, leading the woman to spin a further half turn (180°).

Woman Spin a half turn (180°) to end with your back to the man.

5

COUNT – QUICK

Man Lower the right arm, leading the woman to spin a final half turn (180°).

Woman Spin a final half turn (180°) to end facing the man and relax.

6–7

COUNT – QUICK, QUICK

Man Dance the back, replace steps.

Woman Dance the back, replace steps.

The man must lead these moves correctly and not wait for the woman to complete the spins on her own. By raising and lowering his arm on the appropriate counts, he will assist the woman to turn in time. The woman should allow the man to lead her to make three spins. Keep the feet apart and legs braced throughout.

Jig Walks

This classy figure has its origins in the wild moves of the Lindy Hop. It is equally at home in Boogie-woogie and Rock 'n' Roll and can look quite stunning. However, most dancers learn very quickly how to dance it properly and avoid damage during the simultaneous kicking between their partner's legs. The figure can be preceded by something as simple as the Basic Jive, ending on a close facing position.

1

COUNT – QUICK

Man Holding the woman quite close to you, lift the left knee and kick the left foot out and downwards, keeping the foot loose. Your left leg will be above the woman's right leg during the kick.

Woman The man's adoption of a close hold indicates that you will be dancing the Jig Walks. Lift the right knee and kick the right foot out and downwards, keeping the foot loose. Your right leg will be below the man's left leg during the kick.

COUNT – QUICK

2

Man Step onto the left foot.

Woman Step onto the right foot.

COUNT – QUICK

3

Man Lift the right knee and kick the right foot out and downward, keeping the foot loose.

Woman Lift the left knee and kick the left foot out and downward, keeping the foot loose.

COUNT – QUICK

4

Man Step onto the right foot. Retention of the close hold will communicate to the woman that you will continue with another four counts of the Jig Walks. Otherwise, continue clearly into the back, replace steps.

Woman Step onto the right foot,

Once you have practised this figure, you can enjoy dancing the multiple Jig Walks, rotating them on the spot in a clockwise direction. To continue into your basic programme after the back, replace steps, simply dance a Basic Jive.

JIVE: jig walks

169

International Standard Partner Dances

Together with the International Latin-American dances, the International Standard Partner Dances form the basis of the dance programme at conventional dance schools. Courses and classes generally include both styles and both styles are usually featured at party nights. Many schools will teach the Social Foxtrot, Waltz and Quickstep first in order to develop basic skills. With that experience, the Modern Tango and Slow Foxtrot may then be approached from a position of strength.

For those with a busy or erratic lifestyle, private lessons offer a cost-effective and convenient way of tailoring tuition to the dancer's individual requirements. For further details, call your local dance school.

In most countries, keen dancers have the opportunity to mark their progress through a system of periodic and graded amateur tests. These are conducted by an examiner appointed by the dance teachers' organisation to which the teacher is affiliated. The tests are never compulsory but a successful result gives satisfaction and builds confidence.

The media often misrepresent Standard Dancing as very formal and perhaps even a little stuffy. In reality, the dances themselves are neither. Dances are merely patterns of movements performed to a musical rhythm. It is the dancers and the occasion which define how formal or informal the dancing event. In my experience, the vast majority of dancers are fun people who love life and just want a great time getting out there onto the dance floor to enjoy themselves. If not already, you too will be one of them.

On the Floor

The dance floor, whether crowded or not, is a very valuable asset and should be treated, like its users, with the utmost respect.

Always walk around the edge of the floor and never across it, especially while people are dancing. The sudden emergence of a bystander trying to dodge dancers can cause chaos on the floor and is an unnecessary and discourteous hazard to the dancers.

When taking to the floor, it is important to avoid causing problems to the dancers who are already there. Since men normally start a dance facing the outside of the room, it may seem quite natural for them to walk onto the floor backwards while their attention is focused on their partner. As this will cause a hindrance to the dancers, it is far better to approach the floor and assess the flow of floor traffic before taking up your starting position with due consideration to the other dancers.

When leaving the floor, especially during the course of a dance, the same consideration should be shown. If you are finishing during the dance, you should dance to the edge of the floor, leave the floor at that point and walk back around the perimeter to return to your seat.

Take up the starting position only when you have assessed the situation on the dance floor. Do not dance onto the floor as this may hinder other dancers.

The Dance Floor

Before you begin the steps, here are some basic ways of orientating yourself in the room.

- The flow of the floor traffic (the dancers) will be in an anticlockwise (counterclockwise) direction around the room.
- The orientation of the dancers will be described in relation to the nearest wall, the centre line of the floor and in terms of zigs and zags.

Going with the flow

Assuming that the room is rectangular, stand adjacent to any wall, making sure the wall is on the man's right and the woman's left. The man will now be in a position to move forward with the flow of floor traffic and the woman to move backwards. In some steps, the man will face against the flow of traffic with the wall on his left-hand side. The overall movement of the figure being danced will, however, continue to go with the flow.

The centre line

Still in the same position, the centre line of the room will be on the man's left and the woman's right.

Zigs and zags

A diagonal line, which we will call a "zig", extends from the centre line to the wall parallel to it at an angle of approximately 45°. Another diagonal line, a "zag", extends from the wall to the centre line at an angle of approximately 45°. In the Basic Waltz and Quickstep, the man moves forward along the zigs and backwards along the zags in order to "tack" along the room. Conversely, the woman moves backwards along the zigs and forward along the zags, opposite her partner, as they both travel with the flow.

same method. Remember that, as you dance around the room, you will encounter corners and will need to accommodate them.

Cornering

When you turn a corner, you will orientate yourself using the new wall and the centre line, which is always parallel to the wall you are using. The zigs and zags run along the diagonals between the new centre line and the new wall as before. The flow will, of course, flow around the corner.

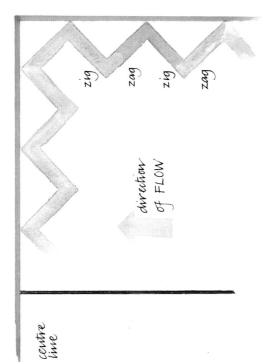

centre line

zig   zag   zig   zag

direction of FLOW

The diagram illustrates the main ways in which the dancers orientate themselves in the room. You can start to get used to this by practising at home.

Waltz Music

Waltz music is organized with three beats to each bar of music. The Basic Waltz is also organized into sections of three steps. Each step therefore corresponds to a single beat of music. Musically, the first beat in each bar is accentuated or emphasized and it is on this beat that you should start to dance. While the beat is giving a count of 1-2-3, you should be dancing the walk-side-close movements of the Basic Waltz.

The time signature of a waltz is 3/4 with a tempo currently recommended internationally as 30 bars per minute. This means that it takes only two seconds to dance each section of the Waltz. This is in fact a relatively easy pace which you can really enjoy.

The Hold

When taking up a hold for the Waltz, Quickstep and Slow Foxtrot, the man takes the woman's right hand in his left hand and draws her to him. This enables him to place her slightly to his right. When in the correct position, the buttons on the man's shirt should be opposite the woman's right shoulder.

To take up the hold, the man presents his left hand as if he is a policeman stopping traffic. The woman then places the hooked middle finger of her right hand between the thumb and forefinger of the man's left hand, palm to palm. Next, the woman places her forefinger and third finger on top of her middle finger and finally rests her little finger on top of the others, curling her thumb around the man's thumb. The joined hands should be held just below eye-level with the hand-hold and arms firm but not rigid. The man now places the fingertips of his left hand along the edge of the woman's right hand with the fingers pointing to the floor. In this way, the underside of both the man's left wrist and the woman's right wrist are facing the floor. When you start to dance, this will considerably enhance stability and make leading much easier.

The hold (front view).

The man cups the woman's left shoulder blade with his right hand, with the fingertips ideally placed against the woman's spine. The woman straightens the fingers of her left hand but allows the thumb to extend out in its normal position. She then places her left hand on the man's upper arm with a straight and flat wrist. It is unnecessary for her third and little fingers to be resting on the man's arm. Both the man and the woman should hold their elbows slightly forward of their backs and a little away from the body. The shoulders should be relaxed, never tensed or hunched.

The man and woman should both stand upright, lifting the diaphragm to produce a good posture. The man and woman

The hold (rear view).

The woman indicates tactical problems with a slight pressure of the left hand.

maintain lower diaphragm and upper stomach contact throughout much of the dance. They should hold their heads a little to the left and with the chin up. The weight of the head can have an adverse effect on balance if it is not held in the desired position. Do not look at your feet. The man's back and arms provide a "frame" in which the woman is held. A good frame is essential for good dancing and good leading.

The hold and starting position often feel too rigid to a first-time dancer for fluidity of movement, but with a little practice, a good but relaxed posture and hold can be developed. This is one of the main skills which characterize a partner who is easy to dance with. The frame created by the man's arms and reinforced by his back and diaphragm should be held still and firm, that is to say that the arms should never move independently of the body. Once this is achieved, the woman will be able to feel a clear lead.

Much of the process of leading is not something which the man does actively but is rather the result of clear and positive dancing. The best leading is the sort which leaves the woman no other option but to dance what the man intends without her really having to think about it. Once the woman has to work at following, the enjoyment is largely lost for her. The woman should accept the man's lead and not try to guess what he will do next and commit herself to a course of action which might be the wrong one.

The woman has a responsibility when she is moving forward and the man is moving back. Since she is the one who can see where the couple are moving, she must indicate to the man if they are about to dance into a problem. She can do this by squeezing the thumb and middle finger of her left hand and then allowing the man to lead his evasive manoeuvre.

This position shows the frame created by the man's arms. The arms, back and diaphragm all move with one another — no element moves independently. This provides the frame with which to lead the woman.

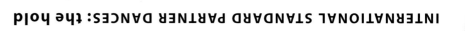

Legs and Feet

It may seem surprising to leave comment on these until last. However, we dance with the whole of our bodies and, once the body is working properly, the feet and legs will often largely take care of themselves. Knees are very important and you will feel more comfortable, relaxed and in control if you can keep your knees flexed at all times. Dancing, in a basic sense, is not so very different from walking and yet it is so often the case that someone who can walk perfectly well feels challenged when taking a normal walk forward, simply because they are "dancing" and not walking down the street.

Try not to get too far away from your partner or worry about stepping on their feet. As the woman is positioned slightly to the man's right, when he walks forward with the right foot his foot will go between the woman's feet. When he walks forward with the left foot he will be walking outside the woman. The same occurs when the woman is moving forward and the man is moving backwards. Using this helpful technique, there is very little chance of treading on a partner's foot unless you create a gap between you.

Above and right: When taking a step, move your foot into position and then remember to move your body weight directly onto that foot.

Taking a step

When taking a step, move your foot into position and then remember to move your body weight onto that foot.

Which foot to start with

Some teachers teach the Waltz or Quickstep starting with the left foot for the man. Logic suggests that when we are moving forward and want to initiate a turn to the right, we do this by curving the right foot forward. This is a good move to start with because the woman can feel the curve and instinctively knows that, because she is moving backwards, it is natural for her to start moving back with her left foot. If the man were to start with his left foot moving forward and dance no turn, the woman would not have a clear lead.

Left: Try not to get too far away from your partner or worry about stepping on his or her feet. As the woman is positioned slightly to the man's right, when he walks forward with the right foot his foot will go between the woman's feet.

Right: When the man walks forward with the left foot he will be walking outside the woman. The same occurs when the woman is moving forward and the man is moving backwards. Using this technique, there is little chance of treading on a partner's foot.

Floorcraft

Your positioning on the floor and how you progress around it may be likened to driving in a flow of traffic. The skill, experience and thinking ahead necessary to negotiate the other dancers are called floorcraft.

As you get used to dancing around the room it will become apparent that there is more to floorcraft than may at first be obvious. The ability to avoid problems and read the situation ahead of you are both attributes of a good dancer. This ability develops with practice but can be acquired more easily by following a few guidelines, the responsibility for which lies mainly with the man.

• It is extremely important to adhere to the given orientation in the room. If you allow yourself to wander from the prescribed path, it will be very difficult to get back to it.

• If you are following a couple around a corner, stay behind and on the wall side of them. By the time you reach their position, they will usually have moved on.

• Avoid dancing across a corner if a couple are already in the corner. You risk them running into you as they exit the corner.

• Women, even though trying to help, should not attempt to lead the man.

All the figures described in this book have been selected not only for their attractiveness as easily enjoyable figures but also for their usefulness as floorcraft figures. As your repertoire grows, so will your ability first to avoid problems and then to escape from any further difficulties.

Floorcraft skills basically entail manoeuvring around obstacles, rather like negotiating through traffic. As you become accustomed to moving around the dance floor, your style will become more relaxed and flowing.

Social Foxtrot

Basic Movement

For many, the ability just to get on to the dance floor and move around it comfortably, confidently and inconspicuously is a worthy aim in itself. This version of the Foxtrot provides an easily repeatable basic movement which first-time dancers can quickly enjoy dancing. Despite being designated a Foxtrot, this dance has been designed to be enjoyed to a wide and varied range of music: from Blues to Quickstep, from Tango to Rock 'n' Roll and even some current chart music. In fact, you can dance the Social Foxtrot to almost any tune with a 2/4 or 4/4 time signature, which means virtually any dance music except that in Waltz-time. The tempo, though, will vary according to the particular style of music.

Take up the Standard Ballroom hold but, for this dance, you can afford to make it a little more informal and relaxed. The Social Foxtrot is a compact dance, ideal for crowded floors, so keep all the steps small. Start on a zig. The man is standing on his right foot, feet together, and the woman corresponds, standing on her left foot.

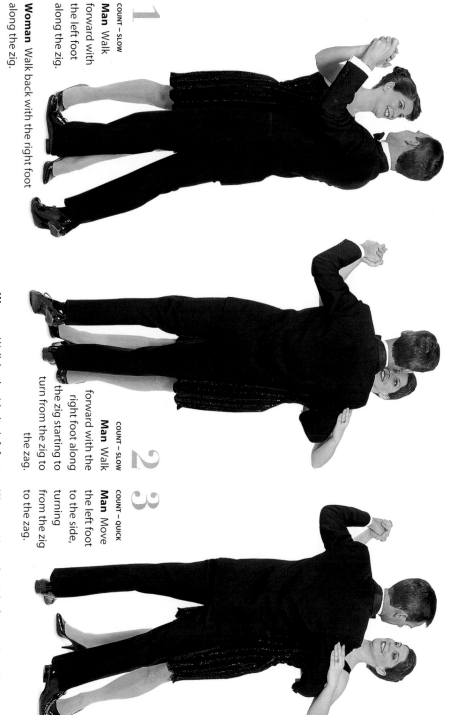

1

COUNT – SLOW
Man Walk forward with the left foot along the zig.

Woman Walk back with the right foot along the zig.

2

COUNT – SLOW
Man Walk forward with the right foot along the zig starting to turn from the zig to the zag.

Woman Walk back with the left foot along the zig starting to walk from the zig to the zag.

3

COUNT – QUICK
Man Move the left foot to the side, turning from the zig to the zag.

Woman Move the right foot to the side, a small step, turning from the zig to the zag.

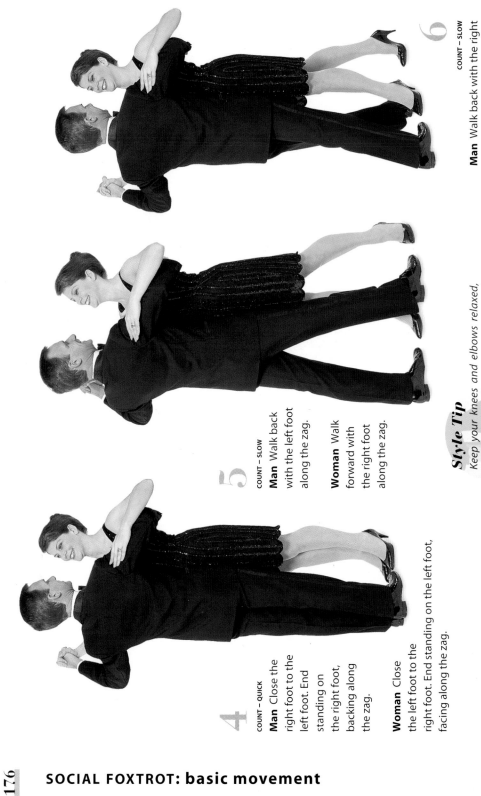

4
COUNT – QUICK

Man Close the right foot to the left foot. End standing on the right foot, backing along the zag.

Woman Close the left foot to the right foot. End standing on the left foot, facing along the zag.

5
COUNT – SLOW

Man Walk back with the left foot along the zag.

Woman Walk forward with the right foot along the zag.

6
COUNT – SLOW

Man Walk back with the right foot along the zag.

Woman Walk forward with the left foot along the zag.

Style Tip
Keep your knees and elbows relaxed, take small and comfortable steps throughout, and enjoy feeling and expressing the rhythm.

7
COUNT – QUICK

Man Move the left foot to the side, small step, turning from the zag to the zig.

Woman Move the right foot to the side, turning from the zag to the zig.

8
COUNT – QUICK

Man Close the right foot to the left foot. End standing on the zig.

Woman Close the left foot to the right foot. End standing on the zig.

The Basic Movement can now be repeated continuously. Curve the Basic Movement comfortably to ease you around corners. This is best done by the man on Step 6, by curving his right foot slightly inwards as he takes this foot back.

SOCIAL FOXTROT: basic movement

Reverse Pivot Turn

Having mastered the Basic Movement, you will soon want to include a new but easy move. The Reverse Pivot Turn is a simple but effective move which will help you to avoid bumping into other dancers ahead of you and one which you will also find helpful for manoeuvring around corners. "Reverse" simply means a turn to the left and does not imply any special type of backward move. Start as for the Basic Movement.

1
COUNT – SLOW

Man Walk forward with the left foot, but check the movement by relaxing the knee. Leave the right foot behind you.

Woman Walk back with the right foot.

2
COUNT – SLOW

Man Rock back smoothly onto your right foot. Keep your right hand firmly in place, to ensure that the woman remains with you.

Woman Rock forward smoothly onto your left foot.

3
COUNT – QUICK

Man Move the left foot to the side, small step, making about a quarter turn (90°) anticlockwise (counterclockwise).

Woman Move the right foot to the side, turning with the man.

4
COUNT – QUICK

Man Close the right foot to the left foot. End standing on the right foot.

Woman Close the left foot to the right foot. End standing on the left foot.

When using the Reverse Pivot Turn at a corner, you only need to dance the move once to end in your starting position on the new wall. However, when using the Reverse Pivot Turn to avoid other couples, you may repeat the move several times. For example, dancing the Reverse Pivot Turn four times will leave you in exactly the same place as when you started the manoeuvre, allowing other floor traffic ahead of you to clear.

Natural Pivot Turn

In this sense, "natural" just means a turn which goes to the right, that is, clockwise. With a little practice, this move can be added quickly to your repertoire. It is especially useful at corners and for combining with the Reverse Pivot Turn to give the feeling of fluent movement around the floor. Start as before.

1
COUNT – SLOW

Man Walk forward with the left foot along the zig.

Woman Walk back with the right foot.

In the orientation given below, you will be dancing the Natural Pivot Turn around a corner.

Combination
Try dancing the Natural Pivot Turn but along the side of the room. You will then end on a zig, ready to move towards the centre line of the room. Next, dance three Reverse Pivot Turns to leave you back in your starting position.

2
COUNT – SLOW

Man Walk forward with the right foot, starting to turn right.

Woman Walk back with the left foot, starting to turn right.

Notes
Dancers often feel that Steps 5–6 are a little like a rocking movement which helps the turn.

3
COUNT – QUICK

Man Move the left foot to the side, turning right to end backing around the room.

Woman Move the right foot to the side, small step, turning right to end facing into the room.

4
COUNT – QUICK

Man Close the right foot to the left foot. End standing on the right foot, backing around the room.

Woman Close the left foot to the right foot. End standing on the left foot, facing into the room.

5
COUNT – SLOW

Man Walk back onto the left foot, turning in the toes to continue turning to the right.

Woman Walk forward onto the right foot, turning to the right.

6
COUNT – SLOW

Man Walk forward onto the right foot, continuing to turn to the right to move onto the zig of the new wall.

Woman Walk back onto the left foot, continuing to turn to the right to move onto the zig of the new wall.

7
COUNT – QUICK

Man Move the left foot to the side, continuing to turn right to end on the zag.

Woman Move the right foot to the side, small step, continuing to turn right to end on the zag.

8
COUNT – QUICK

Man Close the right foot to the left foot. End standing on the right foot on the zag.

Woman Close the left foot to the right foot. End standing on the left foot on the zag.

Continue with steps 5–8 of the Basic Movement.

Side-Step Move

Now try a great figure for temporarily slowing down your progress along the room. It is very flexible and can be danced after either Steps 1–2 or Steps 7–8 of the Basic Movement, turning them less so that the man is facing squarely to the wall. The man is standing on his right foot and the woman is standing on her left foot.

1

COUNT – QUICK

Man Left foot to the side.

Woman Right foot to the side.

2

COUNT – QUICK

Man Tap or touch the right foot next to the left foot.

Woman Tap or touch the left foot next to the right foot.

3

COUNT – QUICK

Man Move the right foot to the side.

Woman Move the left foot to the side.

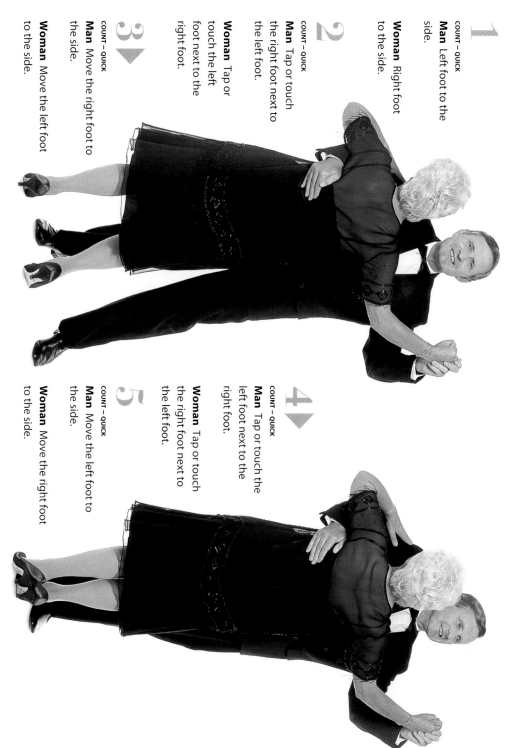

4

COUNT – QUICK

Man Tap or touch the left foot next to the right foot.

Woman Tap or touch the right foot next to the left foot.

5

COUNT – QUICK

Man Move the left foot to the side.

Woman Move the right foot to the side.

6

COUNT – QUICK

Man Close the right foot to the left foot. End standing on the right foot.

Woman Close the left foot to the right foot. End standing on the left foot.

7

COUNT – QUICK

Man Move the left foot to the side.

Woman Move the right foot to the side.

8

COUNT – QUICK

Man Tap or touch the right foot next to the left foot.

Woman Tap or touch the left foot next to the right foot.

9

COUNT – QUICK

Man Move the right foot to the side.

Woman Move the left foot to side.

10

COUNT – QUICK

Man Tap or touch the left foot next to the right foot.

Woman Tap or touch the right foot next to the left foot.

The man continues with the Basic Movement, but curving the first step onto the zig to lead the woman into the next move and return to the normal alignment.

Social Dancing: Do's and Don'ts

Courtesy may seem at first to be an old-fashioned idea to be discussing in a book about modern dancing. Yet politeness and consideration for others is timeless and always appreciated. Here are a few broad guidelines which, if followed, will contribute much to enjoying your dance time and to others enjoying theirs.

While it is quite normal in some dance clubs to dance with different partners, it is only fair to dance at least the first and last dance with the partner with whom you arrived.

Before asking the woman to dance, it is wise for the man to watch her dancing first with someone else and take note of what she is doing so he won't cause embarrassment by launching into a series of death-defying moves if this is her first dance event. The same applies to a partner whom you have never seen before. Start with basics and build up gradually. If your partner finds something difficult, smile with her and enjoy something she can do. Do not try to show off – no one, least of all a new partner, will appreciate it. If you visit a dance event without a partner, and many do, avoid trying to monopolise one partner. If things work out, you can always make a date to visit again as a couple.

Women should note that it often takes a lot of courage for a man to ask them for a dance. If a man does ask you to dance with him, be flattered and agree to dance. If the partner really is not to your liking, you can make your gentle excuses should he ask you again but, at least, you have done him the courtesy of allowing him a dance with you. If you are shy or a beginner, the man will appreciate your modesty in confiding this to him so that he should not embarrass you by launching into his personal "burn out" programme. Similarly, the man may introduce himself as a beginner when he asks a woman to dance with him.

When taking to the floor, it is important to avoid causing problems for other dancers. Since, in the ballroom dances, the man normally starts a dance facing the wall, it may seem natural for him to walk onto the floor backwards while his attention is focused on his partner. This creates an irritating and unnecessary hazard for other dancers. It is far better to approach the floor and assess the flow of floor traffic before taking up your start position with due consideration for other dancers.

Show consideration for others on the floor and especially so when it is crowded. Avoid dancing moves which take up a lot of room if there is not the room to dance them. If you keep bumping into other dancers, it's

time to cool it. In any case, it's much nicer to dance close to your partner when the floor is full – and it is a great opportunity for conversation.

When the dance has finished, thank your partner and leave him or her the option of dancing the next dance with you. It should not be an automatic assumption. If you are leaving the floor, the man should escort his partner at least to the edge of the floor if not back to her seat. When leaving the floor, especially during the course of a dance, the same consideration should be shown. If you are finishing before the music has ended in a travelling dance, you should dance to the edge of the floor and leave the floor at that point.

Under no circumstances should drinks be taken onto the floor. Not only are they likely to be spilled spoiling the floor but broken glass on a dance floor is extraordinarily dangerous. If you have to pass the floor on the way from the bar, wait until the dance has finished or find a better spot. Smoking on the dance floor is dangerous and the height of ignorance; an absolute no-no.

Remember that a little consideration can go a long way and is always welcome.

What to Wear

Social dance events happen across a wide spectrum of social levels ad hence degrees of formality or informality. Generally, weekday dances tend to be more casual than Friday or Saturday events. If you are not sure, you should check with the event organiser.

A staggering variety of specially designed dance shoes is now readily available through specialist dancewear suppliers and schools. The designs will be attractive and fashionable but well suited for the purpose, offering foot protection whilst being cool, light and often featuring a silvered-suede non-slip sole. Trainers or sneakers should, however, be avoided, as they not only make the feet hot but also make turning both difficult and dangerous. This can result in sprained or even broken ankles. Your specialist supplier will be pleased to give specific advice appropriate to your chosen dance style.

Right: Clothes that are both stylish and appropriate for your chosen dance style will improve your performance as well as your appearance.

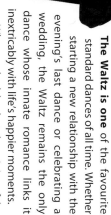

Waltz

The Waltz is one of the favourite standard dances of all time. Whether starting a new relationship with the evening's last dance or celebrating a wedding, the Waltz remains the only dance whose innate romance links it inextricably with life's happier moments.

When we look back at the origins of the Waltz, we discover a dance that has adapted in a remarkable way to changing fashions over the course of its history; a history that has spanned two centuries. The dance that came to symbolize romance started life towards the end of the 18th century as an Austro-German folk dance called the Ländler. It was characterized by the rotary gyrations of men and women dancing together as partners. In the early years of the 19th

century, the Waltz took the controversial step of adopting a hold in which the man's right hand was placed around the lady's waist. The great debate concerning the dubious morality of the Waltz continued until the Russian Czar, Alexander, gave the dance the royal seal of approval when he was observed openly dancing and enjoying the Waltz in public. The enormous popularity of the Viennese Waltzes composed and played by the Strauss family through the latter half of the 19th century ensured that, by the century's end, the Waltz had reached the pinnacle of popularity.

By the time of the First World War, a new generation of dancers was looking for a more natural, less stylized way of dancing the Waltz. A revolution in the Waltz style had started to take place with the advent of another dance called the Boston, in which the dancers employed a "modern" closer hold, danced hip to hip and at a more leisurely pace. Although the Boston had virtually disappeared by the outbreak of the War, it was one of the influences on the new-style Waltz.

In 1914 the craze for the Foxtrot spread from America all over Europe, overshadowing the Waltz, which was still perceived to have Germanic associations.

In 1921, with the Waltz all but extinct, *The Dancing Times* called a conference of dance teachers in London to discuss the pressing issues of the day. One of these was the decline in popularity of the Waltz during the war and the confusion arising out of the lack of standard technique. From this conference came the standard "Walk-Side-Close" technique danced today, which characterizes the Modern Waltz. Because these fundamental developments took place in England, the Standard Waltz is sometimes known as the English Waltz. With its newer, more natural feel, the dance soon re-established itself as one of the most popular social dances in the ballroom and became one of the best loved "standard" international dances.

Based on the techniques defined during the 1920s and cultivated through the 1930s, the Waltz has continued to develop through the 20th century giving rise to an astonishing variety of graceful figures and combinations for the enjoyment of those who dance it. I hope you are now about to become one of them.

Basic Floorcraft

While you and other dancers are dancing around the floor, you should be aware of other couples and their likely direction of travel. Knowing how to avoid problems is a great advantage to a dancer and ways of doing this are described in the Floorcraft tips later in the book. There are, however, a few general rules worth mentioning now.

- *It makes sense for more experienced dancers to give way to less experienced couples.*

- *Whoever sees a potential problem should take action to avoid it. This is usually the couple who are further back in the flow of floor traffic.*

- *Never dance across the centre line of the room into the oncoming flow of floor traffic. With a little practice, the ability to avoid dancing into a problem will itself yield satisfaction and enjoyment.*

Left: The Waltz has adapted to suit changing fashions over two centuries.

The Basic Waltz

Some schools recommend dancing the Waltz in a straight line around the room. This is not incorrect but, as most dancers zigzag along the floor, the straight-line method continually cuts across the path of other dancers and causes problems for everyone. In addition, the character of the Waltz suggests a dance of elegant turns, so we will start with an internationally recognized method of dancing the Basic Waltz which includes a degree of characteristic turn and which also makes it more interesting and enjoyable.

The Basic Waltz described here consists of four sections of three steps to make a short routine of 12 steps. Each section has a Walk, a Side Step and a Close. Start in the hold described previously with the feet together and standing about 4 feet (1.5 metres) away from the edge of the floor to allow sufficient space to dance into. The man is ready to move forward along a zig and the woman to move backwards along it.

Section 1

1

Man Walk forward with the right foot, curving a little to the right (clockwise).

Woman Walk back with the left foot, curving a little to the right (clockwise).

2

Man Turn from the zig to the zag by moving sideways onto the toes of the left foot.

Woman Turn from the zig to the zag by moving a small step sideways onto the toes of the right foot.

3

Man Now, on the zag, close the right foot to the left foot and lower toe-heel onto the right foot.

Woman Now, on the zag, close the left foot to the right foot and lower toe-heel onto the left foot.

Section 2

4

Man Walk back along the zag onto the left foot, with no turn.

Woman Walk forward along the zag onto the right foot, with no turn.

5

Man Move sideways onto the toes of the right foot, with no turn.

Woman Move sideways onto the toes of the left foot, with no turn.

6

Man Close the left foot to the right foot and lower toe-heel onto the left foot.

Woman Close the right foot to the left foot and lower toe-heel onto the right foot.

FLOW

zig

starting position

zag

Sway

Sway is an important feature of a nice, easy and relaxed style. When reaching with the foot, it is quite natural for the body and head to tilt or sway a little away from the reaching foot, acting as a counterbalance. If small steps are taken, sway will hardly be felt but as you get used to dancing the Waltz and start to move more freely, it will enhance your style if you allow yourself to sway a little away from the reaching foot and towards the closing foot.

Section 3

7

Man Walk back with the right foot, curving a little to the left anticlockwise (counterclockwise).

Woman Walk forward with the left foot, curving a little to the left anticlockwise (counterclockwise).

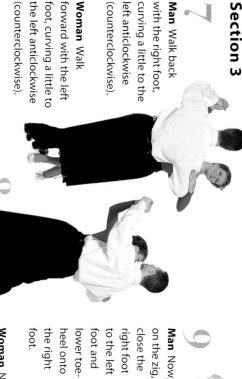

WALL

Man Turn from the zag to the zig by moving sideways onto the toes of the left foot.

8

Woman Turn from the zag to the zig by moving sideways onto the toes of the right foot.

zig

zag

FLOW

Man Now, on the zig, close the right foot to the left foot and lower toe-heel onto the right foot.

9

Woman Now, on the zig, close the left foot to the right foot and lower toe-heel onto the left foot.

Starting position

10

11

12

Notes

- Note how the sections start with alternate feet.
- The sections alternate turning moves and straight moves.
- The overall pattern of the Basic Waltz is a zigzag along the floor.
- It is essential to ensure that the second step in each section moves to the side and does not deteriorate into another walking step.
- Do not be tempted to deviate from the pattern described; accuracy is vital.
- Practise your Waltz, trying to relax and settle down to a steady rhythm. You should find that you are staying in a path just over a metre wide.

Bad tracking?

If you find that you are "tracking" towards the centre or towards the wall, you should check that you are making the same amount of turn to the right and to the left in the turning sections (Sections 1 and 3) to keep you on track.

Section 4

These three steps are only one of four possible examples of a Closed Change Step. A closed change step is any walk-side-close movement without turn. It may move forwards or backwards and may start with either foot.

10

Man Walk forward along the zig onto the left foot, with no turn.

Woman Walk back along the zig onto the right foot, with no turn.

Man Move sideways onto the toes of the right foot, with no turn.

11

Woman Move sideways onto the toes of the left foot, with no turn.

Man Close the left foot to the right foot and lower toe-heel onto the left foot.

12

Woman Close the right foot to the left and lower toe-heel onto the right foot.

You can now repeat the basic 12 steps from the beginning to enjoy waltzing around the room. For the moment, when you reach a corner simply bend the dance around the corner, but make sure that you reorientate yourself as quickly as possible onto the zigs and zags of the new wall. This is best and most comfortably achieved by the man turning to the left more strongly on Step 7.

WALTZ: natural turn around a corner

Natural Turn around a Corner

Once you have settled down to the regular rhythm and pattern of the Basic Waltz, you will soon want to try a move which will help you turn the corner more fluently and comfortably. In standard dancing, any move which turns clockwise is referred to as a "natural" turn, no matter how unnatural it might feel at first. The Natural Turn comprises two sections of three steps. Each section follows the familiar pattern of walk-side-close. Begin as for the Basic Waltz with the feet together. The man is standing on his left foot and the woman on her right foot, about 4 feet (1.5 metres) from the edge of the floor. The man is ready to move forwards along a zig and the woman to move backwards along it.

Section 1

This section comprises the first three steps of the Basic Waltz but turning them a little more.

1

Man Walk forward with the right foot, curving to the right (clockwise).

Woman Walk back with the left foot, curving to the right (clockwise).

2

Man Continue turning and move sideways onto the toes of the left foot.

Woman Continue turning and then move sideways onto the toes of the right foot (a small step).

3

Man Continue turning to end backing into the corner, facing against the flow. Close the right foot to the left foot and lower onto the right foot. (The wall is now on your left.)

Woman Continue turning to end facing down the room with the flow. Close the left foot to the right foot and lower onto the left foot.

Section 2

Continue turning in the same direction as you cut across the corner to end on the zig at the start of the new wall:

4

Man Continue turning clockwise and walk back with the left foot.

Woman Continue turning clockwise and walk forward with the right foot.

5

Man Continue turning clockwise and move sideways onto the toes of the right foot (a small step).

Woman Continue turning clockwise and move sideways onto the toes of the left foot.

6

Man Continue turning clockwise to end on the new wall. Close the left foot to the right foot and lower onto the left foot.

Woman Continue turning clockwise to end on the zig of the new wall. Close the right foot to the left foot and lower onto the right foot.

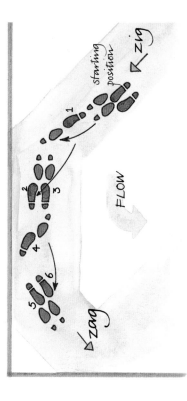

You have now successfully turned the corner and are on a zig ready to dance along the new wall using the familiar Basic Waltz.

zig
zag
zag
zig
starting position
FLOW

Practical tip – Short Steps

On Step 2 for the woman and Step 5 for the man, the dancer should take a slightly shorter step to the side to help their partner turn around them. The person who is dancing backwards into the turn is the one on the "inside" of the turn and should take the shorter steps. This is a very useful tip to remember and try to put into practice throughout the dance.

Fitting the Basic Waltz into the Room

As you dance the Basic Waltz, you may well find that when you want to dance the Natural Turn at a corner you are not quite in the right position; you could be either not quite ready to dance it too early or not ready until too late. As a general rule, it is much better to dance it early, as the later option could see you disappearing off the edge of the floor. With practice, however, you will be able to gauge your progression around the room so that you arrive near the corner in a perfect position to dance the Natural Turn.

It is often assumed, quite wrongly, that this is achieved by increasing the length of the step. This would in fact make the dancing quite uncomfortable. The answer, though slightly more subtle, is no more difficult. The angle of the turns made

during the Basic Waltz can be adjusted to make the dance progress more or progress less along the side of the room. A greater amount of turn will result in more progression and a lesser amount in less progression. An experienced dancer will not worry about reaching the perfect corner in the perfect position until perhaps the last 12 steps of the Basic Waltz, in which the angles can be adjusted to fit the movement into the space available.

Be aware that less experienced dancers often try to dance an extra Basic Waltz when really they ought to have started the Natural Turn or other corner figure. This error often means that the dancer has not planned ahead sufficiently, so it is important to start thinking about the corner as soon as you have danced about two-thirds of the way along the room.

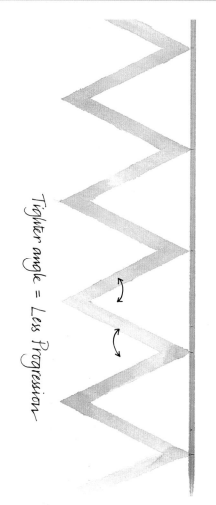

Tighter angle = Less Progression

Wider angle = More Progression

Rise and Fall

Rise and fall is the elevation and lowering which the dancer feels as he or she moves onto the toes of a foot and then relaxes through the knee, ankle and toes to end on a flat foot. In reality, rise and fall is a by-product of the natural swing of the Waltz. A good swing action is something which dedicated competitors strive to achieve over many years of tough coaching and hard practice. The social dancer can also start to enjoy the gentle rising and falling and add considerably to the feeling of the Waltz by following a few simple guidelines.

Right: A walk forward on count 1 will usually be a normal walk, starting with the heel.

Left: A move to the side on count 2 will usually lift onto the toes.

Right: A close on count 3 will usually be accompanied by a lowering (toe to heel) onto the foot that has just moved to close.

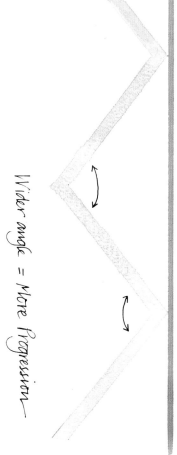

Left: On figures with four steps in one bar of music, for example, a Chassé, the dancer will rise more gradually over the first three steps before lowering gently on the fourth (toe to heel action).

• Occasional exceptions to these guidelines are noted in the appropriate figure if considered relevant to the enjoyment of social dancing. Rise and Fall does not occur in the Social Foxtrot or Modern Tango.

Outside Change

The most useful moves are often the simplest. The Outside Change is a great figure for using as a spacer to extend the Basic Waltz. You can dance the Outside Change immediately after dancing Section 1 of the Basic Waltz. After the Outside Change you will be able to continue by dancing your Basic Waltz again, starting with Section 1 and with the man taking his first step forward with the right foot outside the woman, or by dancing into the Natural Turn around a Corner with the same right foot modification for the man. It can similarly be followed by the Natural Spin Turn which is described later in the book.

1

Man Walk back onto the left foot, still on the zag.

Woman Walk forward onto the right foot.

2

Man Walk back onto the toes of the right foot, still on the zag.

Woman Walk forward onto the toes of the left foot.

3

Man Move sideways onto the left foot, starting to move onto the zig.

Woman Move sideways onto the right foot, starting to move onto the zig.

The move is completed by continuing into the Basic Waltz or Natural Turn around a Corner.

It is important to note that on the first step of the figure following the Outside Change, the man will find it more comfortable and natural to dance outside the woman with his right foot; that is, his right foot will more forward between himself and his partner.

WALL

zig

zag

Starting position

FLOW

1st step of next figure outside partner

1

2

3

Outside Change Ending in Promenade Position

This popular and extremely useful floorcraft variation of the Outside Change is used to overtake slower couples ahead or just to enhance your progress around the room. It includes a new move called the Chassé (pronounced sha-say). Begin by dancing Steps 1 and 2 of the Outside Change as before. On Step 2, the man starts to move his head slightly more to the left than usual and the woman starts to move her head to the right. Then continue as follows.

Man Take a small step to the side along the room by lowering onto the left foot but pointing the left foot along the zig.

Woman Take a small step to the side along the room by lowering onto the right foot but pointing the right foot along the zag. Move the head over to the right.

In this move, the woman does not turn her body. This results in her ending in a slightly open or "promenade" position on Step 3.

black lines show body alignment

WALL

FLOW

Promenade Position

Promenade Position is a very frequently used position in standard dancing. It simply means that the couple has moved into a position in which the distance between the man's left shoulder and the woman's right shoulder is greater than the distance between the man's right shoulder and woman's left. The couple are therefore slightly open on the man's left and the woman's right side. It is crucial that this very slightly open position is not exaggerated to become an almost side-by-side position. In the Promenade Position, the woman will be looking to the right and the man slightly further to the left than normal. When the man uses his right foot and the woman her left foot to take a step in Promenade Position, it will be taken "through the middle" between the dancers and along the same line. Because of the relative positioning of their bodies, the man's foot will go through first. Such a step should be a short one to avoid distorting the top half of the body.

Chassé from Promenade Position

This frequently used move has four steps. These are fitted into the standard three beats of the Waltz by dancing a special count of 1, 2 & 3, where the middle counts of 2 & share the second beat of the music. The man dances this move along a single line parallel to the wall but maintaining the zig alignment. The woman dances this move along a single line parallel to the wall but with the head and body gradually turning left to resume the normal position facing the man.

1

Man Move the right foot forward and across yourself along the line, starting to turn to the left.

Woman Move the left foot forward and across along the line, starting to turn to the left.

2

Man Move onto the toes of the left foot, still progressing along the same line.

Woman Move sideways onto the toes of the right foot, along the same line and continuing to turn left.

&

Man Close the right foot to the left foot, still on the toes.

Woman Close the left foot to the right foot, still on the toes, completing the turn to face the man.

3

Man Move sideways, lowering onto the left foot, along the same line to end on the zig.

Woman Move sideways, lowering onto the right foot, along the same line to end on the zig.

Continue into the Basic Waltz or Natural Turn around a Corner, remembering that on Step 1, the man will walk forward with the right foot outside.

Three Walks Curving to the Right

Imagine you are on a zig ready to dance the Basic Waltz but there is another couple ahead of you. You can dance the Three Walks Curving to the Right instead. By the time you have danced this useful figure, the couple who were just ahead of you will probably have moved on, leaving your path clear.

1

Man Walk forward onto the right foot, starting to curve to the right.

Woman Walk back onto the left foot, starting to curve to the right.

Floorcraft Figures

When you first try out your Basic Waltz at a dance, you will find that one of the man's main preoccupations will be to avoid other dancers on the floor. Sometimes you will find that split-second decisions have to be made to avoid bumping into another couple. It is therefore important that the man leads the woman by making his intentions very clear. He should not and need not physically manoeuvre the woman if he dances his chosen move with clarity. The woman should also try to anticipate possible problems. To stop the man moving backwards into another couple, the woman should squeeze his upper right arm between her left thumb and middle finger as a warning. It is then up to the man to take the avoiding action. It is sensible to choose a figure which will avoid the problem in the simplest way. The easy moves explained here include the Hover Corté, the Whisk and the Checked Natural Turn. These, along with Three Walks Curving to the Right, will help you deal with potential traffic problems.

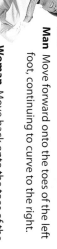

Man 2 Move forward onto the toes of the left foot, continuing to curve to the right.

Woman 2 Move back onto the toes of the right foot, continuing to curve to the right.

Man 3 Walk forward and slightly across yourself with the right foot, lowering onto the right foot outside the woman and continuing to curve to the right to end on the zag. Turn your body a little further to the right on this step.

Woman 3 Walk back a small step, lowering onto the left foot underneath your body, continuing to curve to the right to end on the zag. Turn your body a little further to the right on this step.

Continue by dancing the Outside Change with an important modification. On Step 1, maintain the turned body position of the end of the Three Walks Curving to the Right. The woman takes her first step of the Outside Change outside the man, that is, between herself and her partner, and will start to turn a little to the left to move in line with the man as she continues into Step 2.

Hover Corté

The Hover Corté (pronounced kor-tay) is a standard figure in the Waltz and can be danced after Step 6 of the Basic Waltz, especially if the way ahead is not clear. Start on a zag, having danced Section 2 of the Basic Waltz. The man is standing on his left foot and the woman on her right. Both have their feet together.

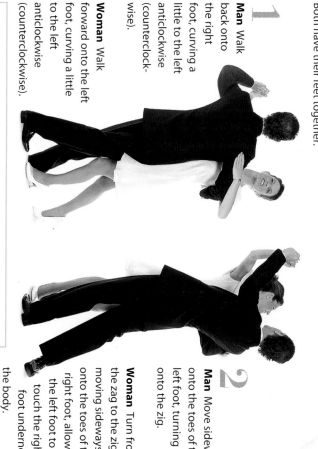

1

Man Walk back onto the right foot, curving a little to the left anticlockwise (counterclockwise).

Woman Walk forward onto the left foot, curving a little to the left anticlockwise (counterclockwise).

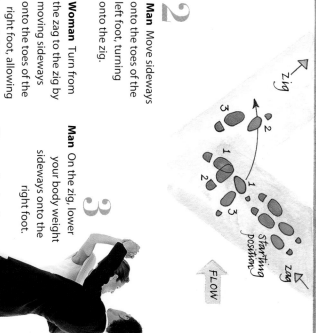

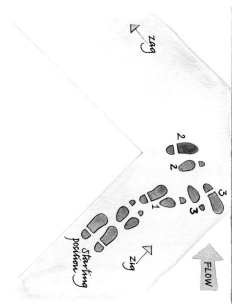

2

Man Move sideways onto the toes of the left foot, turning onto the zig.

Woman Turn from the zag to the zig by moving sideways onto the toes of the right foot, allowing the left foot to touch the right foot underneath the body.

3

Man On the zig, lower your body weight sideways onto the right foot.

Woman On the zig, lower your body weight sideways onto the left foot.

Continue with Section 2 of the Basic Waltz. Dance this without any turn so that you remain on the zig. The woman will take Step 1 forward and across herself and outside the man with the right foot. Then start the Basic Waltz from the beginning.

Whisk

The Whisk is a popular and standard move in the Waltz. A good place to dance the Whisk is after Step 9 (Section 3) of the Basic Waltz. Because the Whisk temporarily halts your progress around the room, it is a good delaying move if another couple is in the path ahead. The couple is on a zig with feet together. The man is standing on his right foot and the woman on her left.

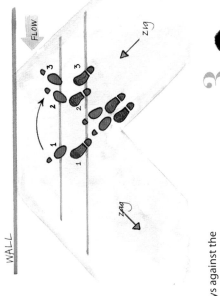

1

Man Walk forward onto the left foot on the zig.

Woman Walk back onto the right foot on the zig.

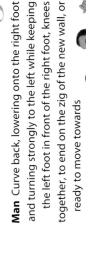

2

Man Move sideways against the flow onto the toes of the right foot, still on the zig.

Woman Move sideways against the flow onto the toes of the left foot, turning from the zig to the zag.

3

Man Lower onto the left foot, crossing it behind the right foot underneath your body and turning your body very slightly to the right.

Woman Lower onto the right foot, crossing it behind the left foot underneath your body.

You are now in a Promenade Position with the woman having opened her right side. Continue with the Chassé from Promenade Position which you danced previously as part of the Outside Change and Chassé from Promenade Position.

Checked Natural Turn with Reverse Pivot

If you are dancing into the Natural Turn around a Corner and you find that the corner is congested with floor traffic immediately ahead of you, you can check the movement into the turn and pivot to the left out of trouble. Start as for the Natural Turn around a Corner.

1

Man Walk forward onto the right foot, starting to turn to the right.

Woman Walk back onto the left foot, starting to turn to the right.

2

Man Move forward onto the toes of the left foot, turning more strongly to the right but keeping your head looking along the zig. Sway a little to the right.

Woman Move back onto the toes of the right foot, turning more strongly to the right. Sway a little to the right and allow your head to move over to the right.

3

Man Curve back, lowering onto the right foot and turning strongly to the left while keeping the left foot in front of the right foot, knees together, to end on the zig of the new wall, or ready to move towards the centre line of the room along the zag.

Woman Move forward, lowering onto the left foot and turning strongly to the left with your knees together. Allow your head to move to the left to resume its normal position. End on the zig of the new wall.

Having negotiated the corner, you can continue to dance into Steps 10–12 (Section 4) of the Basic Waltz or into the Whisk using the Zig of the new wall.

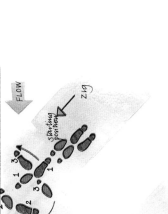

You now have a number of options to help you cope with floor traffic conditions at each stage of the Basic Waltz and at the corner, if you find the way ahead blocked by other dancers.

As you practise, you will find that you will gradually be able to improve your response time to the floor conditions ahead and will increasingly be able to avoid problems by reading the floor. Of course, you don't have to wait until there is a problem to be avoided before you dance these options. You can dance them to hone your floorcraft skills or just to enjoy them as figures in themselves. Practice not only makes perfect, it makes possible. When you are dancing your repertoire of moves with little effort, it is time to try something a little more challenging.

After Section 1:

Outside Change or Outside Change ending in Promenade Position and Chassé from Promenade Position

After Section 2:

Hover Corté

After Section 3:

Whisk and Chassé from Promenade Position

After Section 4:

Three Walks Curving to the Right and Outside Change

Natural Spin Turn

While it is not a basic figure, the Natural Spin Turn has become the international standard method of turning a corner in the Waltz. As a bonus, the Natural Spin Turn is also the standard corner figure in the Quickstep. The figure starts in the same place as the Natural Turn around a Corner. Think of the Natural Spin Turn as having a total of six steps. You have encountered three of them earlier so, with a little patience, you will soon be able to master this simplified version of the Natural Spin Turn. Start by dancing Steps 1–3 of the Natural Turn around a Corner. The man is facing against the flow with his feet together and standing on his right foot. The woman is facing with the flow with her feet together and standing on her left foot.

4

Man Move back onto the left foot, staying down and turning the left foot inwards to make a strong turn to the right. Keep your knees together. (This will feel awkward but only because you are dancing it step by step. At normal speed, the move will flow much more comfortably.)

Woman Move forward onto the right foot, staying down and turning strongly to the right to end on the zig of the new wall. Keep your knees together.

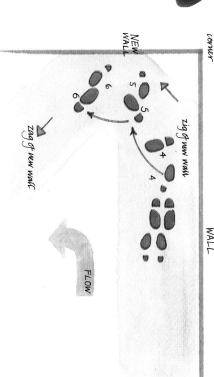

WALTZ: natural spin turn/hover telemark

5

Man Walk forward between the woman's feet onto the right foot on the zig of the new wall. Lift up onto the toes of the right foot and continue turning to the right on the toes of the right foot, keeping the left foot behind.

Woman Move back onto the toes of the left foot on the zig of the new wall, continuing to turn to the right. Bring your right foot back out of the way to touch your left foot.

Floorcraft Tips

If you find the corner blocked as you start the Natural Spin Turn, you can stop the figure by dancing the Checked Natural Turn with Reverse Pivot described earlier.

Style Tip

Some men find it helpful to think of Steps 4–6 as a rock back, a rock forward lifting and a rock back while remembering, of course, to turn. It is a common error for the man to make Step 5 a side step but this must be avoided. It is important for the man to keep his head to the left throughout the figure.

6

Man Relax back onto the left foot away from the corner, having turned onto the zag of the new wall.

Woman Move forward, lowering onto the right foot on the zag of the new wall.

Note that the feet do not close. Continue by dancing straight into Section 3 of the Basic Waltz.

Hover Telemark

The Hover Telemark is a classic figure which is not only extremely useful but also has a superb look and feel and is not difficult to lead. The description of the moves needs to be carefully followed before success will be achieved. Do not confuse the name of this move with the Hover Corté described earlier. Dance this figure after Section 3 of the Basic Waltz. You will now be on a zig with your feet together. The man is standing on his right foot and the woman on her left.

1

Man Walk forward onto the left foot along the zig but turning your body to the left so that you are almost walking across yourself. Relax the knees and look along the zig.

Woman Walk backward onto the right foot along the zig but turning your body to the left so that you are almost walking across yourself. Relax the knees and turn your head well to the left as you feel the clear lead of this figure.

2

Man Move forward along the zig onto the toes of the right foot, turning your body to the right so that it comes square with the feet.

Woman Move back along the zig onto the toes of the left foot, turning your body to the right so that it comes square with the feet. Move your head gradually over to the right to end facing the man.

3

Man Take a small step to the side along the room by lowering onto the left foot and pointing it along the zig in a Promenade Position.

Woman Take a small step to the side along the room by lowering onto the right foot and pointing it along the zag. Move your head over to the right to finish in a Promenade Position.

Continue with the Chassé from Promenade Position.

Open Telemark Group

Now that you have had some practice at combining the figures you have learned and have become familiar with various features of the Waltz, including the Promenade Position, you will certainly want to try a new combination as this move is introduced. Take care and consider the other dancers, as this combination moves you across the flow towards the centre line of the room. First, though, you will need to position yourself ready to dance the Open Telemark.

Section 1

Dance the Natural Spin Turn as you would at a corner and using the same amount of turn, but this time dance it along the side of the room. When you have danced a complete turn (360°), you will end on the zig against the flow.

Section 2

Dance Section 3 of the Basic Waltz to end facing towards the centre line of the room but on the zag. You will have turned a quarter turn (90°) to the left. You are now ready to experience the elegance of the Open Telemark.

1

Man Walk forward onto the left foot along the zag towards the centre line, starting to turn to the left.

Woman Walk back onto the right foot along the zag towards the centre line, starting to turn to the left.

2

Man Move forward onto the toes of the right foot, still along the zag towards the centre line and continuing to turn to the left. End with the right foot to the side, backing the zig.

Woman Close the left foot to the right foot with the left heel in contact with the floor. Continue turning to the left on the heel of the right foot and move your head gradually over to the right as you rise onto the toes of the left foot.

3

Man Continue turning on the right foot and take a small step to the side, lowering onto the left foot and pointing it along the zig in Promenade Position.

Woman Continue turning on the left foot and take a small step to the side, lowering onto the right foot and pointing it along the room in Promenade Position. Your head is now to the right.

Continue with the Chassé from Promenade Position or the Hairpin from Promenade Position.

Hairpin from Promenade Position

The Outside Change, the Whisk, the Hover Telemark and the Open Telemark can or do all end in Promenade Position and would normally be followed by the Chassé from Promenade Position. However, as the route ahead may sometimes be blocked, it is useful to have an alternative course available to you. Here is a superb figure which always looks more difficult than it is, giving professional polish to the Waltz of even moderate dancers. Start by dancing any of the figures listed above, ending in Promenade Position.

1

Man Move the right foot forward and across yourself along the line.

Woman Move the left foot forward and across yourself along the line.

2

Man Move onto the toes of the left foot, pointing them along the zig. Close the woman to your right side by turning your body slightly to the left.

Woman Move sideways onto the toes of the right foot, along the same line but turning strongly to the left to close your right side to the man. Your head resumes its normal left position.

3

Man On the left foot, sway and turn strongly to the right onto the zag. Take a small step forward, lowering onto the right foot outside the woman. Turn your body a little further to the right as you take this step and move your head to the right to look at the woman. Note that the body turn occurs before the step.

Woman Take a small step back, under your body, lowering onto the left foot and turning strongly to the right to end on the zag. Turn your body a little further to the right as you take this step.

Note the strong sway to the right for the man and to the left for the woman on Step 3. Continue into the Outside Change.

Style Tip
The man dances Steps 1–2 along a single line parallel to the wall but maintaining the zig alignment. The woman dances Steps 1–2 along a single line parallel to the wall.

Hairpin from Step 6 of the Basic Waltz

The Hairpin does not have to be danced from the Promenade Position. It can also be started from Step 6 of the Basic Waltz, in which case it is modified as follows. Use it in any situation where the way ahead is blocked and you wish to delay your progress around the room.

1

Man Walk back onto the right foot along the zag.

Woman Walk forward onto the left foot along the zag.

2

Man Move sideways onto the toes of the left foot.

Woman Take a small step sideways onto the toes of the right foot.

3

Man On the left foot, sway and turn a little to the right, still on the zag. Take a small step forward and across yourself, lowering onto the right foot outside the woman. Turn your body a little further to the right as you take this step and move your head to the right to look at the woman.

Woman Take a small step back under your body, lowering onto the left foot and turning a little to the right. Turn your body a little further to the right as you take this step.

Continue as from the Three Walks Curving to the Right.

Hover from Promenade Position

It is always good practice and style to have a floorcraft figure up your sleeve which you can dance if the way ahead is obstructed. This one can be danced after the Whisk, the Outside Change Ending in Promenade Position, the Open Telemark or the Hover Telemark. Steps 2 and 3 are similar to the Hover Corté but the entry is from a Promenade Position.

1
Man Walk forward and across yourself onto the right foot, in Promenade Position.

Woman Walk forward and across yourself onto the left foot, in Promenade Position.

2
Man Take a small step forward onto the toes of the left foot, turning to the left. Lead the "hover" by swaying to the right.

Woman Walk forward onto the toes of the right foot, turning to the left to end facing the man with your feet side by side but apart. Sway to the left and turn your head to the left.

3
Man Move back against the flow line lowering onto the right foot to end facing the zig.

Woman Move forward against the flow line lowering onto the left foot.

> Continue with one of the figures suggested for following the Progressive Chassé to the Right. You may even dance into the Open Impetus Turn from this position. Remember that the next step for the woman will be a forward walk with her right foot outside the man.

Three Walks Curving to the Left

To add interest and flexibility to your Waltz, we will now introduce a move which turns to the left. First dance Section 1 and 2 of the Open Telemark Group. The man is now on the centre line of the room and the woman is opposite. The couple have their feet together. The man is standing on his right foot and the woman her left foot. Although this move ends with the man facing against the flow, as you dance this figure, be careful not to actually move against the flow.

1
Man Walk forward with the left foot, curving to the left.

Woman Walk back with the right foot, curving to the left.

2
Man Walk forward onto the toes of the right foot, still curving and swaying to the left.

Woman Walk back onto the toes of the left foot, still curving and swaying to the left.

3
Man Brushing the left foot past the right foot, walk forward, lowering onto the left foot and continuing to curve.

Woman Brushing the right foot past the left foot, walk back, lowering onto the right foot underneath the body and continuing to curve.

> The figure ends with the man facing against the flow and the woman facing with the flow. By making small adjustments to the amount of turn, you can now dance the Hairpin (as if after step 6 of the Basic Waltz) or the Hover Corté both ending with the man on the zig facing towards the wall. A spectacular continuing move is the Oversway.

Oversway

This classic figure has a number of forms and styles; in this version, the couple come to a temporary halt as the man leads the woman into a turn enhanced by a slightly exaggerated sway. Since the turn is done in place, this move is also useful as a very classy floorcraft figure. Start by dancing the Three Walks Curving to the Left. The man is now facing against the flow, standing on his left foot with feet together. The woman is facing with the flow, standing on her right foot. The Oversway is danced along a line parallel to the wall.

1

Man Walk back along the line onto the right foot.

Woman Walk forward onto the left foot.

2

Man Walk back along the line onto the left foot, relaxing the knee then, on the left foot, start to swivel to the left, with a slight sway to the left, and lead the woman as if you are moving her into Promenade Position.

Woman Walk forward onto the ball of the right foot as if ready to pass the man, leading with your right side, and flex the right knee, leaving the left foot extended behind. On the right foot, swivel to the left with a slight sway to the right. End with your head to the right.

3

Man Still on the left foot, with the knee flexed and increasing the sway to the left slightly, continue to swivel to the left to end facing the wall with the right foot extended to the side but without any weight on it.

Woman Still on the right foot, with the knee flexed and increasing the sway to the right slightly, continue to swivel to the left to end backing the wall with the left foot extended to the side but without any weight on it.

4

Man Still on the left foot with the left knee flexed and the right foot extended to the side, continue to swivel onto the zig, changing the sway from right to left and bringing your left side back a little and pushing forward through the hips.

Woman Still on the right foot with the knee flexed and the left foot extended to the side, continue to swivel onto the zig, changing the sway from right to left and allowing your head to return to the left. The sway to the left should be slightly exaggerated by turning the body a little more to the left.

5

Man Close the right foot to the left foot, then lift onto the toes of the right foot and neutralize the sway, leading the woman into Promenade Position.

Woman Close the left foot to the right foot, then lift onto the toes of the left foot and neutralize the sway as you return your head to the right to end in Promenade Position.

6

Man Take a small step sideways along the room, lowering onto the left foot in Promenade Position.

Woman Take a small step sideways along the room, lowering onto the right foot in Promenade Position.

The best exit is now a Chassé from Promenade Position, though any of the exits suggested for the Promenade Position can be selected.

Swing

A good swing epitomizes the action used by expert dancers of the Waltz. While in the early stages of getting to grips with the Waltz, you will not have much time to think about developing a good action, but sooner or later you will want to enhance your enjoyment and improve your style with a little bit of swing. If you were to suspend a pendulum from the ceiling, then pull it back and release it to fall by the force of gravity, it would travel in an arc along a straight line. You can begin to use such a natural swing in your waltz. In most of the figures in standard dancing, swing acts on alternate sides of the body in each bar of music or set of three steps. Swing can be applied to any figure and here the Natural Turn is used as an example.

Left: As the man turns to the right on Step 2, swing will act on his left side, causing him to rise and helping to propel his left side towards the wall faster than his right side, which has become the centre of the turn.

Right: On Step 3, the swing naturally continues upwards, taking the man's left side with it and causing him rising with the swing's momentum. When the dancer is turning, the swing action will also cause him or her to incline the body towards the centre of the turn – this inclination is called "sway".

Left: On Step 1, the man walks forward with his right foot along the zig.

Style Tip

When dancing with a swing action, Step 2, which is usually a side step, carries the powerful swing momentum and will therefore be longer than Steps 1 or 3.

Swing is responsible for maintaining a proportional amount of turn, alignment, rise and fall, footwork, sway and length of step in many Waltz figures. Swing also leads to a less energetic and more economical way of moving. It is an important ingredient of good dancing and one which your local coach or dance school can help you develop further.

Right: Since swing occurs in a straight line, the feet also use that straight line. Steps 1–3 of the Natural Turn are all taken on the same line (in this example, on the zig), irrespective of the turn and where the feet happen to be facing. On Steps 4–6, each step will be taken on the same floorboard or line parallel with the wall, while the swing will act on the man's right side.

Quickstep

Left: With its lively tempo, the Quickstep is now one of the most popular of ballroom dances.

The Quickstep is one of the two most popular of the International Standard ballroom dances, along with the Waltz. Allegedly, the dance owes its existence to the American comedian Harry Fox, who worked the burlesque theatres of the USA just prior to the First World War. At that time, regulations prohibited semi-clad female performers from moving on stage, and required them to remain in fixed poses in "artistic" tableaux. Fox hit upon the idea of performing a little dance movement around the statically posed women in between jokes. The popular music industry, known as Tin Pan Alley, was soon promoting the music and steps of the "Foxtrot".

The Foxtrot consisted of a slow walk taking two beats of music and a series of quick steps, or trots, each taking a single beat of music. Initially, it relied heavily upon moves from other dances such as the One-step and the Rag, but teachers soon created new figures to meet the demand. By 1915, the Foxtrot reached England and it had soared to new heights of popular acclaim. At this point, the Foxtrot was danced at a tempo of about 32 bars per minute, but in 1916 dancers started to adapt the dance to slower music with a more gliding feel. To differentiate it from the usual, quicker Foxtrot, this slower Foxtrot was initially called the Saunter, and it was this dance which later laid the basis for the Slow Foxtrot.

By the end of the First World War, jazz was coming into its own, expressing the post-war mood of liberation. In the 1920s, the tempo of life quickened, as did the pace of the jazzed-up Foxtrot. By the mid-1920s, dance bands frequently played the Foxtrot at a cracking 50 bars per minute – the Quick Foxtrot. Then, in 1925, the Charleston appeared. While extremely popular as a fad dance, the Charleston lacked long-term

potential. However, in 1927 it was combined with the Quick Foxtrot to result in a dance with the tediously lengthy name of the Q.T.F.T. & C. – the Quick Time Fox Trot and Charleston. The Charleston fell into decline, but its influence lived on in the Q.T.F.T. & C., now renamed the Quickstep.

Through the 1930s and 1940s, the Quickstep's lively character embraced the Big Band Swing sounds. In the 1950s, 1960s and beyond, there were always plenty of foot-tapping tunes and romantic up-tempo melodies for which the Quickstep was the natural dance choice. While the tempo has gradually come down from the athletic 54–56 bars per minute of 1929 to a pleasant 48–50 bars per minute for social dancing in the 1990s, the Quickstep has lost nothing of its lust for life.

At its most advanced, the Quickstep is a combination of body swing movements and syncopated hops, danced at an impressive speed. At its most social, the dance offers a repeatable basic pattern which everyone can enjoy. We hope that you and your partner will embrace the rhythm and swing of what has become the classic Quickstep.

Music

Quickstep music is organized with four beats to each bar of music. The first and third beats are both accentuated by the musicians but the first beat is stronger. It is on the first strong beat that you will take your first step of the dance. You will become familiar with counting the steps of the moves in "Quicks" and "Slows". A "Quick" equates to a single beat of music while a "Slow" equates to two beats. Most of the basic moves in the Quickstep start with a "Slow" count followed by two "Quick" counts.

Some, like the Quarter Turn to the Right, are then completed with a further "Slow" count, while others, such as the Natural Turn, have a different rhythm. Note that, because both the first and third beats are accentuated, you will not necessarily complete a move in a single bar of music. The Quarter Turn to the Right with a count of "Slow-Quick-Quick-Slow" will take 1½ bars of music, while a Natural Turn with a count of "Slow-Quick-Quick-Slow-Slow-Slow" will take 2½ bars of music. You need not be consciously aware of this while you are dancing; it is sufficient to be aware of the "Slows" and "Quicks" of the steps you are dancing.

Musically, the time signature of the Quickstep is 4/4 with a tempo currently recommended internationally at 50 bars per minute, although, for social dancing, Quicksteps can be enjoyed at tempos ranging from 48 to 52 bars per minute. This tempo is a little faster than a brisk walking pace but can seem very fast indeed to start with. However, as you grow more familiar with the Quickstep and remember to take small steps as you dance, the momentum of the moves themselves will help you to cope with the tempo.

Basic Quickstep

The Basic Quickstep described here consists of two sections: a forwards half and a backwards half. Both halves travel along the room in an overall anticlockwise (counterclockwise) direction, with the flow. The side-close-side movement in Steps 2–4 of both halves of the Basic Quickstep is known as a "chassé" (pronounced "sha-say"). Start in the hold described in the introduction to International Standard Partner Dancing, with the feet together and standing about 4½ feet (1.5 metres) away from the edge of the floor to allow sufficient space to dance into. The man is ready to move forward along a zig and the woman to move backwards along it.

Forward Half
Quarter Turn to the Right

1
COUNT – SLOW

Man Walk forward with the right foot along the zig, starting to turn to the right.

Woman Walk back with the left foot along the zig, starting to turn to the right.

2
COUNT – QUICK

Man Move sideways onto the toes of the left foot, travelling along the room but facing the wall.

Woman Move sideways onto the toes of the right foot, travelling along the room but facing the centre line.

3
COUNT – QUICK

Man Close the toes of the right foot to the toes of the left foot, continuing to turn to end on the zag, backing the centre line of the room.

Woman Close the toes of the left foot to the toes of the right foot, continuing to turn to end on the zag.

4
COUNT – SLOW

Man Walk back along the zag towards the centre line, lowering toe-heel onto the left foot.

Woman Walk forward along the zag towards the centre line, lowering toe-heel onto the right foot.

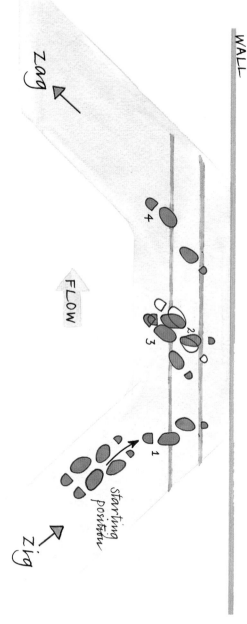

Backward Half

Progressive Chassé

1
COUNT – SLOW

Man Walk back along the zag with the right foot, moving towards the centre line and starting to turn to the left.

Woman Walk forward along the zag with the left foot, moving towards the centre line and starting to turn to the left.

2
COUNT – QUICK

Man Move sideways onto the toes of the left foot, travelling along the room and pointing the left foot along the zig.

Woman Move sideways onto the toes of the right foot, travelling along the room and turning a little to the left to end with your back square to the wall.

3
COUNT – QUICK

Man Close the toes of the right foot to toes of the left foot. End facing the zig.

Woman Close the toes of the left foot to the toes of the right foot, continuing to turn to the left to end backing along a zig.

4
COUNT – SLOW

Man Move sideways, lowering toe-heel onto the left foot to end pointing along the zig.

Woman Move sideways, lowering toe-heel onto the right foot.

Practical Tip

As you try out the Basic Quickstep for the first time, avoid taking big steps. It looks smarter and is more comfortable to keep your steps small and neat.

You can now repeat the Basic Quickstep with one important difference. On each subsequent Step 1 of the Basic Quickstep or other following move, the man will walk forward with his right foot outside the woman's right side. The woman's steps remain the same.

WALL

zag

zig

zag

1st step next figure
outside partner

starting position

1

1

3

3

2

2

4

4

FLOW

centre line

Rise and Fall

Rise and fall is the elevation and lowering which the dancer feels as he or she moves onto the toes of a foot and then relaxes through the knee, ankle and toes to end on a flat foot. Rise and fall will therefore take the dancer both above and below normal height. In reality, rise and fall is a by-product of the natural swing of the Quickstep, giving the dance its speed and flow which have ensured its liveliness and continuing appeal. A good swing action is something which dedicated competitors strive to achieve over many years of rigorous coaching and strenuous practice. Social dancers can also introduce rise and fall and enjoy the improved feeling and appearance of their dance by following a few simple guidelines.

Left: A walk, forward on Step 1 will usually be a normal walk, staying down, though starting to rise at the very end of the step as the body weight rolls over the toes.

Right: A move to the side on Step 2 will usually lift onto the toes.

- *Generally, the dancers will walk, either staying down or lowering on a slow count.*
- *Most "Quick" counts are danced on the toes.*

Right: On figures with four steps in one bar of music, for example, a Chassé, the dancer will rise more gradually over the first three steps before lowering gently on the fourth using a toe–heel action.

Left: On the last step of the bar, whether that is Step 3 or 4, the dancer will usually lower toe–heel onto the flat foot.

Natural Turn Around a Corner

In all the standard dances, including the Quickstep, special figures have been devised to help dancers turn around a corner. Here is one of the easier ones, which will help you to flow easily around the corner and leave you in exactly the right position to continue dancing the Basic Quickstep along the new wall. Start having danced the Basic Quickstep along the wall, and the woman is standing on her right foot ready to move backwards along the zig. You can, of course, start the dance with the Natural Turn at a corner if that is where you take to the floor. This option is depicted here. However, if you are dancing the move after a Basic Quickstep then remember that the man's first step will be outside his partner.

Natural Turn

1

COUNT – SLOW

Man Walk forward with the right foot along the zig starting to turn to the right.

Woman Walk back along the zig with the left foot, starting to turn to the right.

2

COUNT – QUICK

Man Move sideways along the zig onto the toes of the left foot, continuing to turn to the right.

Woman Move sideways along the zig onto the toes of the right foot, continuing to turn to the right.

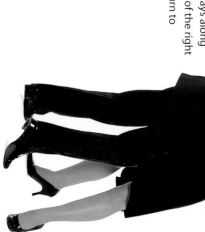

Around a corner

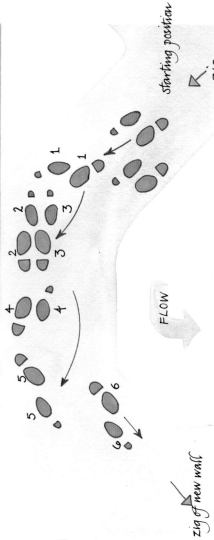

3

COUNT – QUICK

Man Close the toes of the right foot to the toes of the left foot and lower onto the right foot, turning to face against the flow.

Woman Close the toes of the left foot to the toes of the right foot and lower onto the left foot, turning to face with the flow.

4

COUNT – SLOW

Man Walk back with the left foot, continuing to turn to the right and releasing the right toes from the floor but keeping the heel in contact with it.

Woman Walk forward with the right foot, continuing to turn to the right.

5

COUNT – SLOW

Man Pull the right foot back with the heel in contact with the floor, then slide the foot around, continuing to turn to end facing along the zig of the new wall, with the right foot to the side of the left foot and with feet apart.

Woman Move sideways onto the left foot, continuing to turn to the right to face the wall.

6

COUNT – SLOW

Man Walk forward with the left foot along the zig of the new wall.

Woman Walk back with the right foot, continuing to turn to the right to move back along the zig of the new wall.

Starting position

zig

FLOW

WALL

NEW WALL

zig of new wall

Natural Spin Turn

You are already familiar with the Natural Spin Turn as the standard method of turning corners in the Quickstep. In Quickstep, the Natural Spin Turn can be danced after the Basic Quickstep followed by Steps 1–3 of the Natural Turn around a corner remembering that the man takes the first step outside partner. The Natural Spin Turn in Quickstep has a different timing to the Waltz. It is also the standard recognized way of turning corners in the Waltz.

1–3
COUNT – SLOW, QUICK, QUICK
Dance steps 1–3 of the Natural Turn around a Corner.

Dance Tip
When dancing this figure, it is important for the man to keep his head to the left throughout the figure.

4
COUNT – SLOW
Man Move back onto the left foot, turning it inwards to make a strong turn to the right. Keep your knees together. (This will feel awkward at first but only because you are dancing it step by step. At normal speed, the move will flow more comfortably.)

Woman Move forward onto the right foot, turning strongly to the right to end with your back to the zig of the new wall. Keep your knees together.

5
COUNT – SLOW
Man Walk forward between the woman's feet onto the zig of the new wall and lift up onto the toes of the right foot. Continue turning to the right on the toes of the right foot, keeping the left foot behind.

Woman Move back onto the toes of the left foot on the zig of the new wall, continuing to turn to the right. Bring the right foot back out of the way to touch the left foot.

6
COUNT – SLOW
Man Relax back onto the left foot away from the corner, having turned onto the zag of the new wall.

Woman Move forward, towards the centre-line lowering onto the right foot on the zag of the new wall.

Continue by dancing straight into the backward half of the Basic Quickstep – the Progressive Chassé.

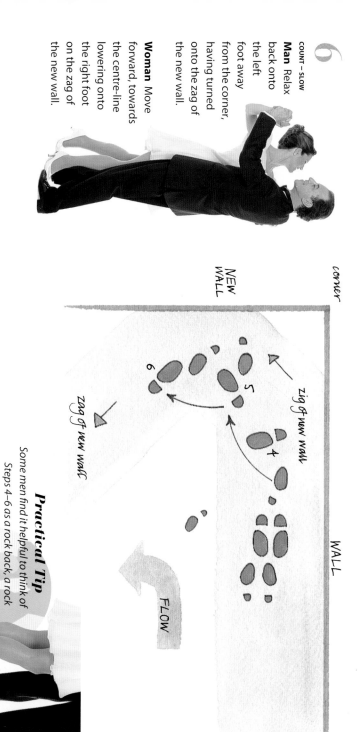

corner

NEW WALL

zig of new wall

zag of new wall

WALL

FLOW

6
5
4
3

Practical Tip
Some men find it helpful to think of Steps 4–6 as a rock back, a rock forward lifting and a rock back while remembering to turn. It is a common error for the man to make Step 5 a side step (shown right).

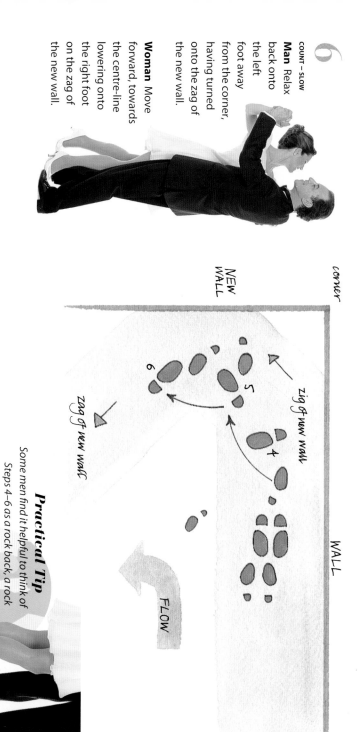

Lock Step

You can now dance a continuous Basic Quickstep with either the Natural Turn or Natural Spin Turn at the corners. The Lock Step will complete your repertoire of international standard Basic Quickstep figures. The name is a little misleading as the feet cross only loosely and do not actually "lock". The steps are the same for both the man and the woman. While the man dances the Forward Lock Step, the woman dances the Backward Lock Step, and vice versa. The man dances the Forward Lock Step and the woman the Backward Lock Step after the Basic Quickstep as a useful spacer for improving positioning prior to dancing one of the corner figures. It can also be inserted between two groups of the Basic Quickstep. As you dance the Lock Step, imagine a line parallel to the wall and dance along it.

Forward Lock Step

Start facing the zig, with feet apart and standing on the left foot. Throughout this move, remain facing along the zig but travelling along the line parallel to the wall.

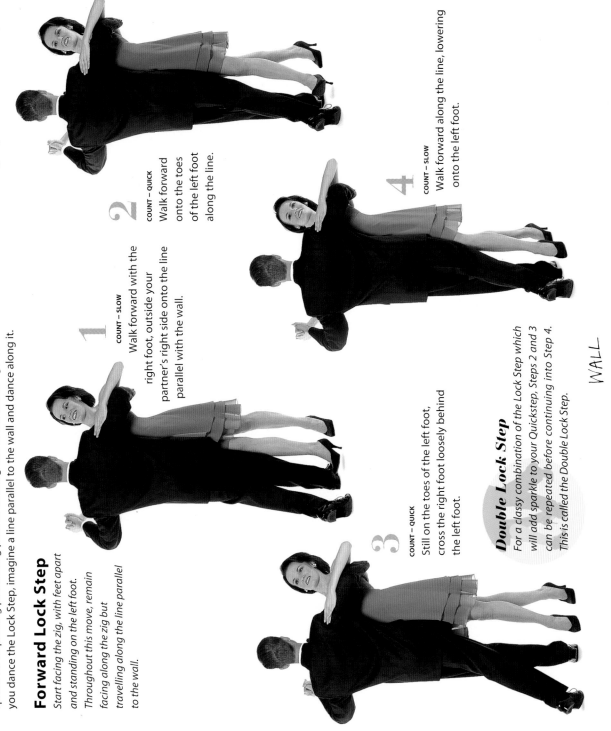

1
COUNT – SLOW
Walk forward with the right foot, outside your partner's right side onto the line parallel with the wall.

2
COUNT – QUICK
Walk forward onto the toes of the left foot along line.

3
COUNT – QUICK
Still on the toes of the left foot, cross the right foot loosely behind the left foot.

4
COUNT – SLOW
Walk forward along the line, lowering onto the left foot.

Double Lock Step

For a classy combination of the Lock Step which will add sparkle to your Quickstep, Steps 2 and 3 can be repeated before continuing into Step 4. This is called the Double Lock Step.

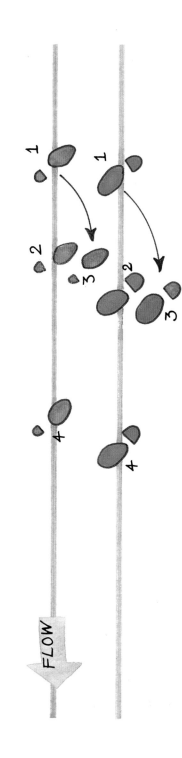

WALL

FLOW

Backward Lock Step

Start backing the zig, with feet apart and standing on the right foot. Throughout this move, remain backing along the zig but travelling along the line parallel to the wall.

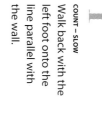

1

COUNT – SLOW

Walk back with the left foot onto the line parallel with the wall.

2

COUNT – QUICK

Walk back onto the toes of the right foot along the line.

3

COUNT – QUICK

Still on the toes of the right foot, cross the left foot loosely in front of the right foot.

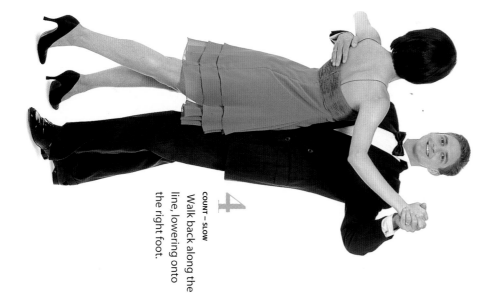

4

COUNT – SLOW

Walk back along the line, lowering onto the right foot.

Fitting the Basic Quickstep into the Room

As you dance the Basic Quickstep, you may well find that when you want to dance the Natural Turn or the Natural Spin Turn at a corner you are not quite in the right position. As a general rule, it is much better to dance the corner figure early, as the later option could see you disappearing off the edge of the floor. With practice, however, there will no longer be a danger of this as you will be able to gauge your progression around the room so that you arrive near the corner in a perfect position to dance around it.

In the Quickstep, the length of the steps should never be increased to the point where the figures and movement become distorted. It is much better to adjust the angles of the zigs and zags during the Basic Quickstep. A greater amount of turn will result in more progression along the floor and a lesser amount in less progression. In addition, figures such as the Lock Step can be used to extend a Basic Quickstep by half as much again to help put you in the right position. Be aware that less experienced dancers often try to dance an extra Basic Quickstep when really they ought to have started the corner figure. This error often results from the dancer not having planned ahead sufficiently, so it is important to start thinking about the corner as soon as you have danced about halfway along the room.

WALL

FLOW

Less Turn = Less Progression

WALL

More Turn = More Progression

Natural Hairpin and Running Finish

Imagine you are on a zig ready to dance the Basic Quickstep or the Lock Step and the way ahead of you is not clear. Now is the time to dance the Natural Hairpin and conclude it with a very stylish flowing movement called the Running Finish, which can also be used later with other figures.

Natural Hairpin

1
COUNT – SLOW

Man Walk forward with the right foot, curving it outside the woman's right side onto the zig, and start turning to the right.

Woman Walk back with the left foot, starting to curve to the right.

2
COUNT – QUICK

Man Move forward onto the toes of the left foot, continuing to curve strongly to the right.

Woman Move back onto the toes of the right foot, continuing to curve strongly to the right.

Style Tip
To help your turn, see how the man will bank or sway to the right and the woman to the left on Steps 2–3.

3

COUNT – QUICK

Man Walk forward, lowering onto the right foot, slightly across yourself and outside the woman, continuing to curve to the right to end facing almost against the flow.

Woman Take a small step back, lowering onto the left foot underneath your body and continuing to curve strongly to the right to end facing almost with the flow.

Running Finish

The Running Finish can also be danced after Steps 1–3 of the Natural Turn or the Natural Spin Turn. In this case, Step 2 for the woman will be taken in line with the man. At a corner, simply go with the flow and bend the Running Finish around it.

1

COUNT – SLOW

Man Move back along the zig under your body, starting to turn to the right.

Woman Walk forward with the right foot, outside the man's right side and turning to the right along the zig.

2

COUNT – QUICK

Man Move sideways onto the toes of the right foot facing the centre line and, still turning to the right, sway to the left.

Woman Move sideways onto the toes of the left foot facing the wall and, still turning to the right, sway to the right.

3

COUNT – QUICK

Man Swing your left side forward to face with the flow, swaying to the left, and move forward, lowering onto the left foot.

Woman Swing your right side back to face against the flow, swaying to the right, and take a short step back, lowering onto the right foot.

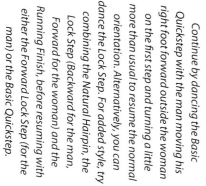

Continue by dancing the Basic Quickstep with the man moving his right foot forward outside the woman on the first step and turning a little more than usual to resume the normal orientation. Alternatively, you can dance the Lock Step, combining the Natural Hairpin, the Lock Step (Backward for the man, Forward for the woman) and the Running Finish, before resuming with either the Forward Lock Step (for the man) or the Basic Quickstep.

Timing Tip
Until you get the hang of this figure, Steps 2 and 3 can be danced as slows.

WALL

FLOW

centre line

starting position

zig

Outside Change

This is another very simple figure but one which has a nice feel to it and which will help add variety to your increasing repertoire of Quickstep moves. It is a good floorcraft move, enabling you to overtake slower couples immediately ahead. In this move, the woman does not turn her body. This results in her ending in a slightly open or "promenade" position on Step 3. You can insert it into your programme after Steps 1–3 of the Natural Turn or the Natural Spin Turn, having reduced the amount of turn ("underturned") a little so that the man ends on a zag facing the wall. The man is standing on his right foot and the woman on her left. Both have their feet together.

1

COUNT – SLOW

Man Walk back with the left foot along the zag.

Woman Walk forward with the right foot.

2

COUNT – QUICK

Man Walk back onto the toes of the right foot, still on the zag, starting to turn to the left.

Woman Walk forward onto the toes of the left foot.

3

COUNT – QUICK

Man Take a small step to the side along the room by lowering onto the left foot to end facing the wall in Promenade Position, with the left foot pointing along the zig.

Woman Take a small step to the side along the room by lowering onto the right foot, pointing it down the room and moving your head to the right to end in Promenade Position.

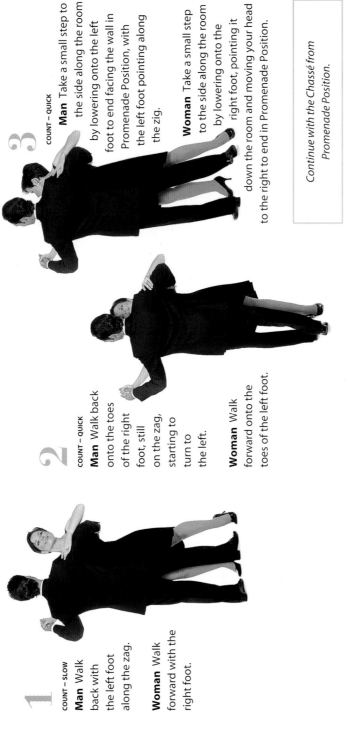

Continue with the Chassé from Promenade Position.

Chassé from Promenade Position

A Chassé is simply a side-close-side movement, and you have already danced this in the Basic Quickstep. Here, the Chassé is danced from the Promenade Position following the Outside Change. The dancers move along a line parallel to the wall but maintaining their zig alignment. In addition, the woman gradually moves her head to the left as she resumes her normal position facing the man.

1

COUNT – SLOW

Man Take a short step forward and across yourself with the right foot, along the line.

Woman Walk forward and across yourself with the left foot, along the line and starting to turn to the left.

2

COUNT – QUICK

Man Move onto the toes of the left foot, still progressing along the same line.

Woman Move sideways onto the toes of the right foot, along the same line and continuing to turn to the left.

3

COUNT – QUICK

Man Close the toes of the right foot to the toes of the left foot.

Woman Close the toes of the left foot to the toes of the right foot, completing the turn to face the man.

4

COUNT – SLOW

Man Move sideways, lowering onto the left foot along the same line to end on the zig.

Woman Move sideways, lowering onto the right foot along the same line to end on the zig.

Continue into the Basic Quickstep, the Natural Turn around a Corner or the Natural Spin Turn, remembering that on Step 1 of the next figure, the man will walk forward with the right foot outside the woman.

WALL

FLOW

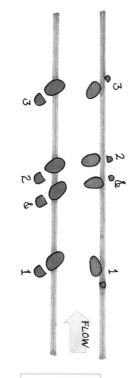

Hover Corté

You can dance the Hover Corté immediately after the Forward Half of the Basic Quickstep (the Quarter Turn to the Right) if your path into the Backward Half (the Progressive Chassé) is blocked. The man is standing on his left foot and the woman on her right, with feet apart.

1

COUNT – SLOW

Man Walk back along the zag with the right foot, starting to turn to the left.

Woman Walk forward along the zag with the left foot, starting to turn to the left.

2

COUNT – SLOW

Man Move sideways onto the toes of the left foot, turning onto the zig and swaying to the right.

Woman Move sideways onto the toes of the right foot, turning onto the zig and swaying to the left.

3

COUNT – SLOW

Man On the zig, lower your body weight sideways onto the right foot.

Woman On the zig, lower your body weight sideways onto the left foot.

Having successfully avoided the problem on the dance floor, continue as follows on the next page.

4

COUNT – SLOW

Man Walk back with the left foot, moving temporarily against the flow.

Woman Walk forward with the right foot, outside the man's right side and moving temporarily against the flow.

5

COUNT – QUICK

Man Move sideways onto the toes of the right foot, swaying to the left.

Woman Move sideways onto the toes of the left foot, swaying to the right.

6

COUNT – QUICK

Man Standing on the toes, close the left foot to the right foot and lower onto the left foot, still swaying to the left. End on the zig.

Woman Standing on the toes, close the right foot to the left foot and lower onto the right foot, still swaying to the right. End on the zig.

Continue into the Basic Quickstep, the Natural Turn, the Natural Spin Turn or the Natural Hairpin, remembering that on Step 1 of the next figure, the man will walk forward with the right foot outside the woman.

Natural Turn with Hesitation

This is a useful variation of the Natural Turn, which can be danced near the beginning or middle of a wall and which combines well with other figures described later in the book. Start by dancing the first three steps of the Natural Turn around a Corner.

1–3

Dance steps 1–3 of the Natural Turn around a Corner.

4

COUNT – SLOW

Man Walk back with the left foot, continuing to turn to the right and releasing the right toes from the floor but keeping the heel in contact with it.

Woman Walk forward with the right foot, continuing to turn to the right.

5

COUNT – SLOW

Man Pull the right foot back with the heel in contact with the floor, then slide the foot around to end to the side of the left foot, with feet apart. Continue turning to the right to end facing along the zag towards the centre line.

Woman Move sideways onto the left foot, staying down with flexed knees and continuing to turn to the right to end on the zag facing the wall.

6

COUNT – SLOW

Man Slide the left foot to close to the right foot but remain standing on the right foot.

Woman Slide the right foot to close to the left foot but remain standing on the left foot.

Continue with the Progressive Chassé to the Right, the Chassé Reverse Turn or the Quick Open Reverse Turn, which are described later.

Chassé Reverse Turn

This is a short but useful figure which follows the Natural Turn with Hesitation described earlier. In dancing terminology, "reverse" simply refers to a turn to the left. It does not mean that the figure moves backwards. The man is standing on his right foot and the woman on her left with the feet almost closed. The man is facing the centre line along the zag and the woman is backing the centre line along the zag.

1

COUNT – SLOW

Man Walk forward with the left foot, along the zag towards the centre line, starting to turn to the left.

Woman Walk back with the right foot, along the zag towards the centre line, starting to turn to the left.

2

COUNT – QUICK

Man Move sideways onto the toes of the right foot, continuing to turn to the left. Sway to the left.

Woman Move sideways onto the toes of the left foot, continuing to turn to the left. Sway to the right.

Sway:

Sway is rather like the banking of a motorcyclist travelling around a bend in the road. It is an important feature of a nice, easy and relaxed style. When dancing a section of Quickstep which has only three steps in the bar, for example, a walk-side-close movement during a turn, it is quite natural for the body and head to tilt or sway a little away from the reaching foot to act as a counter-balance. Natural sway will occur on Steps 2–3 of the Natural Turn in the Swing Dances, to the right for the man and to the left for the woman. Sway is therefore an essential feature of balancing comfortably as you dance.

3

COUNT – QUICK

Man Close the left foot to the right foot and lower onto the left foot. Continue to sway to the left and turn to end facing against the flow.

Woman Close the right foot to the left foot and lower onto the right foot. Continue to sway to the right and turn to end facing with the flow.

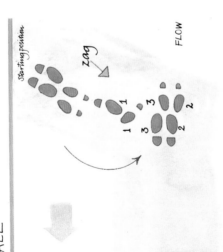

Style Tip

The man will curve his left foot into this move to help lead the turn while the woman takes a shorter step on Step 2 to help the man move around her. The important thing is to keep the flow moving through the turn and allow it to run out into the following chassé.

Continue with the Progressive Chassé (the Backward Half of the Basic Quickstep) but turning it a little more than usual to resume its normal orientation.

WALL

Starting position

zag

centre line

FLOW

Progressive Chassé to the Right

Following the Natural Turn with Hesitation, this figure can move you quickly and easily along the floor with the flow around the room. The Chassé, as usual, is danced along an imaginary line parallel to the wall.

1

COUNT – SLOW

Man Walk forward onto the left foot, starting to turn to the left.

Woman Walk back onto the right foot, starting to turn to the left.

2

COUNT – QUICK

Man Move sideways along the line onto the toes of the right foot, continuing to turn to the left to end with your back square to the wall.

Woman Move sideways along the line onto the toes of the left foot, continuing to turn to face the wall.

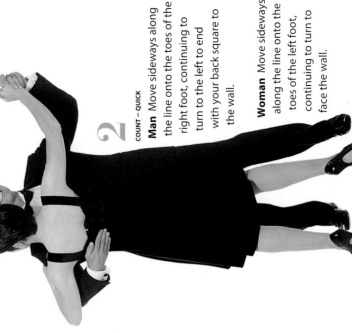

3

COUNT – QUICK

Man Close the toes of the left foot to the toes of the right foot, continuing to turn to the left to end backing along the zig.

Woman Close the toes of the right foot to the toes of the left foot, continuing to turn to the left to end facing along the zig.

You can now continue with a super-smooth ending: either dance the Backward Lock Step followed by the Running Finish or go straight into the Running Finish.

4

COUNT – SLOW

Man Move sideways, still along the line, lowering onto the right foot.

Woman Move sideways, still along the line, lowering onto the left foot.

V-6 Combination

When a figure combination becomes popular, it often becomes a set piece in the dance. The V-6 combines the Backward Lock Step with a modified Outside Change. As the name suggests, the figure makes a "V" pattern, which makes it ideal to dance along the short side of the floor.

The Entry

Dance the Natural Spin Turn around a Corner at the end of a long side and finish it with the man backing the new centre line along a zag. Alternatively, dance Steps 1–3 of the Natural Spin Turn, starting on the short side (after a Natural Turn around a Corner) and underturning the move to 90° to end backing the new centre line along a zag.

Backward Lock Step

If you danced the Natural Spin Turn as the entry, now dance Steps 2–4 of the Lock Step (Backward for the man and Forward for the woman), moving towards the centre line of the short side of the floor. If the alternative entry of Steps 1–3 of the Natural Turn has been used, then dance Steps 1–4 of the Lock Step (Backward for the man and Forward for the woman), with the woman taking her first step in line with the man.

Outside Change

The Outside Change is now modified to fit the different context in which it is danced.

1

COUNT – SLOW

Man Walk back with the left foot underneath your body, along the zag.

Woman Walk forward with the right foot outside the man's right side.

2

COUNT – QUICK

Man Walk back onto the toes of the right foot, still on the zag and starting to turn to the left.

Woman Walk forward onto the toes of the left foot, starting to turn to the left.

Lock Step Exit

The best exit to this combination is for the man to dance the Forward Lock Step and the woman to dance the Backward Lock Step. The angle at the point of the "V" may be adjusted so that the V-6 can be fitted exactly into the short side of many ballrooms. If you find that this is the case, you can return to your programme by dancing into one of the corner figures, such as the Natural Spin Turn, remembering that the first step of the following figure for the man will be outside his partner. Otherwise, continue into the Basic Quickstep or a "natural" figure.

3

COUNT – QUICK

Man Take a small step to the side along the room by lowering onto the left foot to end facing the wall, with the left foot pointing along the zig.

Woman Take a small step to the side along the room by lowering onto the right foot to end backing the wall.

Summary of Counts for the V-6 Combination

Natural Spin Turn	Slow, Quick, Quick, Slow, Slow, Slow
Steps 2–4 of the Backward Lock Step (man) and Forward Lock Step (woman)	Quick, Quick, Slow
Modified Outside Change	Slow, Quick, Quick
Forward Lock Step (man) and Backward Lock Step (woman)	Slow, Quick, Quick, Slow

If the alternative entry is used, the count will be:

Steps 1–3 of the Natural Spin Turn	Slow, Quick, Quick
Steps 1–4 of the Lock Step	Slow, Quick, Quick, Slow

Tipple Chassé Around a Corner

Now that you are building up a repertoire of useful and enjoyable figures, you can combine parts of the moves you already know with a new element in a popular and attractive group – the Tipple Chassé. This is a very flexible figure and, in the first combination, you can use it around a corner. Remember to allow sufficient room ahead of you to dance the figure. For the entry, start by dancing Steps 1-3 of the Natural Turn around a Corner or the Natural Spin Turn.

Entry

The man is now facing against the flow with his feet together and standing on his right foot. The woman is facing with the flow with her feet together and standing on her left foot.

1

COUNT – SLOW

Man Walk back with the left foot, starting to turn to the right.

Woman Walk forward with the right foot, starting to turn to the right.

2

COUNT – QUICK

Man Move sideways onto the toes of the right foot, completing a quarter (90°) turn to the right to face with the flow along the new wall. Sway to the right and look past the woman's left shoulder.

Woman Move sideways onto the toes of the left foot, completing a quarter (90°) turn to the right to face against the flow along the new wall and swaying to the left.

Style Tip
The man should dance this section taking small steps.

3

COUNT – QUICK

Man Close the toes of the left foot to the toes of the right foot, still swaying to the right.

Woman Close the toes of the right foot to the toes of the left foot, still swaying to the left.

4

COUNT – SLOW

Man Move sideways onto the toes of the right foot, swaying to the right and turning onto the zig of the new wall.

Woman Move sideways onto the toes of the left foot, swaying to the left and turning onto the zig of the new wall.

Variation

When you have practised the standard Tipple Chassé, you can develop it further by introducing the Backward Lock Step for the man and the Forward Lock Step for the woman between the Entry and the Tipple Chassé. The woman must make some modifications to ensure that the move goes smoothly:

• take Step 1 of the Forward Lock Step in line with the man.

• take Step 1 of the Tipple Chassé outside the man's right side. The count for this Lock Step will be the usual slow, quick, quick, slow.

Continue along the zig of the new wall by dancing Steps 2–4 of the Forward Lock Step for the man and the Backward Lock Step for the woman. The man will move his left side forward and the woman her right side back as they move into the Lock Step.

Tipple Chassé along the Room

In this combination, the Tipple Chassé is used in a different position. This time, you will be dancing it along the side of the room.

Entry

Dance the Progressive Chassé to the Right, followed by the Backward Lock Step for the man and the Forward Lock Step for the woman, along the zig.

1

COUNT – SLOW

Man Walk back with the left foot, starting to turn to the right.

Woman Walk forward with the right foot, outside the man's right side, starting to turn to the right.

2

COUNT – QUICK

Man Move sideways onto the toes of the right foot, turning to the right. Sway to the right and look past the woman's left shoulder.

Woman Move sideways onto the toes of the left foot, turning to the right and swaying to the left.

Style Tip

The man should dance this section taking small steps.

3

COUNT – QUICK

Man Close the toes of the left foot to the toes of the right foot, still swaying and looking to the right.

Woman Close the toes of the right foot to the toes of the left foot, still swaying to the left.

4

COUNT – SLOW

Man Move sideways onto the toes of the right foot, swaying to the right and turning onto the zig.

Woman Move sideways onto the toes of the left foot, swaying to the left and turning onto the zig.

Continue by dancing Steps 2–4 of the Forward Lock Step for the man and the Backward Lock Step for the woman. The man will move his left side forward and the woman her right side back as they move into the Lock Step.

Modern Tango

The "Modern" in Modern Tango differentiates it from the original and authentic style of Argentine Tango. By the early 1930s, the Tango had been so changed from the original style in order to conform with the conventions of the ballroom, that it had developed into a completely different and quite separate dance.

The Modern Tango established itself as one of the standard dances of the ballroom and as a compulsory dance for Standard Championships. The hard, arrogant style of the Tango in competition dancing belies its essentially romantic nature when danced in a social setting. For competitive dancing, the infamous and affected Tango head-flicks have become the established style, but these are not necessary just to enjoy dancing the Modern Tango for the fun and pleasure it can bring.

The Modern Tango does, however, use a very different technique to the other Standard dances, and we must first explore some of these differences. They exist because, unlike the other Standard dances, the Tango is not a "swing dance". The power and impetus come from the legs rather than from the body swing of the Waltz, Quickstep or Slow Foxtrot. There is therefore no sway, rise or fall, and the Tango is danced flat and into the floor. This actually makes it easier to learn for first-time dancers. The hold is also different.

Music Suggestions

"La Cumparsita" must be the world's best-known and best-loved Tango. The James Last version of "Adios Pampa Mia", written by two of the masters of Tango composition, is my personal favourite, though it does need slowing down slightly for dancing. Klaus Hallen's arrangement of "Verano Porteño" is an excellent version of an authentic Argentinian Tango. Many Tango compilation albums exist, but be careful to choose one which specifies that it is for dancing rather than for listening. Those recorded by the Japanese orchestra of Hisao Sudou are very good and are readily available from specialist dealers worldwide.

The Tango Hold & Feet Positions

Take up a normal ballroom hold. Now, allowing the feet to swivel on the spot, twist the body and feet a little to the left. The result of twisting the body and legs to the left will mean that the right foot will be slightly behind the left foot, so that the inside edge of the ball of the right foot nestles against the instep of the left foot. Both knees will be flexed. The man's right hand will now be a little further around the woman's back – the man lowers his right hand a little. The woman places her left hand *under* the man's upper right arm, ensuring that her fingers are straight. The man's lower left and the woman's lower right arm are flattened slightly towards the floor.

The Hold & Feet Position seen from behind.

The Hold & Feet Position seen in front.

 MODERN TANGO: the tango hold & feet positions   **217**

The Tango Walks

The method of walking in Tango has become an important and integral feature of the dance. Due to the slightly twisted starting position:

- any walk forward with the left foot will be taken slightly across the body.

- any walk back with the left foot will be taken with the left side of the body moving with the moving foot.

- any walk forward with the right foot will be taken with the right side of the body advancing with the moving foot.

- any walk back with the right foot will be taken slightly across the body.

This means that a series of forward walks would quite naturally curve a little to the left. If the walks are made to go in a straight line, the effect and feel will be of a slight crabbing action. This may seem strange at first but it will soon become an integral part of the dance for you.

Forward walk with the left foot.

Backward walk with the left foot.

Forward walk with the right foot.

Backward walk with the right foot.

Timing and Rhythm

The time signature of the Modern Tango is officially 2/4 but many Tangos are also arranged to a 4/4 time signature. This need not concern the social dancer, who can recognize a Tango by its march-like rhythm. The tempo or speed of the dance is normally 32–33 bars per minute.

The basic rhythm of the Modern Tango is Quick-Quick-Slow, but many moves either incorporate or are often preceded by two preparatory Slow walks.

The Tango Action

The "action" merely describes the type or style of movement used. In Tango, it is important to "place" the feet. That is to say that the feet are picked up and placed gently but firmly in position. They are not slid along the floor and they should never be stamped down. When releasing a foot from the floor, the heel should be released first and then the rest of the foot peeled off. All forward walks will be with a heel. In side movements, the inside edge of the foot will usually contact the floor first and then the body weight will be rolled on to the foot. When closing, the foot will be flat.

Much is made of the Tango "staccato" action. It is true that experienced dancers do enhance the appearance and style of the Tango by a sharp action, but the ways of doing this are often misunderstood by less-experienced dancers. The staccato action is a result of a sharp movement which stops suddenly and clearly. The effect, though, is greater than reality, because the abrupt and clear stopping of the movement causes the spectator's eye to continue following the track of the movement for a fraction of a second. This is interpreted by the brain with an over-compensation for what has actually happened. Thus, the staccato action is a clever visual illusion and, like the head-flicks, should be explored under the guidance of an experienced instructor. Dancers who don't develop this skill under expert guidance tend to produce an exaggerated effect which is less than flattering to their dancing.

Leading

As in the other Standard Partner dances, the man establishes a frame with his hold. If the man's arms are held in place and are not allowed to move independently of the body, the woman will be held in the frame and will have little option but to follow the man's intentions. While both dancers' movements are strong, the man must never push or pull the woman into a move or position.

The Rock Turn

To start your Tango, we will use a gentle basic move which includes two easy turns. The couple start on the zig as normal, having first adopted the special Tango hold. The man is standing, feet together, on the right foot and the woman, feet together, on her left foot. Be sure to use the Tango Walk technique and the appropriate action.

1
COUNT – SLOW

Man Walk forward with the left foot along the zig.

Woman Walk back with the right foot.

2
COUNT – SLOW

Man Walk forward with the right foot along the zig.

Woman Walk back with the left foot.

3
COUNT – QUICK

Man Rock back onto the left foot.

Woman Rock forward on to the right foot.

4
COUNT – QUICK

Man Rock forward onto the right foot.

Woman Rock back onto the left foot.

5
COUNT – SLOW

Man Walk back onto the left foot.

Woman Walk forward onto the right foot.

6
COUNT – QUICK

Man Walk back onto the right foot starting to turn left.

Woman Walk forward onto the left foot, starting to turn left.

7
COUNT – QUICK

Man Left foot to the side onto the zig.

Woman Right foot to the side onto the zig.

8
COUNT – SLOW

Man Close the right foot to the left foot, to end standing on the right foot on the zig.

Woman Close the left foot to the right foot, to end standing on the left foot on the zig.

Between Steps 2–5, gradually turn right to end on the zag.

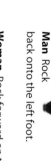

You can now repeat the move as often as you like as you progress around the room. At a corner, dance the same move but miss out the turn over Steps 2–5 and you will end on the zig of the new wall. When you feel comfortable with the Rock Turn, it's time to try out the Progressive Link.

MAN
WOMAN

FLOW

zig
zag
zig
zag
zig

The Progressive Link and Closed Promenade

This is one of the classic moves of the Modern Tango. It is the Progressive Link which, for competitors, incorporates the famous head-flick, but here, we can enjoy a less ostentatious version. Start in the same position as for the Rock Turn.

The Progressive Link

1

COUNT – QUICK

Man Walk forward with the left foot along the zig.

Woman Walk back onto the right foot along the zig and, on the right foot, swivel a little to the right, turning the head to look along the room.

2

COUNT – QUICK

Man Step sideways onto the right foot, turning the body to face the wall. End in Promenade Position.

Woman Step sideways and back onto the left foot to end in Promenade Position, with the head to the right.

Promenade Position is explained fully in the Waltz section.

Style Point

To enhance the feel and appearance of the Progressive Link, the man may suggest added emphasis to the move by looking across the woman's left shoulder on Step 1 before returning his head to the left to look along the room on Step 2. When this decoration is exaggerated and emphasized, it results in the head-flick previously mentioned.

The Closed Promenade

It is conventional in Tango terminology, but confusing for students, to name Modern Tango moves in the reverse order to the sequence in which they happen. A Closed Promenade can therefore be more appropriately explained as a Promenade movement with a Close. Here's how to do it. The dancers have completed the Progressive Link by achieving a Promenade Position. In the Closed Promenade, the dancers move from that Promenade Position back to a closed or normal position.

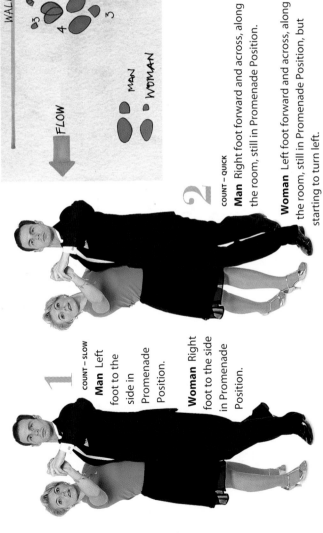

1

COUNT – SLOW

Man Left foot to the side in Promenade Position.

Woman Right foot to the side in Promenade Position.

2

COUNT – QUICK

Man Right foot forward and across, along the room, still in Promenade Position.

Woman Left foot forward and across, along the room, still in Promenade Position, but starting to turn left.

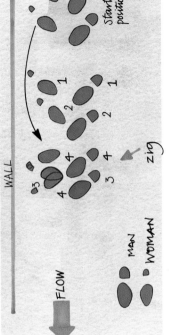

During this move, the woman gradually turns to the left to end facing the man. The woman gradually returns her head to left over the move.

3
COUNT – QUICK

Man Move the left foot to the side on to the zig.

Woman Turning left to face the man, move the right foot along the room.

4
COUNT – SLOW

Man Close the right foot to the left foot on the zig.

Woman Facing the man, close the left foot to the right foot.

Topical Tip
It is helpful for the dancers to think of themselves travelling along a set of tramlines. The man travels along one and the woman along the other. Each takes his or her own steps precisely on that tramline.

The Progressive Link and Closed Promenade can now be alternated with the Rock Turn. If, however, you find you are gradually dancing closer to the wall, you can remedy this problem by changing the angle of the entry into the Rock Turn to be more shallow, and by increasing its first turn more to the right. It's fun building up your experience by experimenting.

The Combination Reverse Turn

We now need to put together a short amalgamation of moves which, individually, would consist of the progressive side step, right foot walk and reverse turn, woman outside, closed finish. This combination will take you away from the wall and towards the centre line of the room as you progress along it, making a turn to the left. After the previous figures, this will add balance to the overall look and feel of your Tango. Let's now break down the combination into its constituent parts and build them up together. The dancers start in the normal position.

The Progressive Side Step
In this move, you will turn a quarter turn (90°) to the left over its three steps. Starting on the zig, you will therefore end on the zag, facing the centre line of the room.

1
COUNT – QUICK

Man Walk forward with the left foot, starting to curve to the left.

Woman Walk back with the left foot, starting to curve to the left.

2
COUNT – QUICK

Man Move the right foot to the side and slightly back, continuing the curve to the left.

Woman Move the right foot to the side and slightly forward, continuing the curve to the left.

3
COUNT – SLOW

Man Walk forward with the left foot onto the zag, towards the centre line of the room.

Woman Walk back with the right foot onto the zag, towards the centre line of the room.

The Reverse Turn

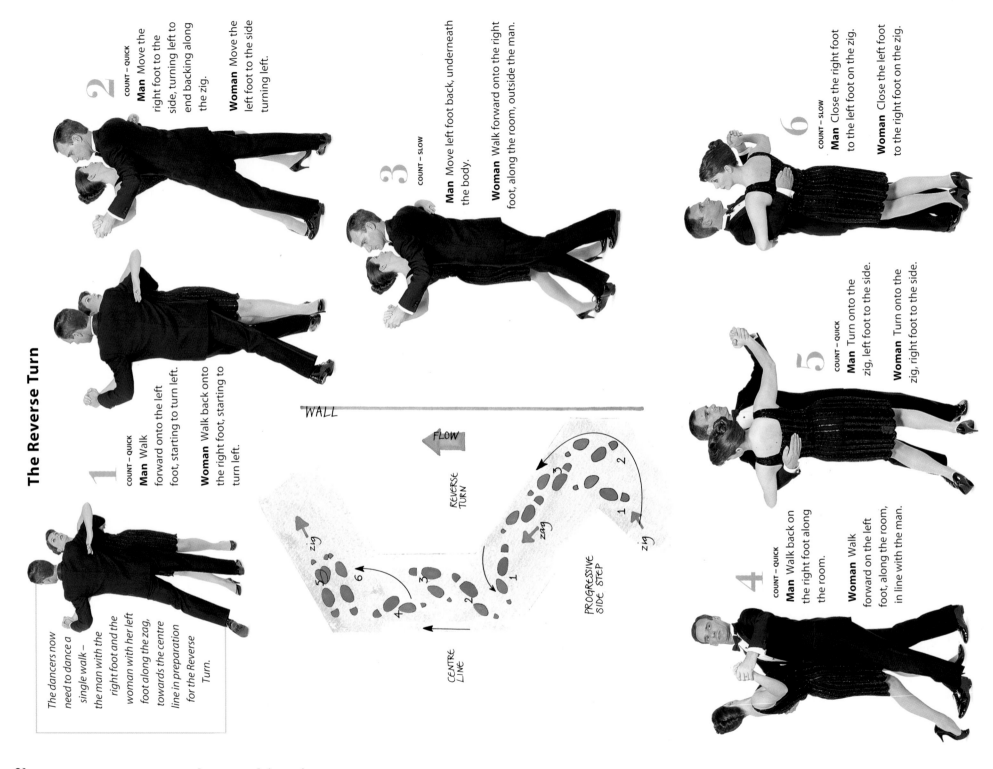

The dancers now need to dance a single walk – the man with the right foot and the woman with her left foot along the zag, towards the centre line in preparation for the Reverse Turn.

1
COUNT – QUICK

Man Walk forward onto the left foot, starting to turn left.

Woman Walk back onto the right foot, starting to turn left.

2
COUNT – QUICK

Man Move the right foot to the side, turning left to end backing along the zig.

Woman Move the left foot to the side turning left.

3
COUNT – SLOW

Man Move left foot back, underneath the body.

Woman Walk forward onto the right foot, along the room, outside the man.

4
COUNT – QUICK

Man Walk back on the right foot along the room.

Woman Walk forward on the left foot, along the room, in line with the man.

5
COUNT – QUICK

Man Turn onto the zig, left foot to the side.

Woman Turn onto the zig, right foot to the side.

6
COUNT – SLOW

Man Close the right foot to the left foot on the zig.

Woman Close the left foot to the right foot on the zig.

WALL

FLOW

REVERSE TURN

zig

zag

zig

PROGRESSIVE SIDE STEP

CENTRE LINE

The Reverse Turn Variation

When **basic figures or moves** are modified, they are called variations. Here is a variation of the Reverse Turn which will add extra verve to the basic figure. The variation comes in the second part of the Reverse Turn, so you can dance Steps 1–4 as normal.

5
COUNT – QUICK
Man Left foot to the side facing the wall.

Woman Right foot to the side facing the centre line.

Note that the count on Steps 5–6 is split so that the two steps are danced in just one beat of music. Continue from the Promenade Position with the Closed Promenade that you danced earlier, following the Progressive Link.

6
COUNT – &
Man Close the right foot to the left foot.

Woman Close the left foot to the right foot.

7
COUNT – SLOW
Man Tap or touch the left foot to the side moving into Promenade Position, looking along the room.

Woman Tap or touch the right foot to the side moving into Promenade Position, looking along the room.

The Brush Tap

You have already used the Progressive Side Step and a Walk to manoeuvre from the zig on to the zag, ready to dance the Reverse Turn. The nature of that move makes it inherently cautious. Here is an alternative which is much bolder and more confident – the Brush Tap. Start as you would for the Progressive Side Step. Start on the zig in the starting position. The man is standing on his right foot and the woman on her left foot.

1
COUNT – QUICK
Man Walk forward onto the left foot, starting to curve to the left.

Woman Walk back on to the right foot, starting to curve to the left.

2
COUNT – QUICK
Man Walk forward and sideways, onto the right foot, continuing to curve to the left to end on the zag, ready to move forward towards the centre line.

Woman Walk back and side onto the left foot, continuing to curve to the left to end backing along the zag, towards the centre line.

The best effect is achieved by keeping the head and upper body still during the Brush Tap on Steps 3–4. It is a mistake to try and embellish the move with any head movements because they detract from the sharpness of movement in the feet, making the move look untidy. Continue with two Tango Walks into the Reverse Turn, or with the Reverse Turn Variation.

4

COUNT – SLOW

Man Touch the left foot to the side, without weight.

Woman Touch the right foot to the side, without weight.

3

COUNT – &

Man Bring the left foot to touch the right foot.

Woman Bring the right foot to touch the left foot.

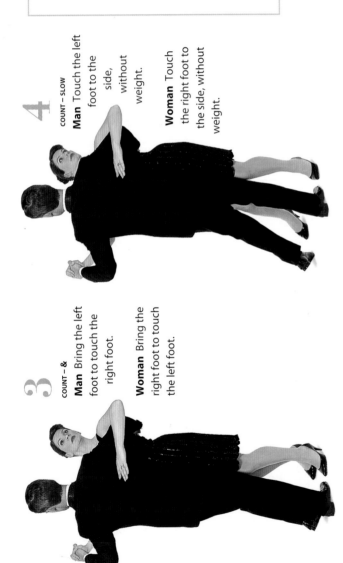

Cornering

Care should be taken to choose an appropriate way of turning around corners in the Modern Tango. A Reverse Turn should never be used, as it not only distorts the shape of the figure but is extremely uncomfortable for the woman. The Rock Turn is an excellent figure to use, when no turn is made over Steps 2–5. This will be comfortable for both the man and the woman. The Progressive Side Step, followed by a right-foot Walk for the man and a left-foot Walk for the woman to a count of "Slow" is another useful way of turning a corner. This can then be followed at the start of the new side by the Rock Turn, the Progressive Link or by another Progressive Side Step as part of the Combination Reverse Turn. Another useful figure to choose at a corner is the Four Step.

The Four Step at a Corner

This is a neat and compact move which is excellent to use at a corner. Start near to the corner on a zig. The man is standing on his right foot, feet together, and the woman on her left foot, feet together.

1

COUNT – QUICK

Man Walk forward with the left foot, starting to turn left.

Woman Walk back with the right foot, starting to turn left.

2

COUNT – QUICK

Man Move to the side and slightly back on to the right foot, completing a quarter turn to the left, to end on the zig of the new wall.

Woman Move to the side and slightly forward onto the left foot, along the zag.

Style Tip

Advanced dancers will sharpen up the Four Step by splitting the beat on Step 1, to dance the Walk on the first part and the turn on the second part of the beat.

The Four Step Along the Side of the Room

The Four Step's versatility also enables it to be danced along the side of the room where it has become a standard figure. Start in the normal position on a zig.

COUNT – QUICK 1

Man Walk forward with the left foot along the zig.

Woman Walk back with the right foot along the zig.

COUNT – QUICK 2

Man Move to the side and slightly back onto the right foot along the zag towards the wall.

Woman Move to the side and slightly forward onto the left foot along the zag.

COUNT – QUICK 3

Man Walk back underneath the body onto the left foot.

Woman Walk forward with the right foot outside the man's right side.

COUNT – QUICK 4

Man Close the right foot to the left foot and end in Promenade Position with the head to the right.

Woman Swivelling a quarter turn (90°) to right on the right foot, close the left foot to the right foot, moving the head to the right, to end in Promenade Position.

Continue along the new wall by dancing the Closed Promenade.

3

COUNT – QUICK

Man Walk back underneath the body onto the left foot.

Woman Walk forward with the right foot outside the man's right side.

4

COUNT – QUICK

Man Close the right foot to the left foot and end in Promenade Position.

Woman Swivelling a quarter turn (90°) to the right on the right foot, close the left foot to the right foot, moving the head to right to end in Promenade Position.

You are now ready to move from Promenade Position along the zag towards the centre line. You can achieve this with the Closed Promenade, ending with the man facing along the zag towards the centre line of the room. The man should then take a small step on step 3 and follow with the Reverse Turn. Alternatively, try the smart Promenade Link.

The Promenade Link

The Promenade Link should not be confused with the Progressive Link, which is a completely different figure. We shall use the Promenade Link as a snappy way of moving from Promenade Position to a normal position, having danced the Four Step along the side of the room. Start in Promenade Position on the zag, ready to move towards the centre line of the room. The man is on his right foot and the woman on her left foot.

1

COUNT – SLOW

Man Move sideways along the zag onto the left foot, still in Promenade Position.

Woman Move sideways along the zag onto the right foot, still in Promenade Position.

2

COUNT – QUICK

Man Walk forward and across onto the right foot, starting to turn left.

Woman Walk forward and across on to the left foot, starting to turn left and closing the body towards the man.

3

COUNT – QUICK

Man Touch the left foot to the side without weight, knees together, turning to end facing along the zag towards the centre line.

Woman Touch the right foot to the side without weight, knees together, turning to end facing the man with the head to the left.

Continue either straight into the Reverse Turn, or two Walks into the Reverse Turn or Reverse Turn Variation.

The Outside Swivel

You now have, in your repertoire, a variety of ways of dancing into the Reverse Turn and Reverse Turn Variation. Let us now explore a classy option that you can enjoy instead of the Reverse Turn.

1

COUNT – QUICK

Man Walk forward onto the left foot, starting to turn left.

Woman Walk back onto the right foot, starting to turn left.

2

COUNT – QUICK

Man Right foot to the side, turning left to end backing along the zig.

Woman Move sideways on to the left foot, still turning left.

3

COUNT – SLOW

Man Move back onto the left foot underneath the body along the zag and, swivelling on the left foot, slide the right foot left until it's pointing along the zig towards the wall.

Woman Walk forward onto the right foot outside the man's right side. Then, bring the left foot to the right foot and swivel a quarter turn to the right on the right foot.

Conclude the move by dancing Steps 2–3 of the Promenade Link so that the man ends on the zig, facing the wall. It is important for the woman not to take too big a walk on Step 3 and for the couple to keep the move reasonably compact. A nice figure to follow the Outside Swivel is the Progressive Link and Closed Promenade. At a corner, dance either the Four Step or the Rock Turn as described earlier.

The Five Step

The Five Step is one of the most flexible, compact and useful figures in the Modern Tango and is full of character and style. One of the most popular places to include the Five Step is instead of the Reverse Turn or Outside Swivel. Start as for a Reverse Turn or Outside Swivel.

1

COUNT – QUICK

Man Walk forward onto the left foot, starting to turn left.

Woman Walk back onto the right foot, starting to turn left.

2

COUNT – QUICK

Man Move the right foot to the side, turning left to end backing along the zig.

Woman Move sideways onto the left foot, still turning left.

3

COUNT – QUICK

Man Move back onto the left foot along the zag, leading the woman to dance outside your right side.

Woman Walk forward onto the right foot outside the man's right side, along the zag.

4

COUNT – QUICK

Man Move back onto the right foot along the zag, leading the woman to dance in line. Turn the body slightly to the left and turn the head to look to the right over the woman's left shoulder.

Woman Walk forward on to the left foot in line with the man, still along the zag.

5

COUNT – SLOW

Man Touch the left foot to the side, without weight, leading the woman into Promenade Position, and turning the head smartly to the left to look along the zig.

Woman Touch the right foot to the side without weight, moving into Promenade Position and turning the head smartly to the right to look along the zig.

Continue with the Promenade Link ending with the man facing along the zig towards the wall. The Five Step can also be substituted for the Four Step by reducing the amount of turn to correspond with the pattern of the Four Step.

The Four Step Photo Figure

This is a fabulous figure and one which develops the Four Step into a photo opportunity. The distinctive "X"-line, which is the highlight of the move, is one which top dancers often use for competitions and which photographers love to capture, as it just exudes the look, feel and character of Modern Tango. Dance the Four Step along the side of the room as previously described.

The "X"-line

The couple achieve the "X" line on Step 5. It is so called because the lines through the bodies and legs form an "X".

5

COUNT – SLOW

Man Flex the right knee and sharply move the left foot out to point to the side, without weight, at right angles to the zag line, and leading the woman to turn slightly to her right.

Woman Flex the left knee and sharply move the right foot out to point back and to the side, without weight, at right angles to the zag line and turning slightly to the right.

6

COUNT – SLOW

Man Retaining a flexed right knee, move the extended left foot back in a circular movement "Rondé". When it is behind the right foot, move back onto the left foot, a small step, along the zag towards the wall.

Woman Retaining a flexed left knee, move the extended right foot back in a circular movement "Rondé", and when it is behind the left foot, move back onto the right foot, a small step, along the zag towards the wall.

Special Effects

Great special effects can be used in the Modern Tango to create the atmosphere of the dance. Perhaps surprisingly, with a little bit of know-how, many of these effects are quite easy to put into practice.

Stillness is the Essence of Tango

If other floor traffic is blocking your route, stop and remain perfectly still. Do not attempt to move again until your path is clear. Dancers often find it difficult just to stop and remain still but, in the original Argentine Tango, pauses formed an integral and essential part of the dance, and these can be used very effectively in the Modern Tango too.

Moving into Promenade Position with Panache

Imagine you are in your normal starting position and another couple is obstructing your intended path towards the wall. You can wait, or you can move sharply into Promenade Position and then progress down the room.

1

COUNT – &

Man Extend and point the left foot forward and slightly across, leg straight, without weight, and looking to the right over the woman's left shoulder.

Woman Extend and point the right foot back and slightly beneath the body, leg straight, without weight. Turn the head a little more to the left than normal.

2

COUNT – SLOW

Man Bring the left foot sharply back to touch to the side, without weight, in Promenade Position.

Woman Bring the right foot sharply forward to touch to the side, without weight, in Promenade Position and turn the head sharply to the right.

7

COUNT – &

Man Close the right foot sharply to the left foot, turning square to the woman.

Woman Close the left foot sharply to the right foot, turning square to the man.

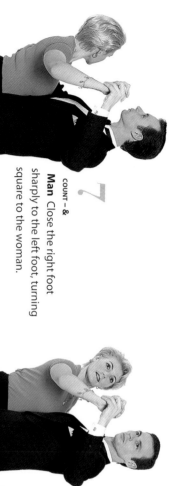

8

COUNT – SLOW

Man Touch the left foot to the side, without weight, and turn the head to the right in Promenade Position.

Woman Touch the right foot to the side, without weight, and turn the head to the left in Promenade Position.

Continue with *Closed Promenade, moving along the zag towards the centre line or with the Promenade Link.*

The Promenade Chassé

The Promenade Chassé is a very effective way of moving along the room in Promenade Position while creating a special effect. Start and finish in Promenade Position and keep the knees flexed throughout.

1
COUNT – QUICK

Man Move sideways onto the left foot in Promenade Position.

Woman Move sideways onto the right foot in Promenade Position.

2
COUNT – QUICK

Man Close the right foot to the left foot in Promenade Position.

Woman Close the left foot to the right foot in Promenade Position.

3
COUNT – QUICK

Man Repeat Steps 1–2.

Woman Repeat Steps 1–2.

4
COUNT – SLOW

Man Touch the left foot to the side without weight, and in Promenade Position.

Woman Touch the right foot to the side, without weight, and in Promenade Position.

Polishing up a Pause in Promenade

When in Promenade Position and the way ahead is not clear, you can make a feature of the delay as follows.

1
COUNT – SLOW

Man Move back underneath the body onto the left foot.

Woman Move back underneath the body onto the right foot.

2
COUNT – &

Man Close the right foot sharply to the left foot, turning square to the woman.

Woman Close the left foot sharply to the right foot, turning square to the man.

3
COUNT – SLOW

Man Touch the left foot to the side, without weight, and turn the head to the left in Promenade Position.

Woman Touch the right foot to the side, without weight, and turn the head to the right in Promenade Position.

Slow Foxtrot

The Slow Foxtrot, as its name suggests, is the slower version of the Foxtrot. The quicker version of the Foxtrot evolved into the Quickstep, and the background to both dances is described in the Quickstep chapter. The Slow Foxtrot is a beautiful, romantic dance which has become the classic swing dance of the ballroom and the dance to which ballroom dancers most aspire. However, the simple, graceful lines of the Slow Foxtrot belie the technical understanding, dance experience and physical skill required to produce them. It is customary and advisable, therefore, for dancers discovering the Slow Foxtrot to have previously mastered the basics of the Waltz and Quickstep. Practice not only makes perfect, it makes possible and, with repeated practice, the sheer delight of this dance's understated and sophisticated elegance comes ever closer.

The Slow Foxtrot is undoubtedly more of a challenging dance than the other Standard Partner dances. However, with a growing understanding, a lot of application and not a little practice, you will be surprised at how much you can achieve and how great the rewards are. Contact your local qualified dance teacher for further help in enjoying the Slow Foxtrot.

Timing and Rhythm

The Slow Foxtrot has a gentle tempo of 30 bars per minute, a time signature of 4/4 and a steady rhythm of Slow-Quick-Quick, where a Slow equals two beats and a Quick equals one.

Music Suggestions

Slow Foxtrot engenders the best of swing, like "On the Sunny Side of the Street", and contemporary favourites like "This Business of Love" from the hit movie The Mask. Romantic ballads such as "Nice 'n' Easy" by Frank Sinatra and Hugo Strasser's superb version of "Autumn Leaves" "Der Schleier Viel" are also classic Slow Foxtrots. Whatever your musical taste, you will be able to indulge it by consulting your specialist dance music supplier.

A Short Programme

The Slow Foxtrot, unlike the Waltz, Quickstep and Social Foxtrot, does not have a simple, enjoyable, repeatable basic move, so we must first build up a short programme of 12 steps, consisting of the Feather Finish, the Three Step and the Impetus Turn.

The Feather Finish

It may seem odd to start a dance with a Feather Finish, but this is simply the ending of another figure which we shall encounter later. Take up the standard hold. The man is standing on his left foot, feet together on the zig and the woman on her right foot, feet together.

1

COUNT – SLOW

Man Walk back onto the right foot and extend the left foot to rest sideways along the zag.

Woman Walk forward onto the left foot and extend the right foot to rest sideways along the zag.

Sway

Sway is the natural inclination of the body as a result of swing. It helps to give a nice, easy, relaxed style to the movement. When reaching to make a step on one foot, the body will naturally tend to incline in order to counterbalance itself. In Slow Foxtrot, the swing will generally alternate from one side of the body to the other over three steps. At the changeover point from one swing to another, there will be no sway. The sway pattern of Slow Foxtrot will therefore generally be straight-right-right, straight-left-left and will then repeat. Exceptions to the sway pattern will occur on certain types of turns, such as the Impetus Turn.

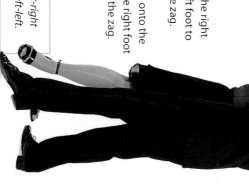

Man's Sway – straight-right-right
Woman's Sway – straight-left-left.

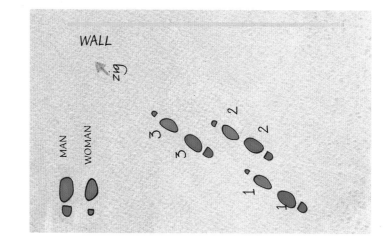

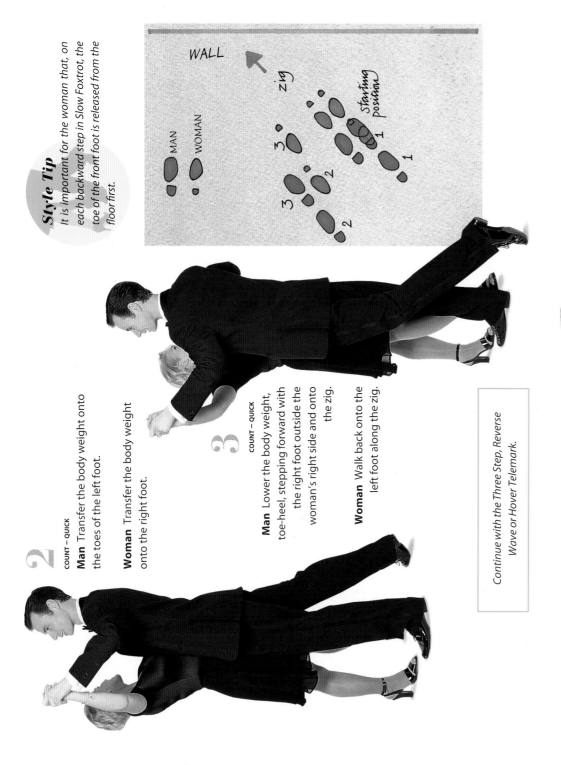

Style Tip
It is important for the woman that, on each backward step in Slow Foxtrot, the toe of the front foot is released from the floor first.

2

COUNT – QUICK

Man Transfer the body weight onto the toes of the left foot.

Woman Transfer the body weight onto the right foot.

3

COUNT – QUICK

Man Lower the body weight, toe-heel, stepping forward with the right foot outside the woman's right side and onto the zig.

Woman Walk back onto the left foot along the zig.

Continue with the Three Step, Reverse Wave or Hover Telemark.

The Three Step

1

COUNT – SLOW

Man Walk forward onto the left foot in-line with the woman and swing the right foot forward along the zig.

Woman Walk back onto the left foot, releasing the toe of the front foot.

Man's Sway – straight-left-left
Woman's Sway – straight-right-right

SLOW FOXTROT: the feather finish/the three step

The Impetus Turn

2
COUNT – QUICK

Man Transfer the body weight forward onto the right foot and lift from the heel onto the toes of the right foot.

Woman Walk back onto the right foot, releasing the toe of the front foot.

3
COUNT – QUICK

Man Lower the body weight stepping forward, toe-heel, onto the left foot along the zig.

Woman Walk back onto the left foot, releasing the toe of the front foot.

Continue into the Impetus or Open Impetus Turn.

1
COUNT – SLOW

Man Walk forward onto the right foot starting to turn right and swing the left foot forward along the zig.

Woman Walk back onto the left foot, starting to turn right.

Man's Sway – straight-right-right, straight-left-straight
Woman's Sway – straight-left-left, straight-right-straight

Cornering

In your Short Programme, you should aim to dance into a corner using the Impetus Turn. As you exit the corner, the man will be on the zag of the new wall, backing the centre line. As you start your Short Programme again, the couple will need to make a quarter turn (90°) to the left over Steps 1-2 of the Feather Finish.

2
COUNT – QUICK

Man Transfer the body weight onto the toes of the left foot turning right to end backing along the room.

Woman Pull the right heel back in contact with the floor to close to the left foot. On the left heel and with the feet together, make a three-eighths turn (135°) to the right to end facing along the room and lift onto the toes of the right foot.

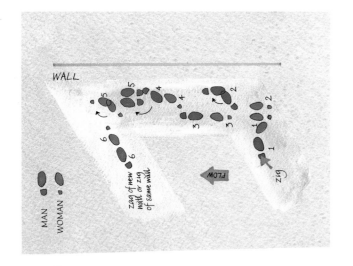

WALL

MAN
WOMAN

FLOW

zig

zag of new wall or zig of same wall

3

COUNT – QUICK

Man Walk back onto the right foot, lowering toe-heel.

Woman Walk forward onto the left foot, in-line with the man, lowering toe-heel.

4

COUNT – SLOW

Man Walk back onto the left foot, starting to turn right.

Woman Walk forward onto the right foot, starting to turn right and swing the left foot forward past the man.

5

COUNT – QUICK

Man Pull the right heel back in contact with the floor, to close to the left foot. On the left heel and with the feet together, make a three-eighths turn (135°) to the right to end on the zag facing the centre line of the room and lift onto the toes of the right foot.

Woman Still turning right, transfer the body weight sideways onto the toes of the left foot and bring the right back to touch or brush the side of the left foot completing a three-eighths turn (135°) to end on the zag, backing the centre line.

6

COUNT – QUICK

Man Continuing to turn on the right foot, step to the side and slightly back lowering the body weight, toe-heel, onto the left foot to end on the zig, backing the centre line.

Woman Still turning on the toes of the left foot, step diagonally forward onto the right foot, lowering toe-heel, to end on the zig, facing the centre line.

Continue with the Feather Finish.

This Short Programme, consisting of the Feather Finish – Three Step – Impetus Turn, can then be repeated and danced continuously. The angles of the zigs and zags can be adjusted to provide more or less progression around the floor and to gauge the approach to a corner.

Improving the Smoothness

Many dancers' desire to dance well is translated into physical effort. Try to keep the dance relaxed and avoid over-dancing. The length of the steps is important in maintaining smoothness. Generally, over three steps, the relative length of the steps will be short-long-short, corresponding to a step-swing-step-step action. On the first step, the dancer takes a step and develops the swing by moving the other foot ready for the second step on the quick count. The swing is resolved and neutralized in Step 3 as it moves from acting on one side of the body to the other. In some moves, such as a heel turn (Steps 1–3 Impetus Turn as woman, or Steps 4–6 as man), the person dancing the heel turn cannot take a long second step, but the other person will.

SLOW FOXTROT: the impetus turn

Reverse Turn

In dancing, a "reverse" turn simply means a turn made to the left. We can introduce the Reverse Turn directly into your Short Programme. Start by dancing the Feather Finish just as before but turning it a quarter turn (90°) to the left, to end with the man on the zag facing the centre line. You are now ready to dance the Reverse Turn.

1
COUNT – SLOW

Man Walk forward onto the left foot in-line with the woman, starting to turn left and swing the right foot forward along the zag.

Woman Walk back onto the right foot, starting to turn left.

2
COUNT – QUICK

Man Transfer the body-weight forward onto the toes of the right foot, turning left to end backing along the room.

Woman Pull the left heel back in contact with the floor, to close to the right foot. On the right heel and with the feet together, turn to end facing along the room and lift onto the toes of the left foot.

3
COUNT – QUICK

Man Walk back onto the left foot, lowering toe-heel.

Woman Walk forward onto the right foot, in-line with the man, lowering toe-heel.

4
COUNT – SLOW

Man Walk back onto the right foot, starting to turn left and swing the left foot back.

Woman Walk forward onto the left foot, starting to turn left and swing the right foot forward.

Man's Sway – straight-left-left, straight-right-right
Woman's Sway – straight-right-right, straight-left-left

5
COUNT – QUICK

Man Transfer the body weight sideways onto the toes of the left foot onto the zig.

Woman Transfer the body weight sideways onto the right foot, toe-heel, still turning to the left.

6
COUNT – QUICK

Man Step forward with the right foot outside the woman's right side, lowering, toe-heel, on the zig.

Woman Walk back onto the left foot, a little under the body, moving back along the zig towards the wall.

You are now in the same position as you originally were at the end of the Feather Finish. Continue with the Three Step, the Reverse Wave or the Hover Telemark.

Natural Weave

An excellent Slow Foxtrot figure which enables the dancers to change direction quickly and move along the floor out of traffic problems is the Natural Weave. It is danced after the Three Step. The man is standing on his left foot on the zig, ready to move towards the wall. The woman is standing on her right foot.

1

COUNT – SLOW

Man Walk forward onto the right foot, starting to turn right.

Woman Walk back onto the left foot, starting to turn right.

2

COUNT – QUICK

Man Move sideways onto the toes of the left foot, making nearly a quarter turn (90°) to the right onto the zag.

Woman Pull the right heel back in contact with the floor to close to the left foot. On the left heel and with the feet together, make a quarter turn (90°) to the right and lift onto the toes of the right foot.

3

COUNT – QUICK

Man Move back onto the toes of the right foot along the zag, allowing the body to turn to face almost against the flow.

Woman Move forward onto the toes of the left foot along the zag, allowing the body to turn to face almost along the room.

*Man's Sway – straight-right-straight, left-straight-right-right
Woman's Sway – straight-left-straight, right-straight-left-left*

Combining the Figures for Different Dance Floors

By dancing the Short Programme, the Extended Programme which includes the Reverse Turn, and the Natural Weave, you will soon learn how far around the room each series of moves will take you. You can now build your experience by practising various combinations to suit the size of any dance floor. For example, on a medium-size rectangular floor, you might start at the beginning of a long side and dance the Extended Programme including the Reverse Turn, to arrive two-thirds of the way along the long side. The Short Programme would then complete the long side and another Short Programme would take you across the short side. Alternatively, the long side might consist of the Feather Finish – Reverse Turn – Three Step – Natural Weave – Three Step – Impetus Turn.

4

COUNT – QUICK

Man Move back underneath the body onto the toes of the left foot.

Woman Move forward and a little across yourself onto the toes of the right foot, to step along the zag outside the man's right side.

5

COUNT – QUICK

Man Move back onto the toes of the right foot, starting to turn left.

Woman Move forward onto the toes of the left foot, starting to turn left.

6

COUNT – QUICK

Man Move sideways onto the toes of the left foot, turning onto the zig.

Woman Move sideways onto the right foot, still turning left, toe-heel.

7

COUNT – SLOW

Man Step forward onto the right foot outside the woman, lowering toe-heel.

Woman Move the left foot back slightly underneath the body along the zig.

The Curved Three Step

The Three Walks Curving to Left used in the Waltz can also be danced in the Slow Foxtrot instead of Steps 1–3 of the Reverse Turn. Use the standard Slow-Quick-Quick timing and continue with Steps 4–6 of the Reverse Turn. It is also a very good entry, if underturned, to the Reverse Wave, omitting Steps 1–3 of the Reverse Turn.

Continue with the Three Step, Reverse Wave or Hover Telemark.

Reverse Wave

The Reverse Wave is one of the most elegant and versatile moves in the Slow Foxtrot. A nice combination is to dance the Curved Three Step, underturning it so that the man ends backing along a zig. The standard entry for the Reverse Wave, though, is to dance it immediately after the Reverse Turn. This superb combination uses some of the moves with which you are already familiar. Start by dancing the Reverse Turn. Then, dance Steps 1–3 of the Reverse Turn, again starting with the man facing the wall on the zig and over-turning the move to half a turn, to end with the man backing the wall on the zig. The extra amount of turn can make this move a little tricky. It is important for the woman to take a small step on Step 1 and for the man not to try to rush or force the turn.

1
COUNT – SLOW

Man Walk back onto the right foot, starting to curve to the left.

Woman Walk forward onto the left foot and swing the right foot forward, starting to curve to the left.

2
COUNT – QUICK

Man Walk back onto the toes of the left foot, continuing to curve to the left.

Woman Transfer the body-weight forward onto the right foot and lift from the heel onto the toes of the right foot, continuing a gradual curve to the left.

3
COUNT – QUICK

Man Walk back onto the right foot, completing the curve to the left to end backing along the room.

Woman Lower the body weight stepping forward, toe-heel, onto the left foot, completing the curve to the left to end facing along the room.

Continue with Steps 4–6 of the Impetus Turn or the Open Impetus Turn. You can also dance the Natural Turn.

Man's Sway – straight-right-right
Woman's Sway – straight-left-left

The Feather Step

Many dancers often use the Feather Step to start the Slow Foxtrot and as an entry into the Reverse Turn. The man is standing on his left foot on a zag, facing the centre-line of the room. The woman is standing on her right foot on a zag, backing the centre line of the room.

1
COUNT – SLOW

Man Walk forward onto the right foot and swing the left foot forward along the zag.

Woman Walk back onto the left foot and start to move the right foot back, releasing the toe first.

2
COUNT – QUICK

Man Allow the swing to continue to bring the body-weight onto the toes of the left foot, and to turn the body a little to the right.

Woman Walk back onto the right foot and start to move the left foot back, releasing the toe first and allowing the body to turn slightly to right.

3
COUNT – QUICK

Man Step forward and slightly across onto the right foot outside the woman's right side, and lower toe-heel.

Woman Walk back and slightly underneath the body onto the left foot and start to move the right foot back, releasing the toe first.

Continue into the Reverse Turn, Curved Three Step, the Open Telemark or the Quick Open Reverse Turn variations.

Man's Sway – straight-right-right
Woman's Sway – straight-left-left

The Natural Turn at a Corner

When the Feather Step is used to start the Slow Foxtrot, a move called the Natural Turn is often used at a corner as a way of getting into it. The Natural Turn can be used instead of the Impetus Turn. First, as you approach the corner, dance Steps 1–3 of the Impetus Turn. The man is now backing along the room and is back on his right foot. The woman is facing along the room and is forward on her left foot.

Woman Walk forward onto the right foot.

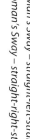

1
COUNT – SLOW

Man Walk back onto the left foot, starting to pull the right heel back in contact with the floor.

Man's Sway – straight-left-straight
Woman's Sway – straight-right-straight

The couple should stay down over these three steps and should avoid rushing the three "slow" counts of the move.

2
COUNT – SLOW

Man Keeping the feet a little apart, pull the right foot to the side and, making one-eighth of a turn (45°) to the right, end standing on the right foot facing along the zag of the new wall, towards the centre line.

Woman Move sideways onto the left foot, turning a little to right, and drag the right foot to touch the left foot.

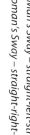

3
COUNT – SLOW

Man Walk forward onto the left foot along the zig, towards the centre line.

Woman Walk back onto the right foot.

Combining the Natural Turn with Other Moves

You can now continue with a Feather Step at the beginning of the new side. It is also possible to miss out the last step of the Natural Turn and dance straight into the Reverse Turn or the Curved Three Step. A nice combination is to dance Steps 1–2 of the Natural Turn, to end at the beginning of the new side. Then dance Steps 1–3 of the Reverse Turn, making only a quarter of a turn (90°), to end with the man backing along the zig. Follow straight into the Reverse Wave.

The Natural Turn can also be danced along the side of the room using three-eighths of a turn (135°), to end with the man facing along the zag towards the centre line. You would then follow the move with any of the combinations recommended above.

The Open Telemark

The Open Telemark is a very elegant and satisfying way of moving into Promenade Position in the Slow Foxtrot. It is also a very useful way of changing direction towards the wall, but still moving along the room instead of dancing a Reverse Turn. Start with the man on the zag, facing the centre line of the room. The man is standing on the right foot and the woman her left foot.

1
COUNT – SLOW

Man Transfer the body-weight forward onto the toes of the right foot, turning left to end backing along the zag.

Woman Pull the left heel back in contact with the floor to close to the right foot. On the right heel and with the feet together, turn to end facing along the room, and lift onto the toes of the left foot. Start to move the head over to the right.

2
COUNT – QUICK

Man Walk forward onto the left foot in-line with the woman, starting to turn left, and swing the right foot forward along the zag.

Woman Walk back onto the right foot, starting to turn left.

3
COUNT – QUICK

Man Point the left foot along the zig and lower onto it, toe-heel, in Promenade Position.

Woman Point the right foot along the zig and lower onto it, toe-heel, in Promenade Position with the head to the right.

Continue with either a Feather Ending from Promenade Position or a Passing Natural Turn. The Open Telemark can also be overturned to end along the room. Follow with the Wing and Syncopated Progressive Chassé to the right and the Weave Ending, ended facing along the zig towards the wall.

Man's Sway – straight-left-straight
Woman's Sway – straight-right-straight

The Feather Ending from Promenade Position

This is a very practical exit from Promenade Position which should be in everyone's Slow Foxtrot repertoire. Start in Promenade Position, having danced, for example, an Open Telemark.

1
COUNT – SLOW

Man Walk forward and across onto the right foot along the zig and in Promenade Position, starting to swing the left foot forward.

Woman Walk forward and across onto the left foot along the zig and in Promenade Position, starting to turn to the left.

Man's Sway – straight-right-right
Woman's Sway – straight-left-left

The Passing Natural Turn

The Passing Natural Turn is the standard entry for the classy Outside Swivel and a range of other moves which your dance coach would be pleased to show you. First, dance the Open Telemark as described earlier then follow it with the Passing Natural Turn.

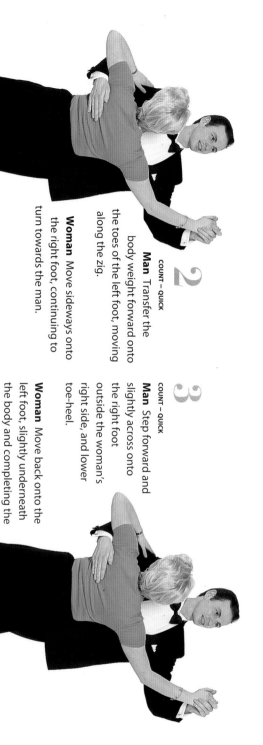

2
COUNT – QUICK

Man Transfer the body weight forward onto the toes of the left foot, moving the right foot outside the woman's right side, and lower toe-heel.

Woman Move sideways onto the right foot, continuing to turn towards the man.

3
COUNT – QUICK

Man Step forward and slightly across onto the right foot along the zig towards the wall, bringing the right side of the body back with the right foot.

Woman Move back onto the left foot, slightly underneath the body and completing the turn to face the man.

Continue with the Three Step or Reverse Wave, remembering to dance steps 1–3 of the Reverse Turn.

1
COUNT – SLOW

Man Walk forward and across onto the right foot in Promenade Position, along the zig, starting to turn to the right, to end facing along the zag towards the wall. Swing the left foot forward towards the zag.

Woman Walk forward and across onto the left foot along the zig and in Promenade Position.

It will feel a little as though the man is cutting across the woman but she should avoid impeding the woman's progress along the zig.

2
COUNT – QUICK

Man Move the body weight forward onto the toes of the left foot and continue turning, to back along the room.

Woman Move forward along the zig, between the man's feet, onto the toes of the right foot.

Man and Woman – No Sway

3
COUNT – QUICK

Man Move back, lowering toe-heel, onto the right foot along the zig towards the wall, bringing the right side of the body back with the right foot.

Woman Step forward, along the zig, lowering toe-heel onto the left foot, bringing the left side of the body forward with the left foot.

Continue into the Outside Swivel.

The Outside Swivel

The stylish move continues from the Open Telemark and Passing Natural Turn combination. It is a standard and popular Slow Foxtrot figure which I am confident you will enjoy.

1

COUNT – SLOW

Man Move back along the zig, slightly underneath the body, onto the left foot with the toe turned inwards. Allow the right foot to cross loosely in front of the left foot, still in contact with the floor. On the left foot, swivel a quarter turn (90°) to the right to end on the zag towards the centre line. Lead the woman to turn right to end in Promenade Position.

Woman Walk forward and across onto the right foot along the zig and outside the man's right side. Bring the left foot to the right foot and, on the right foot, swivel to the right to end on the zag towards the centre line. Don't rush this step.

Man and Woman – No Sway.

Continue with the Feather Ending from Promenade Position moving along the zag towards the centre line, or with the Weave or the Wing.

The Open Impetus Turn

You have already been enjoying the Impetus Turn as part of your basic Slow Foxtrot. Now we introduce some modifications to end the figure in Promenade position, and give an opportunity to develop extra style in the shape of the move. The Open Impetus Turn is danced along the side of the room. Start by dancing Steps 1-3 of Impetus Turn.

4

COUNT – SLOW

Man Walk back onto the left foot, starting to turn right.

Woman Walk forward onto the right foot, starting to turn right and swing the left foot forward past the man.

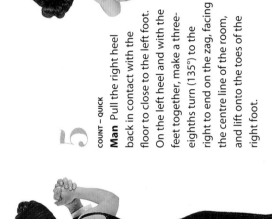

5

COUNT – QUICK

Man Pull the right heel back in contact with the floor to close to the left foot. On the left heel and with the feet together, make a three-eighths turn (135°) to the right to end on the zag, facing the centre line of the room, and lift onto the toes of the right foot.

Woman Still turning right, transfer the body weight sideways onto the toes of the left foot and bring the right foot back to touch or brush the side of the left foot on the zag.

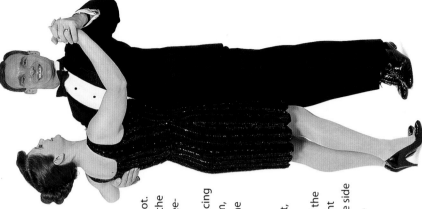

Man's Sway – straight-right-straight
Woman's Sway – straight-left-straight

6

COUNT – QUICK

Man Continuing to turn on the right foot to face along the room, take a small step along the zag towards the centre line, lowering the body-weight, toe-heel, onto the left foot in Promenade Position.

Woman Still turning on the toes of the left foot, take a small step onto the toes of the right foot along the zag towards the centre line, then lower, toe-heel, onto the right foot in Promenade Position.

Continue with the Feather Ending, the Weave or the Wing. If danced at a corner, it is possible to dance straight into a Passing Natural Turn and Outside Swivel at the beginning of the new side.

Using your Head

Normally, the man's head will remain to the left. However, to add extra style, the man may look to the right over the woman's left shoulder as he sways and turns to the right on Steps 4 and 5. As the couple lift onto the toes, the man and the woman will synchronize the movement of their heads into Promenade Position.

4a
COUNT – SLOW

5a
COUNT – QUICK

The Weave

The Weave has become one of the international standard moves in the Slow Foxtrot and this version is designed to be danced after the Open Impetus Turn or the Outside Swivel. The couple are in Promenade Position ready to move along the zag towards the centre line. The man is standing on the left foot and the woman on the right foot.

1
COUNT – SLOW

Man Walk forward and across onto the right foot along the zag towards the centre line in Promenade Position.

Woman Walk forward and across onto the left foot along the zag, towards the centre line, in Promenade Position.

2
COUNT – QUICK

Man Take a small step forward onto the toes of the left foot along the zag between the woman's feet, starting to turn to the left.

Woman Turning to left across the man, move sideways onto the toes of the right foot, backing the centre line along the zag.

Man's Sway – straight-straight-left-left, straight-right-right
Woman's Sway – straight-straight-right-right, straight-left-left

3
COUNT – QUICK

Man Move sideways onto the the toes of the right foot, turning left to end backing the zig towards the wall.

Woman Move sideways onto the the toes of the left foot, turning to the left to face down the room.

4
COUNT – QUICK

Man Move back onto the toes of the left foot slightly underneath the body, turning to back down the room.

Woman Step forward and across outside the man's right side, onto the toes of the right foot.

5
COUNT – QUICK

Man Move back onto the toes of the right foot, backing down the room, still turning to the left.

Woman Step forward onto the toes of the left foot in-line with the man, and continuing to turn to the left.

The Wing and Syncopated Progressive Chassé to Right with a Weave Ending

The best dancers always have an alternative move ready to dance should the way ahead become blocked by other floor traffic. Imagine you have just danced an Open Impetus Turn or an Outside Swivel, and you are unable to move towards the centre line because of other floor traffic. Now is the time to dance the Wing in which the man halts the couple's progress to lead the woman to dance three walks around him, to finish on his left side – the opposite to normal – now that's Floorcraft with Flair!

The Wing

1

COUNT – SLOW

Man Walk forward and across onto the right foot in Promenade Position along the zag towards the centre-line, starting to turn to the left.

Woman Walk forward onto the left foot, starting to turn left around the man.

Continue with the Three Step, Steps 1–3 of the Reverse Turn & Reverse Wave or the Hover Telemark.

6

COUNT – QUICK

Man Still turning to the left, point the left foot along the zig and transfer the body weight onto the toes of the left foot.

Woman Move sideways onto the right foot, turning left to back the wall.

7

COUNT – QUICK

Man Step forward and across onto the toes of the right foot on the zig, outside the woman's right side, and lower toe-heel.

Woman Move back slightly underneath the body onto the left foot, along the zig towards the wall.

Man's Sway – straight-right-right
Woman's Sway – straight-left-left

Style Tip

As the woman walks around the man, it is important for her to keep her right side forward to maintain contact with the man. The woman gradually turns her head to the left over the move.

3

COUNT – QUICK

Man Still on the right foot, continue to swivel to left to complete a quarter turn (90°) drawing the left foot to close to the right foot without weight. End standing on the right foot.

Woman Lowering toe-heel onto the left foot, walk forward between yourself and the man's left side.

Continue with the Syncopated Progressive Chassé to Right.

2

COUNT – QUICK

Man Standing on the right foot, swivel slowly to the left, drawing the left foot in contact with the floor towards the right foot but without putting any weight onto the left foot.

Woman Walk forward onto the toes of the right foot, continuing to move around the man.

The Syncopated Progressive Chassé to Right

While a Chassé is a common figure in the Waltz and Quickstep, it is less common in the Slow Foxtrot. This gives the move a degree of surprise and adds a little unexpected highlight in the middle of the combination. The Chassé moves along the zag towards the centre-line of the room.

Man & Woman – No Sway

1

COUNT – SLOW

Man Walk forward onto the left foot outside the woman's left side, starting to turn to the left and swing the right foot along the zag.

Woman Move back onto the right foot, starting to turn left and swing the left foot back along the zag.

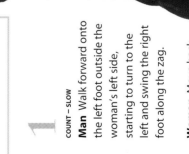

2

COUNT – QUICK

Man Move sideways onto the toes of the right foot along the zag, still turning to the left.

Woman Move sideways onto the toes of the left foot along the zag, still turning to the left.

The Quick Open Reverse Turn with Turning Cross

3
COUNT – &

Man Close the toes of the left foot to the toes of the right foot still turning to the left.

Woman Close the toes of the right foot to the toes of the left foot still turning to the left.

4
COUNT – QUICK

Man Move sideways and slightly back onto the toes of the right foot along the zag, still turning to the left to back down the room.

Woman Move to the side and slightly forward onto the toes of the left foot along the zag, still turning left to face down the room.

Continue with Steps 4–7 of the Weave.

The Quick Open Reverse Turn

The Quick Open Reverse Turn is a standard move in itself. To dance the basic Quick Open Reverse Turn, dance Steps 1–3 of the figure as described below, then Steps 5–7 of the Weave.

The Quick Open Reverse Turn with Turning Cross

We are now going to upgrade the Quick Open Reverse Turn to climax with a crossing action. I always associate this move with my one time coach, former World Ballroom Champion, Len Armstrong, whose powerful movement and control perfectly suited this figure. I hope it suits you too Start as if ready to dance the standard Reverse Turn.

Man's Sway – straight-left-left, straight-right-right
Woman's Sway – straight-right-right, straight-left-left

1
COUNT – SLOW

Man Walk forward onto the left foot in-line with the woman and along the zag, towards the centre line, starting to turn left and swing the right foot forward along the zag.

Woman Walk back onto the right foot along the zag towards the centre line, starting to turn left, and swing the left foot back along the zag.

2
COUNT – QUICK

Man Transfer the body weight forward onto the toes of the right foot, turning left to end backing along the zig.

Woman Point the toes of the left foot along the room and transfer the body weight onto the toes of the left foot, turning to the left.

3
COUNT – &

Man Move back underneath the body onto the toes of the left foot, continuing to turn left to back down the room.

Woman Step forward and across onto the toes of the right foot, along the room and outside the man's right side.

The Hover Telemark

The Hover Telemark is a super move in both the Waltz and Slow Foxtrot. It is described in the Waltz section, but you can dance it in exactly the same way in the Slow Foxtrot, using the standard Slow Foxtrot timing of Slow-Quick-Quick.

Continue with the Passing Natural & Outside Swivel or Feather Ending in Promenade Position.

Continue with the Open Telemark, which you will need to turn a little more than normal, or underturn the Quick Open Reverse Turn with Turning Cross, to end facing along the zig towards the wall, and dance the Hover Telemark.

4

COUNT – QUICK

Man Move back onto the right foot, turning to back along the zag towards the centre line, and lowering momentarily.

Woman Move forward onto the left foot in-line with the man, turning to the left on the zag towards the centre line and lowering momentarily.

5

COUNT – SLOW

Man Point the toes of the left foot along the room, and turning to face along the zig, transfer the body weight onto the toes of the left foot.

Woman Move sideways onto the toes of the right foot, still turning to the left to end backing the zig.

6

COUNT – &

Man Cross the right foot, lowering it behind the left foot and continue turning to end facing along the room.

Woman Cross the left foot, lowering it in front of the right foot and continue turning, to end backing down the room.

Viennese Waltz

The elegance and charm of the Viennese Waltz conjures up spectacular images of gracious balls in the great houses and palaces of the European nobility, yet the Waltz started life as the "Ländler" an Austrian folkdance. The Viennese Waltz continues as a specified dance in Championship competitions, where the competitors exhibit their graceful fluency, stamina and control at speed, as they rotate around the floor to a quick tempo of 60 bars per minute.

Despite this image of a fast, dizzy and demanding dance, the Waltz never lost its common appeal and versions of it remain among the most popular of social dances, particularly in Europe.

Here, we explore the simplified social version, which is neither strenuous nor vertigo-inducing. For social dancers, the Waltz is transformed into a beautiful, lilting version which everyone can enjoy, whatever their level of ability.

In the Championship version of the Viennese Waltz, the competitors dance one step to each beat of music. In this popular social version, the simple moves comprise one gentle swing action to each bar of music, giving the dance the delightful lilting feel but without the speed of its competition counterpart. The dance should still progress around the room, albeit at a gentler pace.

Basic Natural Lilt Step

Start on a zig. The man is standing on his left foot, feet together, while the woman is standing on her right foot, feet together. Each step starts on the first beat of each new bar of music and the move is taken over the whole bar. The next step is therefore taken on the first beat of the following bar of music.

1

Man Walk forward with the right foot, starting to turn to the right. Allow the left foot to swing forward towards the right foot.

Woman Walk back with the left foot, starting to turn right. Allow the right foot to swing back towards the left foot.

2

Man Walk back with the left foot, continuing to turn right. Allow the right foot to swing back towards the left foot.

Woman Walk forward with the right foot, continuing to turn to the right. Allow the left foot to swing forward towards the right foot.

The Basic Natural Lilt Step can be repeated several times so that a gradual turn to the right is made.

Basic Reverse Lilt Step

This move gradually turns the dancers to the left. It is conventionally started when the man is on a zag, ready to move forward towards the centre line of the room. The man is standing on his right foot, having completed a Basic Natural Lilt Step, and the woman is standing on her left foot.

1

Man Walk forward with the left foot, starting to turn to the left. Allow the right foot to swing forward towards the left foot.

Woman Walk back with the right foot, starting to turn left. Allow the left foot to swing back towards the right foot.

2

Man Walk back with the right foot, continuing to turn left. Allow the left foot to swing back towards the right foot.

Woman Walk forward with the left foot, continuing to turn left. Allow the right foot to swing forward towards the left foot.

The Basic Reverse Lilt Step can be repeated several times so that a gradual turn to the left is made. It is conventional to complete the series of Basic Reverse Lilt Steps on a zig so that the Basic Natural Lilt Step may follow.

Stationary Lilt Step

It is always important to be courteous to other dancers on the floor and good dancers will always give way to less experienced ones. It may therefore be good practice temporarily to interrupt your progress in deference to other floor traffic. This is simple with the Stationary Lilt Step, which is danced on the spot with a sideways lilting action. It may be danced as often as is necessary, and in any position, before continuing with the original desired move. The move can start with either foot, but here we shall try it starting with the man's right foot. Start therefore as for the Basic Natural Lilt Step.

1

Man Move sideways on to the right foot, allowing the left foot to swing towards the right foot.

Woman Move sideways on to the left foot, allowing the right foot to swing towards the left foot.

2

Man Move sideways on to the left foot, allowing the right foot to swing towards the left foot.

Woman Move sideways on to the right foot, allowing the left foot to swing towards the right foot.

Sequence Dancing

Sequence Dancing is very popular in the UK and, in Australia, where it is called New Vogue dancing. Old Time Sequence dances employ the old ballet feet positions. Modern Sequence dances are based on Modern or Standard Ballroom dances, and Latin-American Sequence dances are based on the Latin-American dances. Each dance is generally choreographed into a standard 16-bar routine. Each routine or sequence is given a name: this becomes the dance, which may be repeated several times during the piece of music. The dancers all start at the same time and dance the same sequence of moves until the music ends. Sequence Dancing tends to reduce the need for technique and leading and is particularly popular with older social dancers, who enjoy the music and social atmosphere without the need to work at producing a high level of dancing. There is a constant supply of new dances, so when the dancers become bored with one they simply move on to another.

One of the drawbacks, though, is that there are now tens of thousands of Sequence dances listed, and different Sequence Dance clubs may share only a few dances in their common repertoire. If you plan to go to a Sequence Dance club or to go on a Sequence Dance holiday, check first which dances will be played. It is not acceptable to dance any dance other than the one that has been announced. As a reminder, most Sequence Dance "leaders" will first dance the sequence through before the dancers themselves take to the floor. Sequence dances that have become classics include the "Mayfair Quickstep", the "Saunter Together", the "Tango Serida", the "Melody Foxtrot" and the "Square Tango".

To exit, there are four options:

1 When the man is standing on his left foot, exit forwards with the Basic Natural Lilt Step.

2 When the man is standing on his left foot, exit backwards with Step 2 of the Basic Reverse Lilt Step.

3 When the man is standing on his right foot, exit forwards with Basic Reverse Lilt Step.

4 When the man is standing on his right foot, exit backwards with Step 2 of the Basic Natural Lilt Step.

Further information

It is to be hoped that this book has inspired you to dance, whether at a Latin club, a private social event or a company dinner. With the moves you have learned in this book you will soon be out on the floor dancing so why not join other who share your interests? Look up your local dance school or call a dance club in your area. Your teacher will be able to give you personal guidance to help you refine your technique and you will be surprised by how quickly you progress. Remember that most people find dancing a little difficult at first but, given a little time, patience and practice, you will soon have learned to dance, which is a lifetime's reward for such a small investment.

International Dance Teachers' Association
International House, 76 Bennett Road,
Brighton BN2 5JL
Telephone: 44 (0) 1273 685652
Email: idta@fastnet.co.uk

The World Dance and Dance Sport Council and The British Dance Council
Terpsichore House, 240 Merton Road,
London SW19 4FQ
Telephone: 44 (0) 181 545 0223

National Dance Council of America
24556 Mando Drive,
Laguna Niguel,
Ca. 92677 USA
Telephone/Fax: 1 714 643 9700

American Ballroom Company
PO Box 453605, Miami,
Fl. 33245/3605 USA
Telephone: 1 305 442 1288

Australian Dancing Board
49 Links Road, Adross 6153,
Western Australia
Telephone: 9 364 3553

New Zealand Council of Ballroom Dancing
PO Box 37-342, Parnell,
Auckland, New Zealand
Telephone: 9 3034 650

South African
National Council of Ballroom Dancing
7 Woodside, 8 Park Lane,
Kloof, Natal,
South Africa 3610
Telephone: 31 764 3732

Canadian Dance Teacher's Association
94 Boulevard Lavesque,
Pont Viau, Laval,
Quebec H7G ICI Canada
Telephone: 514 669 6984

LINE DANCING
Country Western Dance Council UK
8 Wick Lane, Felpham,
Bognor Regis, West Sussex, PO22 8QG
Telephone: 44 (0) 1243 585545/01278 792233

UCWDC
United Country Western Dance Council
PO Box 21007, Albuquerque,
NM 87154 USA
Telephone: 1 505 293 0123

National Teachers' Association
PO Box 39, Ekron,
Ky. 40117 0039 USA
Telephone: 1 502 828 8887

Acknowledgements

The author and publisher would like to thank the following for their contribution to this book:

Tanya Janes AIDTA, MGPTD for her invaluable Salsa expertise; Karina Rebello for her insights into the authentic detail of Lambada and Samba Reggae; Simon Selmon and Derek Young, F&Exam. UKA for their expert advice on Lindy Hop and Rock 'n' Roll respectively.

Many thanks to the following dancers for their participation in the photographic sequences. Their expertise and enthusiasm were invaluable:

Elaine Bottomer (Four times undefeated World & European Tango Argentino Supreme Champion and All-England Professional Ballroom Championship Grand Finalist), Goran and Nicola Nordin (UK Professional Latin-American Champions), Harm-Jan Schadenberg and Wendy Kroeze (Three-times undefeated Dutch Professional Latin-American Champions), John Byrnes and Jane Lyttleton, (UK Professional Rising Star Latin-American Champions), Mark and Jane Shutlar, Steve and Deborah McCormick, Jeff and Teresa Lindley, Michael Burton, Camilla Laitalia, Trevor and Naomi Ironmonger, Karina Rebello, Berg Dias, Andrew Barrett, Luis Bittencourt, Tanya Janes, Mina di Placido, Phillippe Laue, Julie Glover, Mark Field, Natascha Hall, Katherine Porter, Anny Ho, Ben Ryley, Shahriar Shariat, Debbie Smith, Debbie Watson, Simon Selmon, Helia Lloyd and Dr Eric Sille.

We gratefully acknowledge the kind permission of Sounds Sensational to use references from Tango Argentino: The Technique and Video by Paul Bottomer and for their co-operation in the preparation of this publication. Paul Bottomer, 6 Dove Grove, Egginton, Derbyshire, DE65 6HH, England and Sounds Sensational, 38 Katherine Drive, Toton, Nottingham, NG9 6JB, England. Fax: 01159 038888 Email: tango@innotts.co.uk

Many thanks to Supadance International for supplying dance shoes for photography.

Dresses were very kindly lent by After 6, Consortium, Pineapple, Tadashi and Vera Mont.

Index